CERAMICS OF THE MERV OASIS

PUBLICATIONS OF THE
INSTITUTE OF ARCHAEOLOGY,
UNIVERSITY COLLEGE LONDON

Director of the Institute: Stephen Shennan
Publications Series Editor: Peter J. Ucko

The Institute of Archaeology of University College London is one of the oldest, largest and most prestigious archaeology research facilities in the world. Its extensive publications programme includes the best theory, research, pedagogy and reference materials in archaeology and cognate disciplines, through publishing exemplary work of scholars worldwide. Through its publications, the Institute brings together key areas of theoretical and substantive knowledge, improves archaeological practice and brings archaeological findings to the general public, researchers and practitioners. It also publishes staff research projects, site and survey reports, and conference proceedings. The publications programme, formerly developed in-house or in conjunction with UCL Press, is now produced in partnership with Left Coast Press, Inc. The Institute can be accessed online at http://www.ucl.ac.uk/archaeology.

ENCOUNTERS WITH ANCIENT EGYPT Subseries, Peter J. Ucko, (ed.)
Jean-Marcel Humbert and Clifford Price (eds.), Imhotep Today (2003)
David Jeffreys (ed.), Views of Ancient Egypt since Napoleon Bonaparte: Imperialism,
    Colonialism, and Modern Appropriations (2003)
Sally MacDonald and Michael Rice (eds.), Consuming Ancient Egypt (2003)
Roger Matthews and Cornelia Roemer (eds.), Ancient Perspectives on Egypt (2003)
David O'Connor and Andrew Reid (eds.), Ancient Egypt in Africa (2003)
John Tait (ed.), 'Never had the like occurred': Egypt's View of its Past (2003)
David O'Connor and Stephen Quirke (eds.), Mysterious Lands (2003)
Peter Ucko and Timothy Champion (eds.), The Wisdom of Egypt: Changing Visions
    Through the Ages (2003)

Andrew Gardner (ed.), Agency Uncovered: Archaeological Perspectives (2004)
Okasha El-Daly, Egyptology, The Missing Millennium: Ancient Egypt in Medieval Arabic
    Writing (2005)
Ruth Mace, Clare J. Holden, and Stephen Shennan (eds.), Evolution of Cultural Diversity:
    A Phylogenetic Approach (2005)
Arkadiusz Marciniak, Placing Animals in the Neolithic: Social Zooarchaeology of
    Prehistoric Farming Communities (2005)
Robert Layton, Stephen Shennan, and Peter Stone (eds.), A Future for Archaeology (2006)
Joost Fontein, The Silence of Great Zimbabwe: Contested Landscapes and the Power of
    Heritage (2006)

ARCHAEOLOGY OF MEDIEVAL NOVGOROD Subseries, Mark Brisbane (ed.)
Clive Orton (ed.), Pottery from Medieval Novgorod and its Region (2006)

ANCIENT MERV PROJECT Subseries, Tim Williams (ed.)
Gabriele Puschnigg, Ceramics of the Merv Oasis: Recycling the City (2006)

CERAMICS OF THE
MERV OASIS

RECYCLING THE CITY

Gabriele Puschnigg

**Left Coast
Press** Inc.
Walnut Creek, California

Left Coast
Press Inc.

LEFT COAST PRESS, INC.
1630 North Main Street, #400
Walnut Creek, CA 94596
http://www.LCoastPress.com

ISBN 1-59874–225–6 hardcover
978–1–59874–225–1

Library of Congress Cataloging in Publication Data
Puschnig, Gabriele, 1966–
  Ceramics of the Merv Oasis : recycling the city / Gabriele
Puschnigg.
    p. cm. – (Publications of the Institute of Archaeology,
University College London) (Ancient Merv Project)
  Includes bibliographical references and index.
  ISBN-13: 978–1–59874–225–1 (hardcover : alk. paper)
  ISBN-10: 1–59874–225–6 (hardcover : alk. paper)
  1. Merv (Extinct city) – History. 2. Turkmenistan – Antiquities. I.
Title.
  DK939.5.M47P87 2006
  939'.6–dc22

2006026628

British Library Cataloguing in Publication Data
is available from the British Library

Printed in the United States of America

06 07 08 09 10   5 4 3 2 1

CONTENTS

DETAILED CONTENTS

PREFACE

Throughout the history of archaeological research the choice of specific study areas and methodological approaches has been subject to changes of academic concepts and fashion. Utilitarian pottery has long been regarded as one of the least informative and rewarding themes. Over the years, however, the potential of pottery as an archaeological source material has been recognised and the different aspects of ceramic analysis hold a prominent position within archaeological research today.

Yet little is known about the ceramic production of the Sasanian Empire. On the one hand, this was attributed to the lack of suitable assemblages for examination. On the other, the comparatively indistinct appearance of the plain wares combined with the complex archaeology of the multi-period sites that usually produced Sasanian material delayed progress in the study of Sasanian ceramic industry. In 1993 an exhibition catalogue on Sasanian material culture could justifiably reduce the section on the pottery of this period to a short statement concluding: 'Il n'existe aucune publication spécialisée sur la céramique d'époque sassanide, du fait qu'aucun site sassanide n'a été fouillé de manière extensive. Il est dès lors impossible de reconstituer une typologie de cette céramique dans un cadre chronologique' (Vanden Berghe 1993).

This study is an attempt to contribute to the understanding of Sasanian pottery and its archaeological context. International collaborations in the area which form the focus of this research became feasible only through the changes to the political landscape in the early 1990s. With the breakdown of the Soviet Union the ground was prepared for the current British involvement in the archaeology of Turkmenistan, a territory that was part of the Sasanian Empire. Joint excavations at the city site of Merv produced a large corpus of pottery from Sasanian occupation levels, which forms the basis of the current analysis and also determines its chronological frame.

Excavation techniques and recording methods have changed and developed over the past decades, becoming increasingly aware of the value of mundane objects for the under-standing of daily life in the past. In addition to the fresh archaeological perspective, strat-egies regarding the quantitative analysis of ceramic assemblages were advanced providing the necessary tools for a new approach to the study of Sasanian pottery.

One of the problems found repeatedly in the archaeological literature concerned the identification of vessel forms as Sasanian. Few pottery types seem characteristic for this period, which are often, however, related to non-ceramic shapes inspired by metal ware. Variations in the stylistic expression and pace of development were noticed for different regions, indicating a local aspect of Sasanian ceramic industry which would define it as a regional matter unrelated to the common cultural expression attested for the Sasanian Empire in more representative media, such as silver vessels, glass, stucco or textiles.

In the absence of suitable morphological and stylistic criteria, research focused on the archaeological and stratigraphic evidence. This, however, proved to be equally problem-atic. Sasanian occupation levels are often encountered in urban contexts among a variety of chronologically different horizons. Like many Central Asian sites, Merv is a city built from mudbrick. The highly organic nature of this type of architecture led to a cycle of material reuse adding to the stratigraphic complications of urban archaeology.

In view of these specific problems, analytical options were carefully considered to determine a suitable strategy for the present analysis. Great emphasis was laid on an objective approach to the chronological assessment based primarily on the information gained from the archaeological excavations, in order to avoid the repetition of previous errors.

Despite its distinct quantitative approach, this study should not be seen in isolation. Archaeological fieldwork has a long tradition at Merv and numerous excavations were conducted covering all occupational levels of the city, from its foundation in Achaemenid times up until the Islamic period. Although excavation techniques and theoretical backgrounds are diverse, much valuable information is contained in the publications of earlier projects. The integration of previous work is an important objective, and considerable effort is made to use material from a selected number of relevant excavations in order to supplement the evidence for the stylistic evaluation and to gain an outlook into the preceding and following periods untouched by the recent excavations. Indeed, many of the conclusions reached on the stylistic development of the pottery would not have been possible without the fundamental work undertaken at Merv in Soviet times.

Original trial analyses with the statistical package started, before excavations in the Sasanian domestic quarter were completed. The data set was subsequently amended to include the finds and results of the final two field seasons. Still, the present publication should be regarded as a pilot study of pottery research at Merv. The focus will consequently be on problems of methodology and practical implications. Research questions are centred on chronology and the attempt to identify the factors determinant in the development of form and style.

Other issues of the ceramic research at Merv are covered elsewhere. A comprehensive discussion on aspects of technology, function and trade supported by scientific analyses and including a complete form and fabric catalogue of both Achaemenid to Sasanian and Islamic periods will be the subject of a separate publication, *The Ceramics from Merv* (Puschnigg and Gilbert forthcoming). The pottery repertoire of particular excavation areas will be presented as part of the individual site reports, *Late Sasanian Remains in Erk Kala* and *A Sasanian Residential Quarter in Gyaur Kala* (Simpson (ed.) forthcoming). This series of publications is only a first step towards understanding the wider context of ceramic traditions at Merv, but it is hoped that results will encourage future work.

ACKNOWLEDGEMENTS

Archaeological investigations are rarely done in isolation, but usually involve the intellectual input, work effort and support of a whole group of people. This is all the more relevant for research programmes generated by large international projects similar to the one at Merv. The present study developed over several years parallel to the ongoing fieldwork. Many people have contributed to my work throughout and their help was essential for the completion of this book.

First and foremost I am indebted to Georgina Herrmann, director of the project between 1992 and 2000, for her encouragement and support. I am also grateful to St John Simpson for his useful comments at the early stages of my work. The following institutions and scholarships thankfully provided financial support for my research: the Austrian Ministry of Science and Research, the British Academy, the Graduate School of University College London, the UNESCO Hirayama Fellowship, and the Raymond and Beverly Sackler scholarship in Ancient Iranian Studies.

Among the Turkmen colleagues, I would like to thank in particular Kakamurad Kurbansakhatov, co-director of the Merv project, and Rejeb Dzhaparov, director of the Ancient Merv Archaeological Park, who arranged the work space at the dig house and helped with equipment and organisational problems on a day-to-day basis. I would like to extend my gratitude to Azim Akhmedov for granting me access to his collection of pottery from the final YuTAKE excavations at Merv.

Most important for my research was the support I received from all members of our team during the field seasons. The preparation and processing of the pottery would not have been possible without our local assistants, Gunsha, Enabay and Gulshat Durdieva, and Ogulsheker and Ogulbabay Esenmyradova. Working with masses of archaeological material can be both challenging and discouraging, and throughout all enthusiasm, doubts and despair I benefited most from the expertise and good humour of my close colleagues Sheila Boardman, Pierre Brun, Ann Feuerbach, David Gilbert, Ian Smith and Faith Vardy, who is also partly responsible for the illustrations in this volume.

I am also indebted to the many scholars who helped me with their opinion and advice throughout the different stages of my research. I would like to mention here Genadi Koshelenko, Boris Marshak, Alexander Nikitin, Edvard Rtveladze and Natalya Smirnova, who helped me greatly in deepening my knowledge about neighbouring provinces and gaining access to archive material. In particular, I would like to thank Zamira Usmanova for her generous support with information on previous excavations at Merv and her openness regarding her own work.

For their valuable comments on my original work I am very grateful to Mike Baxter and Ernie Haerrinck, and to Michael Roaf for his constructive criticism. I owe special thanks to Alan Vince for his valuable recommendations, and to Vladimir Zavyalov for his continuous encouragement and advice.

Finally, I would like to thank all those who gave me special support in completing this book, above all Tim Williams, director of the Ancient Merv Project. I am particularly grateful to Clive Orton, who patiently guided me through all matters statistical.

Among those who helped me with their technical expertise, I would like to mention with gratitude Bryan Alvey, specialist for Access databases, Sjoerd van der Linde, who helped me with design issues and maps, and Kate Morton, the pottery illustrator.

LIST OF PLATES

The colour plate section is positioned between pages 26 and 27. Plates 1–5 refer to Chapter 2,
Plates 6–12 refer to Chapter 6 and Plates 13–15 refer to Chapter 7.

LIST OF FIGURES

LIST OF FIGURES

LIST OF TABLES

— PART I —

CONTEXT AND PERSPECTIVE

– 1 –

CERAMICS IN SASANIAN ARCHAEOLOGY

Ceramics constitute the largest group of archaeological finds. Their fragility when complete, and endurance through taphonomic processes once broken, qualify them as a reliable medium for archaeological interpretation. With the development of new analytical methods over the last decades, ceramicists are enabled to contribute to a wide range of questions concerning the understanding of ancient civilisations.

In the field of Sasanian ceramics, however, the stage of research seems far behind compared to subjects such as Greek or Roman pottery. This delay may be explained by the relatively late discovery of the Iranian world to western interest as well as general problems of methodological adjustment.

The archaeology of ancient Persia was never regarded as an independent discipline. Initially, scholars studied the Iranian empires from a Mesopotamian or Greek perspective with a strong emphasis on early dynasties. The research focus shifted only gradually to include later periods. Impressive monuments, such as rock reliefs and palaces, and elite objects generated a strong art-historical interest at first. Advances in Sasanian archaeology, however, have been rather erratic. Different scholarly traditions at work simultaneously, but unsynchronised, and the fundamental changes in the modern political landscape of the countries that now cover the territory of Sasanian Iran have produced a patchwork of evidence. The following brief discussion will highlight different strands of archaeological research that contributed to the current state of knowledge on Sasanian pottery.

ARCHAEOLOGICAL RESEARCH IN IRAN AND IRAQ

Early excavations

During the nineteenth and early twentieth centuries, as excavations were mainly driven by the ambition to uncover legendary sites such as Nineveh, Nimrud or Susa, Sasanian levels were often only briefly documented or simply removed to reach earlier horizons (cf. Huff 1986, 302). As a consequence, many samples of Sasanian ceramics remained initially unstudied, although some material has survived in museum collections (Simpson 1996, 89–94; Moorey 1978). The first scholars to show interest in Parthian and Sasanian assemblages were originally specialists in Islamic art, who sought to understand the stylistic quality of the material and establish possible links between pre-Islamic and Islamic

3

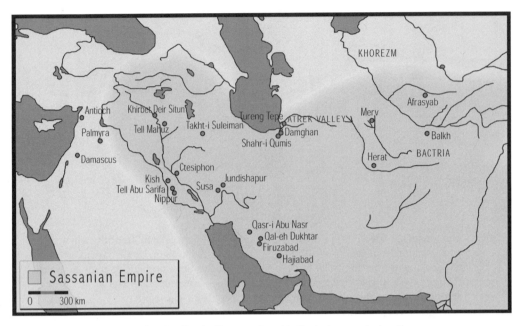

Figure 1.1: The territory of ancient Persia. Sites mentioned in the text are marked on the map.

ceramics. At the time, however, pottery studies still had a strong art-historical inclination, which ultimately proved to be unsuitable to handle the plain and often fragmented material (Sarre 1921; Ettinghausen 1938). A comprehensive survey of Sasanian pottery was first published by the Islamic art historian Richard Ettinghausen as part of Arthur Upham Pope's encyclopaedic work 'A Survey of Persian Art from Prehistoric Times to the Present' (1938, 664–680). Ettinghausen tried to define a pottery sequence based primarily on stylistic considerations (1938, 665). He founded his study on an eclectic assemblage of complete or near-complete vessels, consisting of excavated as well as commercially acquired specimens of sometimes doubtful provenance (Ettinghausen 1938, 664–680). Although Ettinghausen identified three major stages in the pottery development from the Parthian through early Islamic periods (1938, 668), his overall judgement on Sasanian wares remained inconclusive: 'the total repertoire of shapes does not seem to have any consistent quality that might be expressive of the character of the culture' (Ettinghausen 1938, 666).

The interpretation of such late ceramic assemblages proved to be difficult, though, even when processed and examined in the field, as the stratigraphy was frequently disturbed and the material itself inconspicuous (Schmidt 1934). Johann Heinrich Schmidt, a member of the German expedition to Ctesiphon, recognised the problems of establishing a reliable chronology. He found it particularly difficult to use numismatic data for this purpose, as Parthian and Sasanian coins were often found together in the same layer (Schmidt 1934, 22).

Despite the generally systematic excavation techniques, stratigraphic divisions were rather coarse and the level of recording varied greatly (Moorey 1978, 13; cf. Langdon and Harden 1934, 124–130).

A number of ceramic collections from excavations conducted in the 1930s, including

Kish, Qasr-i Abu Nasr and Tell Mahuz, were examined in more detail at a later stage by trained archaeologists (Moorey 1978; Venco Ricciardi 1970; Whitcomb 1985). Inadequate field records and poor stratigraphy, however, frustrated attempts to gain a tighter chronological control (Moorey 1978, 13; Venco Ricciardi 1970, 430).

In this context the material from Qasr-i Abu Nasr near Shiraz is of particular import-ance for Sasanian archaeology. Chosen initially as a supposed Achaemenid settlement, it soon became evident that Qasr-i Abu Nasr was confined to Sasanian and Islamic occupa-tion levels (Whitcomb 1985, 16). Fortunately the excavations continued and revealed an urban centre in the Shiraz plain close to the birthplace of the Sasanian dynasty. The com-paratively high standard of documentation enabled Donald Whitcomb to re-evaluate the excavations of Qasr-i Abu Nasr in great detail and with special regard to the ceramic evidence (Whitcomb 1985). Whitcomb even tried a pottery seriation (by hand) for one of the trenches, although with limited success (Whitcomb 1985, 47f.). A comparative study of ceramic types was not very yielding, as assemblages, particularly the Late Sasanian, seemed subject to local tradition (Whitcomb 1985, 49). This was also observed with the pottery from Tell Mahuz (Venco Ricciardi 1970, 430) and Kish (Moorey 1978, 142).

The 1960s and 1970s

As archaeologists became gradually more aware of the gap in knowledge regarding the post-Seleucid periods, excavations focused increasingly on Parthian and Sasanian levels. Individual research objectives, however, varied, with some teams concentrating on urban development, while others were more interested in monumental architecture.

An Italian team investigated domestic quarters at Choche and tell Baruda near Bagh-dad (Venco Ricciardi 1967, 1984). Both areas form part of a city site, which was originally thought to be Ctesiphon, but is now identified as the Sasanian foundation of Veh Ardashir (Venco Ricciardi 1984, 49). The pottery analysis, however, did not exceed a preliminary stage and was initially restricted to complete or near-complete vessels (Venco Ricciardi 1984, 50). While early Sasanian pottery types seemed still indebted to Parthian traditions, a genuine style emerged in the later phases (Venco Ricciardi 1984, 53).

German archaeologists conducted excavations at Takht-i Suleiman, an important Zoro-astrian ritual centre in Iranian Azerbaijan (Naumann and Huff 1975). The remains of a large sanctuary with fire temple and surrounding structures were discovered. Coin finds provided the dating evidence for the Sasanian occupation levels (Naumann and Huff 1975, 166). In view of the impressive architecture, research focused on building archaeology, while the relating pottery assemblages were presented only briefly in an interim report (Schnyder 1975, 184–188).

In addition to these regular projects, a number of discrete Sasanian sites were explored through rescue operations.

The fieldwork and documentation at Qal-eh Dukhtar in Fars were part of the conserva-tion programme of the Sasanian king Ardashir's palace near Firuzabad (Huff 1978, 117). Stratigraphic observations, copper-alloy coins and epigraphic evidence provided the framework for the chronology of structures and finds (Huff 1978, 125–140). In accordance with the expertise of the German head of team Dietrich Huff, a building archaeologist, research questions again focused on the architectural structure of the site. Apart from a number of unusual inscribed storage jar rims (Gignoux 1978, 148), only a small proportion of the ceramic material was published (Huff 1978, 144–146).

The Iranian salvage project at Hajiabad (1978), in Fars province, resulted in a more detailed account. Excavations of the Sasanian manor house, its vicinity and a surface survey of the surrounding areas produced a substantial amount of pottery (Azarnoush 1994, 184). Due to circumstances beyond his control, Massoud Azarnoush had to rely exclusively on his original notes for a preliminary evaluation of the ceramic evidence, which inevitably left his conclusions impaired (1994, 183). A collective study with tentative chronological assessment appeared in the final publication (Azarnoush 1994, 183–215).

Pottery chronology again formed an important part in the analyses of material from multi-period sites, where Sasanian levels were enclosed in a sequence of continuous occupation. Two French projects should be mentioned in this context.

At Susa Rémy Boucharlat tried to establish a continuous ceramic sequence based on the results of the long-lasting French mission (Boucharlat 1987). Unsolved stratigraphic relationships and the lack of other reliable chronological evidence, however, left the typology for the Sasanian and early Islamic periods rather vague (Boucharlat 1987, 202–203).

Significant levels of Sasanian occupation were also discovered at Tureng Tepe in northeast Iran, where a French team explored the extensive stratigraphic sequence of the mound and its fortification (Boucharlat and Lecomte 1987). The study of relating pottery assemblages concentrated on questions of chronology and regional distribution (Lecomte 1987, 102–114). Absolute dates were obtained by comparative analysis and C14 dates (Lecomte 1987, 44). Some inconsistencies, however, remained concerning the Sasanian part of the sequence, which indicated a remarkable contrast between the high density of ceramic fragments of the earlier (3rd to 5th centuries) phase VIa and the almost void layers of the later (6th to 7th centuries) phase VIb (Lecomte 1987, 103–109). As this later phase seems to be accompanied by considerable restructuring efforts in the fort (Boucharlat and Lecomte 1987, 42f.), such discrepancy may be explained by differences in the formation process, rather than changes in the development of the ceramic assemblage. With regard to the regional study, strong links were shown between Tureng Tepe and Central Asia, especially Khoresm (Lecomte 1987, 113).

What seems common to many of the projects listed above is that their research activities remained unfinished. Instead we are left with a number of preliminary results and interim reports. The premature end to ongoing studies certainly represents a major factor in the persistent deficit of pottery studies dedicated to the Sasanian period. Other reasons appear to be inherent in the conventional approach. Excavation techniques had not changed radically since the large-scale projects of the 1930s; they were merely executed with more care and in awareness of stratigraphic problems. Trenches were still excavated according to artificial layers, while stratigraphic information was gained primarily through sections (Boucharlat and Lecomte 1987, 18–23). In the process of the archaeological interpretation levels were classified into mixed and well-stratified layers, the latter of which formed the basis for the chronological sequence (Boucharlat 1987, 181; Lecomte 1987, 102–114). Yet, in many cases this sequence of 'well-stratified' assemblages seemed inconclusive in terms of the overall typological development as well as the distinct qualities of the pottery from stratigraphically determined phases (Lecomte 1987, 103–109 and pl. 46–61). This may derive equally from the largely unsystematic sampling strategies and the lack of diagnostic features on a primarily utilitarian group of wares.

Surveys

Parallel to excavations a growing number of projects were dedicated to surface artefact surveys. With the rise of 'new archaeology' during the 1950s and 1960s, the focus of archaeological research shifted from the investigation of discrete historical problems or sites to the study of the general evolutionary patterns of ancient civilisations. Projects in this new field tended to span several consecutive periods. The technique of surface surveys was regarded as the optimal tool for such ambitions allowing a relatively large geographical area to be sampled with comparatively limited resources of time and labour. Ceramics formed the material bases of these surveys and served as a chronological indicator. The enormous increase in the amount of pottery to be examined in a short period of time required new techniques of analysis and led to the introduction of statistical methods.

Central Iraq and southwest Iran, including Mesopotamia and the Persian heartland, were found to be rich test grounds for studies concerned with long-term cultural developments (Wenke 1975, 33–34). The American anthropologist Robert McC Adams started the series of surveys with projects in Khuzistan and Asoristan in the 1950s to 1970s (Adams 1962). In the process it became obvious that a valid ceramic sequence for the later periods, especially the Sasanian, was still missing. Consequently, Adams tried to fill this gap and specifically started exploratory soundings in Gundi Shapur, Iranian Khuzistan (Adams and Hansen 1968), and Tell Abu Sarifa, Iraq (Adams 1970). Both sites were chosen for their late and relatively short phases of occupation. Historical evidence and archaeological reconnaissance point to a Sasanian foundation date for Gundi Shapur (Adams and Hansen 1968, 53–54), while Tell Abu Sarifa represents one in a number of apparently Sasanian sites around Nippur (Adams 1970, 87–88). The complexities of mudbrick stratigraphy, however, were still not matched by the archaeological methodology (Adams and Hansen 1968, 55ff.; Adams 1970, 91). Adams conducted a tentative pottery seriation at Tell Abu Sarifa based on the number of occurrences of diagnostic features per level (Adams 1970, 111–114). His absolute chronology has since been revised (Moorey 1978, 123; Simpson 1996, 100).

Other projects focused on the study of inter-site relationships within their survey area based on the use of advanced statistical applications. Robert Wenke evaluated the role of population growth within the cyclical development of early empires (Wenke 1975). In an attempt to assess the diverse economic functions of the various sites from his Khuzistan survey, he tried to highlight the differences within their ceramic assemblages through multi-dimensional scaling (Wenke 1975, 51–54). The lack of a detailed chronology for Parthian and Sasanian ceramics, however, limited these ambitions (Wenke 1975, 54).

The archaeologist and statistician team Edward and Marguerite Keall started a project exploring statistical methods for pottery analysis. They collected material from different 'pottery regions' in Iraq and Iran in order to define interregional groupings for Parthian through Islamic ceramics (Keall and Keall 1981, 60). Similarities between assemblages were examined by Principal Component Analysis (Keall and Keall 1981, 40). Unfortunately the project could not be completed and preliminary results still seemed too tentative to draw further conclusions (Keall and Keall 1981, 68).

A comprehensive salvage programme of surveys and excavations accompanied the vast hydraulic project on the Saddam Dam in Iraq from 1977 to 1987 (Demirji 1987). Although the Sasanian pottery found at a number of sites on this occasion was limited in quantity, the excavations at Khirbet Deir Situn provided a significant assemblage that formed the basis for a comparative analysis of Late Sasanian die-stamped ceramics (Simpson 1996, 99–100). This specific class of pottery appears to represent a small proportion of the Sasanian ceramic repertoire with a strong regional character (Simpson 1996, 101).

Some surveys were also undertaken in the northeastern part of Iran, including the Atrek Valley and Damghan. Roberta Venco Ricciardi, who had already analysed Sasanian ceramic material from Choche, Tell Baruda and Tell Mahuz in Iraq, aimed at assessing the settlement structure of the upper Atrek Valley, an important route of communication from West to East (1980, 52). Insufficient evidence of the pottery chronology in this part of Iran again limited her interpretation regarding the Sasanian period (Venco Ricciardi 1980, 69–72).

Settlement patterns and land use were also at the centre of Kathryn Maurer Trinkaus' study of the Damghan area (Trinkaus 1983). Trinkaus tried to establish her own pottery sequence based on a seriation of specific time-sensitive attributes (Trinkaus 1981, 147). The fundamental chronological framework was provided by a small number of previously excavated sites, which marked the corner points of each phase (Trinkaus 1981, 149). Despite the coarse and tentative nature of her sequence, Trinkaus made some valuable observations:

(a) The rate in stylistic development seems to vary between different vessel types; or in other words, the life span of different vessel types varies (Trinkaus 1986, 44f).

(b) Ceramics of the Sasanian period show features of mass production, resulting in less distinct vessel types of mediocre quality (Trinkaus 1986, 49).

(c) There is a general trend of increase in decoration and complexity in the composition of shapes (Trinkaus 1986, 50).

The current situation

Following the radical changes in the political landscape of the region after 1979, archaeological activities were interrupted at first. Following the Islamic revolution Iran was for a long time virtually inaccessible for western scholars. Over the past decade Iranian missions have resumed archaeological fieldwork and international collaborations are starting again. In Iraq fieldwork decreased during the 1980s and, after minimal activity between the two wars, is currently on hold.

These particular circumstances left research on Sasanian pottery in a frozen state over much of the past two decades. Reviewing the progress made in the years until the late 1970s and 1980s respectively, it becomes clear that despite considerable efforts to define anchor points for a Sasanian ceramic sequence, scholars were ultimately faced with an imbalance between the archaeological problems and methodological deficiencies. Many of the excavated sites showed a continuous sequence of multi-period occupation (cf. Ctesiphon, Susa, Takht-i Suleiman, Tureng Tepe). The Sasanian levels were frequently enclosed between extensive earlier as well as later Islamic occupation. Earlier material was automatically introduced into Sasanian layers through material reuse and recycling processes, while subsequent Islamic activities on their part disturbed the Sasanian occupation levels, destroying many primary deposits. Archaeologists reacted in different ways to this problem. The majority tried to exclude contaminated assemblages from the beginning and focused on 'well-stratified' material including deposits sealed by floor levels or immured material* (Boucharlat 1987, 201–202; Venco Ricciardi 1984, 49). This has sometimes resulted in considerable loss of data (Boucharlat 1987, 181). Others choose sites with a relatively short occupation span to tackle the problem of stratigraphy and pottery distribution (Adams 1970).

Assemblages were mostly subject to typological analyses. Their prime objective was to define the stylistic development of pottery through a ceramic sequence related to strati-graphically determined phases (Boucharlat 1987, 192–209; Lecomte 1987). With an emphasis on the evolutionary aspects of their samples, these studies were unable to assess the depositional or functional role of assemblages, their composition or their relationship to the overall ceramic repertoire.

From their research perspectives and strategies survey projects seemed to favour more progressive analytical techniques. Dependent on the chronological framework provided by stratified material, most of these, however, were impaired by the lack of a valid ceramic sequence. Surface collections naturally could not compensate for excavated assemblages. Most recent contributions to the subject were again concerned with the correlation of survey data and stratified material in a chronological assessment of the Sasanian and Islamic periods in Oman (Kennet 2004). While restricted to fringe areas of the empire, this study, including new approaches to the analysis and presentation of the material, provided valuable pieces of information to a larger mosaic. Ultimately, though, the understanding of Sasanian pottery is still poor (Boucharlat and Haerinck 1992, 306–307).

ARCHAEOLOGICAL RESEARCH AT MERV

Independent and, for most of the time, completely separated from archaeological activities in Iraq and Iran, the history of research unfolded at Merv as part of the exploration of Russian and Soviet Central Asia. In view of the particularities of this development and its significance in relation to the current study, the archaeological research at Merv is considered here in more detail.

After a period of individual uncoordinated efforts the nature of archaeological investi-gations changed fundamentally with the launch of a permanent mission, the Southern Turkmen Archaeological Comprehensive Expedition (YuTAKE), dedicated to the exploration of southern Turkmenistan.

Early exploration

The first information on the ancient city sites of Merv was published by European travel-lers during the nineteenth century, when influence in the area was disputed between the British and Russian empires. The vast landscape of ruins, visible even from a distance, undoubtedly impressed every foreigner and was described in private correspondence by diplomats as well as travel literature (Masson 1980, 11–16).

Archaeological fieldwork beyond general descriptions of physical remains began only after the annexation of Merv by the Russian Empire in 1884 (Masson 1963, 16). Shortly

---

* It should be noted in this context that 'well-stratified' does not correspond to the definition of 'primary' deposits used in urban archaeology in Britain (Carver 1985, 353, 356).

afterwards the military general A V Komarov, who was part of the Transcaspian provincial government, explored the ancient cities on his own initiative as an archaeological enthusiast. In 1885 he undertook a surface survey in Erk and Gyaur Kala, where one hundred of his Cossacks collected cut stones and about 1500 coins (Filanovich 1974, 18; Masson 1963, 16). A shallow trench opened by him in Erk Kala became the first excavation at Merv. Despite the lack of scientific planning and documentation, Komarov's work was a first step towards archaeological exploration. (He published his observations in the local newspaper *Turkestanskie vedomosti*, No. 3, 1886).

Over the following years decisive changes led to a sharp deterioration of the archaeological environment. The compulsory expropriation of the territory around Bayram-Ali, which was incorporated into imperial property, gave way to the destruction of archaeological monuments outside the ancient city walls through agriculture or in order to gain building material (Masson 1963, 19).

In 1890 the Imperial Archaeological Commission finally established an expedition designed to explore the archaeology of the new Transcaspian province and the ancient ruins of Merv in particular (Zhukovsky 1894, 1). The expedition was headed by the orientalist Valentin Alekseevich Zhukovsky, who spent three months at Merv. Part of his project was dedicated to the archaeological investigation of Erk and Gyaur Kala. The sheer scale and complexity of the site, however, overwhelmed Zhukovsky, who was inexperienced in archaeology. He opened three trial trenches in Erk Kala, one on each of three distinct mounds, in an attempt to assess the chronological span of the site. General working conditions, however, with a lack of workforce and shortage of water, restricted the proceedings of his excavations (Zhukovsky 1894, 193). No further analysis of the finds, including pottery, figurines, clay missiles, bone objects, beads and coins, was undertaken. According to his background as an orientalist, Zhukovsky focused on the historical and literary sources about Merv. Since these mainly concern the period from the Arab conquest, he could only reach as far back as the Sasanian period, to which he attributed Gyaur Kala (Zhukovsky 1894, 114).

Not long after this first systematic approach the American Carnegie Institute sent a team to southern Turkmenistan in an independent mission under the geologist Raphael Pumpelly. Pumpelly's interest in Central Asia was related to the 'Aryan problem', which he hoped to solve with the help of geological and archaeological data (Pumpelly 1908, XXV). During the first season in 1903 he realised the importance of settlement patterns to his project and planned to investigate their emergence in southern Turkmenistan. Aware of his own shortcomings in the field of archaeology, he invited a professional, the German archaeologist Hubert Schmidt, to conduct trial excavations in several places. In this respect the American-German excavations of 1904 were the first professional archaeological excavations at Merv, although Schmidt emphasised their preliminary character. Exploratory trenches were opened in Erk and Gyaur Kala along with several soundings to gain additional information on the stratigraphy of the site. The trenches, however, reaching a depth of up to 12m, were designed as deep soundings and were hardly suitable to expose complete structures. This archaeological limitation prevented a profound understanding of the relationships between the several phases reflected in patches of paved floors, mudbrick walls and wells (Schmidt 1908, 188–191). A preliminary analysis of the ceramic material led to the conclusion that the assemblages remained largely unchanged over a depth of more than 12m (Pumpelly 1908, 192), which illustrates the lack of awareness of the mechanisms involved in the formation of this multi-layered site as well as an undifferentiated approach to plain wares. A similar picture was recognised in the numismatic material. Coins found during the excavations ranged from Parthian to Samanid times and often occurred together in the same layer, aggravating a precise dating (Schmidt 1908, 196f.). Schmidt's excavations highlighted the difficulties faced by archaeologists at Merv, but also offered a first corpus of reference material, including pottery, figurines, coins and epigraphic evidence (ostraca, inscribed bones).

After the October revolution Merv became part of the Turkestan Republic and its archaeological remains were supervised by Turkomstaris, the Turkmen Commission for the conservation of ancient monuments (Masson 1963, 10).

In 1937 further excavations were conducted in Erk Kala by the archaeologists A A Marushchenko from Ashkhabad and Boris B Piotrovsky from the Hermitage Museum. Marushchenko undertook excavations at the main mound of Erk Kala, where he revealed a structure of seemingly post-Sasanian times (Masson 1963, 31–32). No original report has been published on this trench, although some documentation was apparently used later by the permanent Mission (Masson 1963, 32).

Piotrovsky was the first to appreciate the stratigraphic complexities of the mudbrick architecture at Merv. He was particularly interested in the earliest levels of occupation, which he saw reflected in pottery fragments that were incorporated in later brickwork in one of Zhukovsky's trenches (Piotrovsky 1949, 36). In order to reach these levels he re-opened Zhukovsky's trench and continued the sounding down to sterile soil (Piotrovsky 1949, 37, 40). Piotrovsky himself classified the project as exploratory and hoped to obtain material comparable to early sites in Turkmenistan and the Caucasus (Piotrovsky 1949, 35).

The YuTAKE

Over the following years a decisive change and restructuring process took place in Central Asian archaeology resulting in the foundation of the YuTAKE (Southern Turkmen Archaeological Comprehensive Expedition). Two factors were mainly responsible for the new research strategy – the personal engagement of Mikhail Evgen'evich Masson and the development of Soviet archaeology.

Masson, who came from an educated Russian family in Samarkand, recognised the need for a systematic approach to archaeology in Central Asia. His main interest focused on pre-Islamic times, which previously had been considered a hopeless territory for archaeologists (Zhukovsky 1894, 114; Schmidt 1908, 196f). Following his proposal, the Academy of Sciences of the Turkmen SSR established a permanent archaeological expedition, the Southern Turkmen Archaeological Comprehensive Expedition (YuTAKE) (Masson 1963, 9). The YuTAKE united both the official guidelines of Soviet archaeology and the objectives of its head and founder – Masson. Its main focus was the study of the Parthian Society, specifically the investigation of the ancient cities of Nisa and Merv. Already from 1940 Masson had been in charge of the newly founded Department of Archaeology at Tashkent University (Masson 1966, 18). In his position as head of both institutions Masson tied the YuTAKE to the university department and established Merv as its field school for his students from Tashkent. Most of the excavations at Merv, indeed, provided the material for their diplomas and Ph.D. theses. Consequently the archaeological exploration of Merv in many ways bears the personal imprint of the teacher Masson.

Excavation techniques

For the first time, excavations at Merv were organised systematically with clearly defined aims and methods. Excavation techniques and documentation were standardised and procedures regularly published in a special series – the Works of YuTAKE (Trudy YuTAKE, Vol. 1, 1951 to Vol. 17, 1981).

Masson formulated and published his methodology as guidelines for his field school, which were in many respects analogous to those followed by contemporary European scholars (Masson 1966). The starting point was the study of topography and the documentation of what Masson called the 'archaeological micro-relief' through ground reconnaissance (Masson 1966, 36). This served as a guide to future excavations. The archaeological reconnaissance of Gyaur Kala was conducted by Masson himself in 1951 (Masson 1966, 7).

Once a place had been chosen, an exploratory sounding was sunk through the archaeological deposits to assess the stratigraphic sequence. If this proved to be promising, a trench was opened in the form of regular squares no larger than 3 × 3m, which were excavated in artificial spits of 50cm. These were standard recommendations that could be modified and refined according to archaeological circumstances (Masson 1966, 39).

Masson personally understood archaeology as a branch of historical science, which was studying 'the development of societies based on their material traces' (Masson 1966, 34). Archaeological observations and finds were only valuable in their function as a historical source. This link between archaeological object and history was perceived as inherent and is often reflected in individual aspects of interpretation. Perhaps as a result of this historical emphasis, Masson's guidelines do not contain any instructions on how to process and analyse archaeological finds, such as pottery and small finds.

Theoretical background

The October Revolution was not confined to political change alone, but profoundly transformed the perception of science and influenced the development of academic subjects. The importance of archaeology in Soviet research was based on the understanding of its value in relation to Marxist ideas on history (Klejn 1997, 25ff). Marx himself showed great interest in history and archaeology as a testing ground for his global theory known as historic materialism (Landshut 1971). This treatise provided the basic concepts for archaeological schools in early Soviet times (Klejn 1997, 29, 153f). The main principle taken from Marxist theory was that history is regarded as a progressive development expressed in changes of social and economic formations. At the heart of this development lies the improvement of the means of production, a concept known as the primacy of production (Klejn 1997, 99). Central Asia was regarded as particularly suitable for the study of historic development, since it provided large multi-period sites showing the various stages of social development on a territory, where large empires interacted with nomadic tribes (Klejn 1997, 43; Masson 1960, 5). Appropriately, the aim of the YuTAKE was the periodisation of the history of Turkmenistan (Ovezov 1970, 6).

Marxist principles were constantly discussed, reshaped and reinterpreted within the various schools and branches of Soviet archaeology. Some concepts received dogmatic value, albeit in a simplified form (Klejn 1997, 30, 157). Thus the progress of historic development was determined as linear, starting with early societies, developing into slave-owning societies and eventually into feudalism (Klejn 1997, 99). The single phases were then immediately correlated with historic periods defined by empires or dynasties, forming a basic chronological reference scheme. For Merv, an equivalent historical model transpires from many contemporary YuTAKE publications. A basic reconstruction is illustrated in Table 1.1.

Research priorities were set according to this pre-defined model and focused on the main evolutionary phases: late Bronze and Iron Age down to the Achaemenid period ≅ 'early societies', Parthian empire ≅ 'slave-owning society' and eleventh to twelfth centuries ≅ 'feudalism' (Ovezov 1970, 6).

YuTAKE excavations at Merv

In concordance with the research tasks, the programme proceeded in several stages. Surface survey and pottery distribution provided the basic outline of the settlement structure. The exploration of the earliest phases, mostly overlain by extensive later deposits, was restricted to soundings, which were intended to determine the boundaries of the first settlement at Merv (Filanovich 1974, 24, 35f). Parthian and early medieval structures were then more closely examined in larger excavations (Filanovich 1974, 21–23). About twenty-five trenches were opened in total, six in Erk Kala and nineteen in Gyaur Kala. Sometimes exploratory soundings were just documented as reference points without further excavation (Filanovich 1974, 21); sometimes several soundings were conducted in the same trench (Filanovich 1974, 67f).

The YuTAKE nomenclature illustrated in Figure 1.2 was not always consistent, but generally follows a basic division between the single parts of the city sites, Erk and Gyaur Kala, and a qualitative differentiation between sounding (S) and trench (T). Some of the soundings with independent numbers were renamed after they had been transformed into a trench.

Architectural plans and their gradual structural alterations were established from the open excavations in squares. Archaeological deposits were roughly subdivided into floors, infills, collapse or rubbish pits. Stratigraphic and chronological information was mostly gained from the sections of the trenches and soundings.

Table 1.1 Model of the historic development in Central Asia as reconstructed from YuTAKE publications.

Progressive historical development as presented in Soviet Central Asian archaeology based on the historical materialism of Karl Marx	*Related periods*
Early agricultural societies	Yaz-depe (largely equalling the Achaemenid period, 6th–4th centuries BC)
Formation of cities	Transitional period expressed in co-occurrences of old and new pottery shapes
Slave-owning society	Seleucid and Parthian Period (3rd century BC–3rd century AD)
Crisis of slave-owning society	Crisis expressed in lower quality of products and decrease of settlement, partly reaching into the Sasanian period
Early feudal society	Sasanian Period (3rd–7th centuries AD)

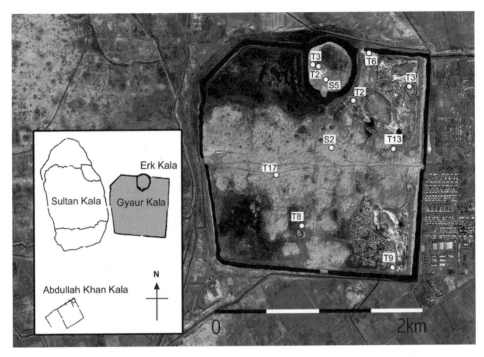

Figure 1.2: Plan of the major YuTAKE excavations.

Artificial spits (cf *Excavation techniques*, above) varied in depth, but seemed to span an average of 25cm. The basic stratigraphic unit for further analysis was the cultural layer; spits, by contrast, were used only as reference points of depth. A cultural layer could comprise several metres and generally described the continuous occupation of one chronological phase (cf. Filanovich 1974, 25ff; Usmanova 1963a, 27ff).

Chronology

The chronological phases were determined by pottery. Piotrovsky had paralleled the earliest pottery shapes found at Merv with vessels from the Anau IV period, named after the Bronze Age type site at the foothills of the Kopet Dag mountains near Ashgabat (Piotrovsky 1949, 37). These formed the beginning of a ceramic sequence based on a qualitative assessment of the pottery assemblages from the single consecutive cultural layers. The variety of shapes present in an assemblage was selectively documented in pottery drawings and served as the basis for the classification of cultural layers. Linked together, these drawings provided an illustrated ceramic sequence. No formal criteria are stated for the selection of ceramic shapes to be drawn and this process was most likely guided by individual perception. From the discussions of ceramic material in the YuTAKE reports it becomes obvious that generally all vessels of an assemblage were regarded as contemporary (Filanovich 1974, 82; Katsuris and Buryakov 1963, 141–146; Usmanova 1963b, 184ff).

Differences between the assemblages were interpreted as chronological development. This resulted in a blurred ceramic typology. Certain vessel types seemed to have a life span of several hundred years (Filanovich 1974, 82), apparently testifying to a rather slow development. Depending on the stratigraphic definition and extent of the cultural layer, this also led to an accumulation of shapes over several phases towards the upper end of the layer, since older vessel forms seemingly remained in use, while new ones had already been introduced (Katsuris and Buryakov 1963, 142–146). The only specialised study on pottery from Merv (Rutkovskaya 1962) was based on an undifferentiated generalisation of the phasing established by individual excavators, and consequently reflects the same inconsistencies regarding the life span and size of assemblages. L M Rutkovskaya took a typological approach in her pottery analysis with detailed descriptions of the shapes and comparative material, which generally provided a useful reference catalogue.

Absolute dates were based on numismatic evidence. The earliest coins found at Merv belong to the Graeco-Bactrian kings of the third century BC. From Parthian times onwards the city had its own mint up to early Islamic times. Coin finds occurred fairly regularly in occupational layers, although in limited numbers. The coins found in a cultural layer determined its absolute date range, the latest coin usually marking the upper end (Filanovich 1974, 54). Thus the lower floor level of a structure in trench 6, where late Parthian and early Sasanian coins were found, was dated to the second to third centuries AD (Katsuris and Buryakov 1963, 146).

Archaeological interpretation

The archaeological interpretation is characterised by two aspects: the development as reflected in the change of material culture through consecutive phases and the social function of the buildings excavated in the various trenches.

The ultimate aim of the phasing procedures was to separate discrete stages that were regarded as representative of the relevant time period and consequently comparable with each other. Once dated, each phase was linked to one of the pre-defined evolutionary stages of society and analysed with regard to its specific role in history. Most prominent in this respect was the Parthian period, which corresponded to the stage of slave-owning society. According to the stratigraphic analysis of the trenches and soundings, Parthian Merv was a blooming city with a flourishing economy and trade (Filanovich 1974, 38). At the end of this period the stratigraphic evidence apparently supported the assumption of a general recession visible in the abandonment of structures, believed to illustrate the so-called crisis of the slave-owning society (cf. Filanovich 1974, 53; Katsuris and Buryakov 1963, 152). Perceived changes in the quality of materials were interpreted in the same way (Filanovich 1974, 67; Rutkovskaya 1962).

Another aspect characteristic of the theoretical background of the archaeological interpretation was an interest in manufacturers and workshops. Kiln or furnace sites were especially targeted to gain information on the organisation of labour and economy, which corresponded to the Marxist principle of the primacy of production. A total of five different production areas were published in YuTAKE reports (Filanovich 1974, 23; Katsuris and Buryakov 1963, 154f; Usmanova 1963, 164).

Outlook

The work of YuTAKE certainly represents a landmark in the archaeological exploration of Soviet Central Asia. Never before has a mammoth project such as this been organised over such a long period of time, lasting almost forty years. Even more remarkable is the highly efficient organisation, which, supported by a favourable merger of a university department and an excavation unit, provided a permanent and stable team of archaeologists from the same school that guaranteed maximum continuity. In its clearly formulated aims and methodology the YuTAKE is exemplary for archaeological programmes.

The problems outlined above resulted from a mismatch of imposed research objectives and archaeological reality. In their practical methodology YuTAKE excavations followed the traditional scheme also used by many projects mentioned in the previous section (cf. Boucharlat 1987). The far-reaching historical inferences, however, seem unjustified considering the limits of stratigraphic information. As far as the struggle for differentiation of the archaeological data is concerned, the YuTAKE shows parallels with some Western survey projects (cf Wenke 1987). In contrast to these, an exploratory approach or negative result, however, was impossible within the regulation of the academic regime. The theoretical model remained unchanged, while the archaeological argumentation appeared overstretched. Most publications still distinguish clearly between the presentation of archaeological situations and finds and their interpretation, and therefore continue to provide a valuable source for new research.

Fieldwork has not stopped after the breakdown of the Soviet Union and archaeological investigations were continued by a number of international teams. In 1992 the International Merv Project (IMP) joined the excavations of the YuTAKE at the site and established a collaboration, which from the closure of the YuTAKE in 1998 until the year 2000 cooperated with the Institute of the History of Turkmenistan. The current Turkmen–British collaboration of the Ancient Merv Project is set up between the Institute of Archaeology, University College London, and the Institute for the Study of the Cultural Heritage of the Peoples of Central Asia, Ashgabat, and the Cultural Ministry of Turkmenistan. During the 1990s an Italian–Turkmen–Russian project conducted a survey of the northern part of the oasis, accomplishing an archaeological map of this area (Gubaev *et al* 1998). This project provided valuable new data, particularly with respect to the earlier phases of occupation in the Merv oasis. South of the oasis Polish–Turkmen excavations at Serakhs uncovered the remains of a Sasanian fire temple and surrounding structures at the site of Mele Hairam (Kaim 2002). These ongoing efforts will further contribute to our understanding of the historical periods at Merv and will help reshape our image of Sasanian archaeology.

– 2 –

THE SETTING

GEOGRAPHICAL SETTING

Ancient Merv is situated in an oasis formed by the delta of the River Murghab flowing north from the Afghan mountains into the Karakum desert (Figure 2.1). From its spring at about 2600m above sea-level the Murghab remains constantly below the zone of permanent snow or glaciers and receives its water solely from seasonal melt and rainfall (Kirsta 1984, 39), which makes the river particularly sensitive to short-term fluctuations in precipitation. Before reaching the Karakum desert, the Murghab is joined by a number of smaller mountain rivers and two more significant tributaries, the Kashan and the Kushka. Both these tributaries and the Murghab are characterised by strong erosive processes, which

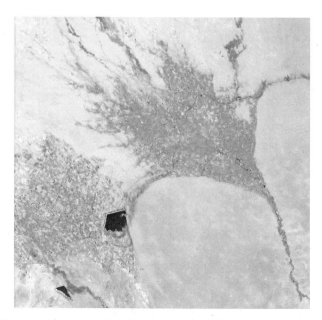

Figure 2.1: Satellite image showing the Merv (right) and Tadjen (left) oases.

were certainly a major factor in the evolution of the oasis. Recent inspections measured the annual alluvial deposits near the town of Takhta Bazar, situated about 200km south of ancient Merv, as 7.6 million tonnes (Kirsta 1984, 39). Changes in the delta system were crucial for the development of settlement patterns in the oasis which appear to have gradually changed over the centuries (Salvatori 1998). Some of the early centres of occupation now lie off the fringe of the oasis (Cremaschi 1998, 18). The correlation between sites of different consecutive periods, however, is not yet fully understood, as evidence from the recent geomorphological survey in the oasis suggests, and may be more complex than first assumed (Salvatori 1998, 57f.). Merv itself is located in the eastern part of the oasis. The ancient site consists of a number of adjacent cities representing discrete phases of occupation, the earliest of which, Erk Kala, dates back to the Late Iron Age (cf Herrmann *et al* 1993, 40). Gradually the city expanded and the citadel was eventually shifted, resulting in the characteristic plan of the site (Figure 2.2). Merv was the principal city of the oasis for the historical periods (Loginov and Nikitin 1993a–c). On the one hand, its location within a fertile oasis on the gateway to Central Asia secured Merv a strategic position in both commercial and military affairs (Herrmann *et al* 1993, 40). Its natural boundaries, on the other hand, led to considerable isolation which would have also affected the traffic of goods with caravans from the adjacent territories. Coming from the Iranian side, the way led first over the Kopet-Dag mountain range and then another 200km through the desert and past the neighbouring oasis of the Tedzhen River. On the northeastern side the River Amu-Darya, the ancient Oxus, provided one of the main arteries in this part of Central Asia. However, the banks of the Amu-Darya are about 200km away from Merv, separated by the Karakum desert. The river valley of the Murghab offered probably better travel conditions coming from the area of Herat to the south. Whatever route travellers may have chosen, the journey to Merv was not an easy one, and its geographical isolation should be taken into account considering the mechanisms of change in the material culture of the city.

HISTORICAL SETTING

For a long time the political landscape of Antiquity was determined by two superpowers – Rome in the West and Persia in the East. After the states of the Diadochi, the successors to Alexander's empire, had waned in power, their territories were rearranged with Rome moving into the eastern Mediterranean and as far as Syria, while the lands held previously by the Seleucids fell into Parthian hands. The Parthians, themselves of eastern Iranian origin, were eventually challenged by one of their own provincial governors, Ardashir, king of Fars, a descendant of Sasan (Wiesehöfer 2001, 153, 169).

The Sasanians were the last of the great dynasties to rule pre-Islamic Iran from AD 224 to the Arab conquest AD 651. Ancient Iran was a vast empire of distinct geographical regions and ethnic communities situated in a vital strategic position for the trade of luxury goods from China and India to the Near East and the Mediterranean. In defence of this position and pressed by the new political situation emerging from the constant migration of peoples along the northern and eastern fringes of Iran, the Persian kings spent much of their time in battle. When Ardashir I established his rule over the whole empire in the first decades of the 3rd century AD, his Parthian predecessors had been engaged in a long-lasting struggle with their Roman neighbours over the common border along the Euphrates. This conflict, which was primarily fought over for control of the rich trading cities in

Syria, continued to dominate the agenda of Sasanian foreign politics for another 200 years (Shaw 2001, 143; Wiesehöfer 2001, 194–195).

Meanwhile at the opposite border of the empire Hunnic and Turcic tribes exerted growing pressure on the eastern frontier, prompting several military campaigns during the fifth and early sixth centuries. Following the submission of the former Kushan kingdom to Sasanian sovereignty in the 3rd century, the Sasanian administration failed to contain the movements of pastoral tribes of various ethnic origins arriving in waves from the Eurasian steppes and forming powerful political alliances on Bactrian territory (Frye 1984, 346–349). The success of the Hephtalites, who repeatedly defeated the Sasanian army and killed King Peroz I in AD 484, is the most renowned episode of this period (Frye 1984, 322; Wiesehöfer 2001, 173).

Early in the seventh century the power balance between the Byzantine and Sasanian empires was overthrown and King Khusro II succeeded in expanding Iranian dominance over Syria and into Egypt. This ambitious war, however, exhausted the military resources of the Sasanian army. Lasting disputes over dynastic succession and internal crises finally prepared the ground for the unforeseen success of the united Arab tribes, who conquered the entire empire in under two decades (Shaw 2001, 163).

The four centuries of Sasanian rule over Iran coincided with the fundamental changes that marked the transition from late Antiquity to early medieval times manifest in a reorientation towards cultural homogeneity, nationalistic movements and an emphasis on religious identity (Gnoli 1989, 162–164). Early on in their reign the Sasanians established a systematically organised Zoroastrian church, which was consciously focused on its Iranian roots (Gnoli 1989, 177–178). The closeness of the court to the Zoroastrian religion, however, did not automatically result in a continuous suppression of other beliefs. Persecutions of minority religions occurred sporadically and were politically motivated, but for most of the time religious practice was relatively liberal and at times even Christians or Jews could become members of the royal family (Fowden 2001, 95).

Indeed, despite its strictly Iranian ideology, the Sasanian Empire probably experienced more demographical fluctuation than its predecessors due to the large-scale deportation and resettlement policy pursued by the king of kings (Christensen 1993, 67–70; Wiesehöfer 2001, 192–194). These programmes unwittingly also led to the spread of minority religions in Iran, specifically Christianity (Schwaigert 1989, 19–20; EncIr VII, 1994, 298f). From the Sasanian viewpoint the deportation of entire populations from the conquered Syrian cities served as a demonstration of power, a punishment, but also constituted an effective means to economically revive certain parts of the empire by importing useful skills specifically in the field of engineering and trade. Many of the impressive irrigation systems and bridges throughout Mesopotamia, Khuzistan and Fars were built by prisoners of war and deportees (Christensen 1993, 68–71, 107–112, 176; Wiesehöfer 2001, 190). This pattern of intense urbanisation suggested by both textual and archaeological evidence is regarded by some scholars as a key area for the understanding of the Sasanian world, at least as far as the southwestern part of the empire is concerned (Wenke and Pyne 1990, 242–243).

Although cities seem to have played an important part with their trade and industrial activities, the Sasanians are not characterised as exponents of an urban culture. On the contrary, their economy and social structure were based increasingly on feudal systems (Gnoli 1989, 157–158; Wiesehöfer 2001, 191–192). During the sixth century a far-reaching programme of administrative, fiscal and military reforms was conceived resulting in a strongly centralised form of government. Parts of these reforms concerned the introduction of a new social class, the *dehqans*, who were landed magnates responsible for tax collection (Tafazzoli 2000, 41, 45). Many aspects of the administrative structures and cultural life of the Late Sasanian Empire survived long into the Islamic period. One of these were the *dehqans*, who not only maintained their status, but moreover became conservators and advocates of Iranian traditions for centuries under Arab domination (Gnoli 1989, 173–174; Tafazzoli 2000, 53–54).

Another facet of this late and 'canonical' phase in Sasanian history was the highly cultured life of the court and open-mindedness widely associated with the king (Wiese-höfer 2001, 216–221). When the Neoplatonic Academy in Athens was closed by the Byzan-tine Emperor Justinian, King Khusro I Anushirvan welcomed its philosophers at his court (Wiesehöfer 2001, 217). Accomplished manners and education were a prerequisite for the aristocratic lifestyle and the kings promoted learned institutions. The medical school in the city of Gundi Shapur was founded in Sasanian times and flourished for centuries, enjoying great fame throughout the Islamic world (Wiesehöfer 2001, 218).

The history of Sasanian Iran finally comes to an end at Merv in the mid-seventh cen-tury. Gradually the Arab army invaded Iran, driving the last king of kings Yazdgard III further and further to the East, where Merv became his final refuge in AD 651. This final chapter of Sasanian history is well illustrated in secondary and tertiary sources. Several different variations are preserved. In the Chronicle Anonymous we just find a brief note that Yazdgard ended his life at Merv (Nöldeke 1893, 33). According to Sebeos, an Armen-ian author of the seventh century, the king was killed by Hephthalite troops which were supposed to help him against the Arabs (Thompson and Howard-Johnston 1999, 135). Arabic sources report that Yazdgard negotiated with the Hephthalite army following advice from the *marzban*, the governor of Merv, Mahoe, who betrayed his king. Yazdgard was murdered by the Hephthalite troops (Marquart 1901, 67).

Apart from its role in the final chapters of pre-Islamic Persia, Merv is hardly mentioned in the literary sources available on Sasanian Iran. The predominant focus on western Iran, explicable by the overwhelming historiographical tradition of the classical world and the exact opposite so far as the Central Asian steppes are concerned, leave Merv at the periphery of the historical conscience of this period.

Merv in Sasanian times

With this background of rather poor and scattered evidence the reconstruction of Merv's historical position under Sasanian rule appears particularly difficult. Apart from the rock inscriptions of the early kings and some of their dignitaries no primary epigraphic or literary sources on the Sasanians and their politics are preserved. Thus our knowledge of the regions in eastern Iran is generally confined to very basic levels. Merv is listed among the provinces ruled by Shapur I (AD 240–272) in the king's inscription on the Ka'ba-i Zardusht at Naqsh-i Rustam in Fars (Wiesehöfer 2001, 184). Although this first official reference is valuable in order to ascertain Merv's political affiliation, it does not provide any help in assessing the province's character and relative significance. In the following section three groups of primary evidence are used in an attempt to elucidate different aspects of the city's life during the Sasanian period.

The evidence

COINS

Numerous coins found at Merv and elsewhere have offered compensation for the lack of primary evidence and consequently hold a very prominent place in the historical study of Central Asia (Rawlinson 1912, xxi). The information we gain from coins is diversified depending on the perspective of our consideration, whether we see them as single specimens or as part of the monetary system.

Within the Sasanian world coins served as money to facilitate the transactions and economic activities of the population at various levels of society. Controlled and issued by the ruler, along with its economic function coinage communicated through images his main ideological concepts to a widespread and heterogeneous audience. In the Roman Empire coin issues were used extensively for political propaganda (Baharal 1996, vii, 6). To a certain extent they fulfilled a similar purpose for the Sasanian king. Sasanian coins usually follow a fairly standardised scheme of representation, which in abbreviated form illustrates the author of the particular issue or king, who is distinguished by his personal crown. Each king carefully designed his own crown, which could even change shape within his reign after an interruption or disturbance of his rule (Göbl 1971, 10f). The reverse shows either a symbol for his justified rule or a reference to the official Zoroastrian religion. Mintmarks are testified in Early Sasanian times only for a small number of minting places, but occur regularly in later Sasanian times. Fortunately the coins minted at Merv are mostly marked for the period studied here, ie the 5th to 7th centuries (Göbl 1971, 25).

During several decades of intensive research conducted in the field of Sasanian numismatics a general typology and classification of coin issues was established, that with minor corrections is still valid today (Alram 1986; Göbl 1967). Greater difficulties occur in evaluating the entire monetary system, since our knowledge is restricted to a limited amount of coin issues from few minting places. Basic patterns of the economic and financial system of the Sasanian state are traceable. Yet its internal structures and payment modalities on all different levels of political, administrative and military organisation remain obscure, including the frequency and circulation of issues.

One major problem affecting the interpretation of numismatic evidence lies in the diverse nature of the sources, being dependent on (often private) collections and the variable progress of archaeological excavations. Specimens that were regarded as worth collecting are mainly higher denominations, ie silver and gold coins. The silver drahm appears to be the Sasanian standard denomination (Göbl 1971, 25), which served also for international transactions, such as payments of tribute as is suggested in literary sources (Wright 1882, § X). Material from collections of mainly unspecified provenance contributes only generally to the knowledge of the monetary system and is usually less accessible for further historical interpretation. In the case of the silver drahm archaeological discoveries outside the Sasanian boundaries help to define its mode of use. Coin finds on Chinese territory indicate that the Hephthalite auxiliary troops employed by Kavad were paid in silver drahms (Thierry 1993, 116–118). Nothing is known, however, about the payment of Sasanian army units (Göbl 1971, 26). In fact the status and organisation of the Sasanian army remain controversial issues. Rather diverse, if not opposing, theoretical positions derive from the different evaluation and use of the available literary evidence. Due to the lack of primary sources, historians are forced to turn to later Arabic and Persian authors such as Al Tabari and Firdausi, whose works rely on lost Pahlavi originals (Rubin 1995,

234ff). However, it is very difficult to filter additions and passages, which might reflect features of a later system (Howard-Johnston 1995, 170–171).

Scholars who follow the Arab sources closely believe that up to the late 5th to the beginning of the 6th century the Persian king did not maintain a standing army (Göbl 1971, 26; Rubin 1995, 279–290). Consequently any military recruitment would automatically result in an increase of coin issues (Göbl 1971, 26). Only with the introduction of far-reaching reforms particularly in the field of logistics could a professional army be established under King Khusro II Anushirwan in the 6th century. This was made possible and financed by the new system of taxation (Rubin 1995, 290–291).

Those who judge the Arabic literature more critically give less weight to the alleged reforms arguing that the obvious balance between the Roman and Sasanian armies indicates an already well-advanced military system on the Sasanian side in earlier times (Howard-Johnston 1995, 160–169). In this case, a strong fluctuation of coin issues would rather be connected to payments outside the Sasanian Empire or changes in economy and monetary policy.

In contrast to the silver coins from collections, those discovered during archaeological excavations are mainly lower copper-alloy denominations that served primarily the local market and did not have such a wide geographical range (Alram 1986, 12; Göbl 1971, 27; MacDowall 1979, 312). Apart from single specimens that occur regularly in archaeological contexts, excavations at Merv have revealed seven hoards of up to thirty-two copper-alloy coins, apparently contents of purses that were deposited for private reasons (Loginov and Nikitin 1993c, 292–294). Since the knowledge of these lower denominations is related to fieldwork, new discoveries might change the numismatic landscape radically.

As mentioned above, many topics concerning the financial system are not yet sufficiently known or studied to allow immediate inferences, although the information gathered by numismatists to date presents a picture of the fluctuations of issues between the rules of different kings. In the case of Merv a reasonable amount of numismatic data collected during extensive archaeological research provides the basis for an evaluation of the local minting activity of the single rulers. Therefore an analysis of the coinage seems justified and has been conducted recently (Loginov and Nikitin 1993a–c).

The numismatic evidence relating to Merv consists of three groups, including (1) issues found and minted at Merv, (2) issues found at Merv but minted in other provinces, and (3) issues minted at Merv but preserved only in collections.

Irregularities of issues released at Merv may have different causes; they probably reflect a reaction to changes in the local market, ie in this case the oasis of Merv (Loginov and Nikitin 1993a, 230). Frequently an increase in coin issues has been related to military activities of the Sasanians (cf Loginov and Nikitin 1993a–c). Locally at Merv the mere presence of an army unit would have resulted in an expansion of copper-alloy denominations in use. These attempts of interpretation must be carefully evaluated with regard to the actual state of archaeological research. The following paragraphs focus on the historic value of numismatic evidence for the city of Merv. All difficulties related to its use as a chronological device will be discussed in the archaeological section (see below).

BUDDHIST TEXTS

A more eloquent source is reflected in two Buddhist manuscripts found at Merv. They were written in Brahmi with black ink on leaves of bark (Vorob'eva-Desyatovskaya 1983, 69).

Both manuscripts were discovered inside ceramic vessels. One was found during archaeological work on the northern facade of the stupa in Gyaur Kala, hidden in the famous 'Merv-vase', a painted amphora-like vessel. Pugachenkova assigns the restoration of the northern part of the building, where the painted vessel was carefully bricked up, to the fifth phase of the stupa now dated according to coin finds in the foundation to the 6th century. Earlier attempts to attribute the stupa to the late Parthian period have proved wrong and have recently been corrected (Pugachenkova and Usmanova 1995, 56ff; Stavisky 1996, 29). Regrettably this manuscript has not been restored or deciphered (Vorob'eva-Desyatovskaya 1983, 69). It is currently stored in the Institute of Restoration of the Russian Ministry of Culture.

The second, a much more extensive manuscript comprising 150 pages, was deposited in a ceramic vessel dated to the 6th to 7th centuries for 'archaeological reasons' (Vorob'eva-Desyatovskaya 1983, 69). Unfortunately the publication does not include a picture or drawing of this second vase, so we know nothing about its shape or original use. The text may be divided into an older part with traces of ancient restoration and a better preserved one in Indian Brahmi (Vorob'eva-Desyatovskaya 1983, 69f). Apart from the manuscript, the ceramic vessel also contained a small stone statuette of a Buddha and bronze coins of Khusro I (531–579) dated to his eighteenth regnal year (Vorob'eva-Desyatovskaya 1983, 69). This vase again appears to have been deliberately set into the brickwork of a second stupa to the east of Gyaur Kala, which unfortunately, due to agricultural cultivation, is completely demolished (Pugachenkova and Usmanova 1995, 76). According to the archaeological reassessment of both sanctuaries, this extramural stupa is believed to belong to the second half of the 6th century (Pugachenkova and Usmanova 1995, 61). Interestingly both manuscripts were deposited in exactly the same way and, it seems, for the same purpose, which we might describe as reliquary function. Although the texts themselves are completely independent from Merv in content, they give an account of the Buddhist community that is the only religion explicitly testified by architectural remains inside the city walls.

SYNODICAL LISTS

The Synodical lists of the 'Nestorian' or Eastern Syriac Church (Chabot 1902) form a collection of acts that contain the rules established and decisions taken at each of the 'Nestorian' Synods. As a sign of approval each bishop present had to sign the act with his name and title. In some cases those who lived too far away and could not attend the Synod sent a personal letter of approval.

These acts were compiled in the 8th century (Gillman and Klimkeit 1999, 209) and are preserved in manuscripts in the Chaldaean Convent at Al-Qosh near Mosul in northern Iraq. Two 'modern' copies are now kept: one complete version in the Vatican library (all three volumes) and a reduced one (only the second volume) in the Bibliothèque Nationale in Paris. The latter provided the basis for Chabot's publication (Chabot 1902).

As far as the signatures of the acts are concerned no doubt has been raised about their authenticity, and they form a most important source with regard to the history of Merv. The relevant signatures were produced by members of the synod, who were resident at Merv. In this respect the Synodical lists bear features of primary evidence. They attest not only to the mere existence of a Christian community in the city at a certain time, but the title of its representative also implies the position of this community within the 'Nestorian'

Church. Research in the field of Sasanian administrative structure further points to a relation between ecclesiastical and state administration (Gyselen 1989).

Historical reconstruction

Sasanian kings started to issue coins at Merv from the beginning of their rule with Ardashir I (AD 224–241) (Loginov and Nikitin 1993a, 226f). The long reign of Shapur II (AD 309–379) is reflected in the large numbers of coins in his name found both in Soviet and IMP excavations at the city. Single issues minted during this period bear the name of a king of Merv under Shapur, giving rise to the assumption that the local mint was also used by the Kushano–Sasanian rulers in charge of Bactria, which had come under Sasanian dominance. Details of the chronology and extent of these Kushano–Sasanian issues, however, are still disputed and no definite answer can be given as to Merv's role within the Kushano–Sasanan administration (Wiesehöfer 2001, 164).

Another extraordinary coin issue is preserved from king Yazdgard I (399–421). The reverse shows a cross in combination with the ribbon (Loginov and Nikitin 1993c, 271f). The ribbon forms part of most crowns of the Sasanian king and as pars *pro toto* gradually developed into a symbol of Sasanian rule (Göbl 1971, 10f). Considering the rather strict concept of Sasanian coin imagery it is quite striking to see a religious symbol apparently alien to the Sasanian king taking such a prominent place. Furthermore, these coins proclaim a relation of the Christian belief with the Sasanian king by combining their symbols, ribbons and cross. Local authorities of minting places apparently enjoyed a certain amount of freedom; still, it seems impossible to release coins whose image would explicitly counteract official policies. Hence the occurrence of this issue seems to mark a change in the relationship between the king and the Christian Church.

Indeed it was under Yazdgard's reign that the first Synod of the Persian Church took place in AD 410 in Seleucia (Chabot 1902, 253–275). At this Synod initial steps of a separation from the Western Church were introduced and confirmed during the following period, which helped to relieve the Christian communities in the Sasanian Empire, since their religious identity had made them allies of the arch-enemy Byzantium in the eyes of the king (Wiesehöfer 2001, 202). The special bronze issue may have signalised the king's approval of the separatist movement in the Iranian Church. During Yazdgard's reign Merv saw an increasing Christian community that under his successor for the first time entered the Synodical record (Chabot 1902, 285). Whether (in the course of a broader political concept) such coins were released in other parts of the empire or whether they present a local peculiarity stimulated by an encouraged Christian community at Merv (cf Loginov and Nikitin 1993c, 272; cf also Göbl 1971, 5) remains unknown for the moment. This issue is so far known only from Merv (Loginov and Nikitin 1993c, 271f).

A number of fifth-century coin issues seem to provide a glimpse of the city's position during the Hephtalite crisis and its related military campaigns. Although not a single coin of Bahram V has to date been found at Merv, a large number of silver specimens known from collections are attributed to the mint of the city. Furthermore, these constitute a high percentage of all Sasanian coins preserved from the reign of Bahram (Loginov and Nikitin 1993c, 272–273). The lack of archaeological data despite intensive surface survey and excavations is remarkable, though it may be explained by the fact that very few drahms have been found by archaeologists in general and there may have been no or only a few copper coins released at Merv during Bahram's reign. As mentioned initially, our knowledge on the circulation of Sasanian copper coins is still very diffuse and we can only assume that the local market survived on earlier issues.

The high percentage of silver coins minted at Merv has been explained by the king's campaigns against the Chionites (Loginov and Nikitin 1993c, 272). These large numbers of drahms, according to numismatic studies, inspired the minting of local issues in Central Asia (Loginov and Nikitin 1993c, 272; MacDowall 1979, 312). Bahram's eastern campaigns are the first in a long series of confrontations with the Chionite or Hephthalite neighbours. Merv appears to have played an important role in this first period of war, providing a huge amount of silver drahms. The money was partly needed for payments agreed to the Chionites or Hephthalites (Neusner 1986, 178). Howard-Johnston (1995, 219) interprets it as proof that the Sasanian army at that time was paid in silver.

During the reign of Bahram's successor Yazdgard II, coins, both silver and bronze, are attested again in the archaeological material from Merv (Loginov and Nikitin 1993c, 273). The political role of Merv within his Hephtalite warfare is not clearly defined. Yazdgard apparently preferred to retreat further into Sasanian territory to organise his war strategy. Possibly Merv appeared too exposed to Hephthalite activities, though the city still minted coins on a modest scale (Loginov and Nikitin 1993c, 273).

An enigmatic issue is attributed approximately to that period, since it occurs together with coins from Yazdgard II and his successor Peroz (Loginov and Nikitin 1993c, 273). This issue is interesting, because it consists of coins which were overstruck showing just a single object that has been described as a 'fork-like device' (Loginov and Nikitin 1993c, 273). The original image is not identifiable. Such an issue appears very unusual, compared to the standardised concept generally assumed for Sasanian coinage (Göbl 1971, 5). Traces of overstriking are even more notable in this respect. These anonymous coins and the irregular issues of Yazdgard II described might suggest that the Sasanian king had lost control over Merv for some time during the 5th century (Zeimal 1996, 246).

Numismatic evidence once more presents the main source of information on Merv for the reign of Peroz (459–484). However, only a few coins have been minted at Merv in the beginning of his reign, while the majority of specimens found at the site probably derive from the mint of Amul, situated in Tabaristan (Loginov and Nikitin 1993c, 273–274). Here again a relation of this phenomenon to the eastern campaigns of the king seems quite close at hand (cf Loginov and Nikitin 1993a–c). In this case, the strategic base may be assumed in Tabaristan: Merv would have served merely as a station en route to the front line. The enduring critical situation at the eastern border with the last battle lost may have caused a further retreat. Merv might still have appeared too unstable or close to the front line to have provided a safe base for a military camp.

With the constant changes in the number and quality of the numismatic evidence it appears difficult at the moment to reach a profound understanding of the situation of Merv in the 5th century. First, we find no coins in the city at all, but sufficient proof for minting activity from examples in various collections. Moreover, we see the influence of these issues reflected in other areas. While local evidence is rather poor, we note many coins from neighbouring Tabaristan, and chronologically, somehow related with this period, a most unusual anonymous issue. At the moment the inequality of this numismatic picture, the differences between data from collections, exclusively silver, and data obtained from archaeological work, mostly bronze, and the lack of comparable material from adjacent areas put a narrow frame to any further evaluation.

The most reasonable conclusion may be to consider that during the 5th century the

Merv coinage reflects the city's rather unstable and changing position. Undoubtedly Merv was at times immediately affected by the struggle between the Sasanian king and the Hephthalites.

A different aspect of the city's life is illustrated by the Nestorian Synods. At the beginning of Bahram's reign for the first time we find a bishop of Merv, Bar Šaba, attending the third Synod presided over by the Catholicos Dadjesus in 424 AD (Chabot 1902, 285–298).

Already during the 4th century the clergy endeavoured to organise the Christian congregations within a metropolitan and patriarchal system (Wiessner 1967, 294). Finally at the Synod of AD 410 the main part of this system seems successfully established and dioceses further away would have gradually been involved (Wiessner 1967, 294–296). This development is to a certain extent reflected in the lists of the first Synods, where we find a bishop for Abashahr in AD 410, and at the third Synod AD 424 also bishops for Merv and Herat (Chabot 1902, 285).

For the rule of Bahram V Gor a certain promotion of the region of Merv is mirrored in the impact of its silver drahms on the Bukhar-khuda coins (Frye 1996, 176) and the integration of the Christian community at Merv into the metropolitan system.

Khusro I 'Anushirvan' is one of the best-known Sasanian kings, due to the fundamental reforms attributed to him concerning administration, army and taxation (Rubin 1995, 234). As mentioned above sigillographic studies showed some parallelism between the dioceses known from the Synods and the provinces mentioned in administrative seal inscriptions (Gyselen 1989, 3). A final conclusion is hampered by the scarcity of evidence, since the signatures often occur without dioceses on the lists, and administrative seals are rather few in number and are concentrated mainly in the West (Gyselen 1989, 3). As far as Merv is concerned Gyselen assumes that this region had two 'shahrs', Merv and Marw-i-rud, parallel to the dioceses in this area (Gyselen 1989, 85).

The development reflected in the Synodical lists of the time seems of significance in this context. David, bishop of Merv, signs the subscription list of Mar Aba's Synod AD 544. A decade later we again find the name David in the Synodical act, this time registered as Metropolitan together with a certain Theodorus bishop of Merv-i-rud (Chabot 1902, 328, 332, 366). If Gyselen's observation is correct, we may assume that Merv gained in importance during this period as shown in its elevation to Metropolitan centre.

This theory is further supported by another argument. The partition of the Sasanian empire into quarters, attributed to Khusro I as part of his comprehensive reform scheme by Armenian and Arab sources (Gnoli 1985, 267f), was long the subject of intense academic disputes. Opinions on this topic ranged from restricted acceptance (Gnoli 1985) to complete rejection as historical fiction (Gignoux 1984). Gignoux has recently revised his opinion on the topic, due to a seal inscription mentioning a 'general (*spahbed*) of the South' (Gignoux 1991, 69). Still further evidence is needed for a closer reconstruction and dating of the military structure indicated by this seal. Moreover, it remains unclear how long the new system worked. We may at least assume now, with some justification, that Merv in the course of these reforms possibly had become one of the four major military centres as suggested in the Syriac legend of the bishop and missionary Bar Šaba, where Merv is named as residence of the '*Aspahid*' (ie general) for Khorasan (Scher 1908–1918, 258; see also Fiey 1979, 76). Situated at the northeastern frontier of the Sasanian Empire it appeared predestined to be an outpost against the East with often changing and unstable political conditions.

Despite the problems of insufficient data a general tendency in the political and

Plate 1: Body sherds with fluted decoration.

Plate 2: Fragments with rows of impressions and wavy combed decoration.

Plate 3: (a) Red slip ware: the fragment on the right shows a finer slip that covers both surfaces; (b) Traces of vertical burnish on the fragment to the left and burnished grid pattern on the inside of a bowl rim.

(b)

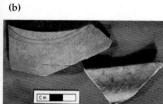

(a)

Plate 4: Two fragments showing the white-red colour change typical for fabric B4.

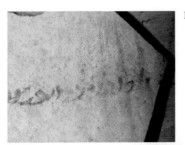

Plate 5: Inscribed sherd.

Plate 6: Handled bowl, semi-complete specimen from MGK5, context no 863.

Plate 7: Trefoil-mouthed jug from MGK5, context no 582.

Plate 8: Body profile of the waisted bowl found in MGK5, context no 911.

Plate 9: Neck–shoulder transition and upper body part of double-handled jars from MGK5, context no 961, height 18.5cm, and context no 842, height 18cm.

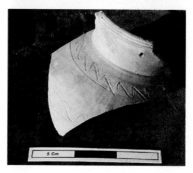

Plate 10: Fragment of a jar with perforated neck from MGK5, context no 850.

Plate 11: Juglet from MGK5, context no 774.

Plate 12: Jug from MGK5, context no 560. Height 25cm.

Plate 13: Specimen of a jar with perforated neck found in Erk Kala, YuTAKE, Trench 2.

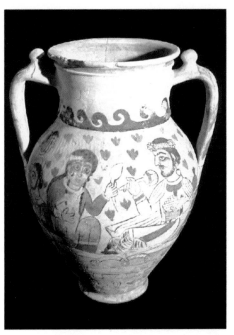

Plate 14: (a) Reconstructed specimen from MEK1, context 40; (b) The painted 'Merv vase' found in the Buddhist stupa, Gyaur Kala, YuTAKE, Trench 9.

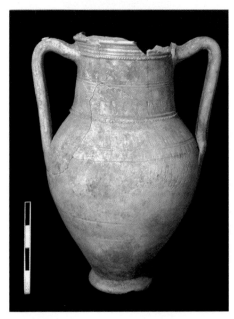

Plate 15: Double-handled jar found accidentally near MGK4.

administrative development of Merv during the 6th century seems visible. The continuous release of coin issues in contrast to the 5th century points to a firmly established concept in financial and economic matters, and shows Merv as part of a tightly organised empire. It is worth noting in this respect that silver denominations began again later in Kavad's reign and were issued up until the end of the reign of Khusro II (590–628). These observations are also reflected in the ecclesiastic organisation that during this century at Merv reached its final shape, maintained far into Islamic times (Fiey 1979, 82ff). Finally, the whole picture appears to fit in perfectly with the framework established for the entire Sasanian state at this time. Politically it seems Merv had reached a stable position and merged into the centralised organisation of the empire.

Another major religion in the city's life during this time was Buddhism. Buddhism first reached the area of Bactria-Tokharistan during the Kushan period in the early centuries AD (Errington and Cribb 1992, 11). The new religion was supported by the Kushan rulers, and many sanctuaries and monasteries were founded (Stavisky 1996, 27). One of the most spectacular of these Buddhist complexes is preserved in Kara-Tepe, near Termez in southern Uzbekistan, with several sanctuaries, caves and a rich epigraphic tradition (Stavisky 1996, 27). With the rise and expansion of the Sasanian Empire in the 3rd century the king of kings subdued the weakened Kushan Empire and later established a semi-independent dynasty there – the Kushano–Sasanians (Frye 1964, 203, 209). In this period of intensive contact between the Sasanian Empire and Bactria-Tokharistan, Buddhism spread to Merv (Stavisky 1996, 26). Building activities for a first sanctuary inside the city walls started soon afterwards. According to numismatic evidence, this sanctuary functioned from the 4th to the 6th century (Pugachenkova and Usmanova 1995, 52, 61).

More detailed information on Buddhist life at Merv, however, is provided by the manuscript found in the second stupa outside the city walls, which is dated slightly later (Vorob'eva-Desyatovskaya 1983, 69). Based on a passage of the colophon listing the Vinaya rules for monastic life (Vorob'eva-Desyatovskaya 1983, 73), the manuscript was assigned to the Buddhist school of the Sarvastivadins (Vorob'eva-Desyatovskaya 1983, 73), a school known in India already from the second Buddhist council, dating to the early 4th century BC (Dutt 1978, 4f). Gradually this school spread from their centre in Mathura to the northwest of India and eventually into Central Asia (Dutt 1978, 10; Vorob'eva-Desyatovskaya 1983, 73). The location of both sanctuaries, one in the southeastern corner of the city, the other outside the walls, suggests a rather segregated social position of the Buddhist community at Merv.

In contrast to the lack of written sources for the previous centuries, we find an explicit reference to Merv for the campaigns of Khusro II 'Parviz' (590–628). Sebeos, the 7th-century Armenian author, reports that after the final defeat of the Hephthalites through the royal general Smbat Bagratuni at the beginning of the 7th century a large part of the army settled in the region of Merv and Marw-i-rud (Thomson and Howard-Johnston 1999, 52–53). Unfortunately any further comparison with numismatic evidence is hampered by the very poor state of the coin finds, so any detailed analysis is impossible (Loginov and Nikitin 1993c, 275).

In the publication of coin finds at Merv, specimens from the period of Khusro II onward are generally grouped as 'Late or Post Sasanian' (Loginov and Nikitin 1993c, 275). Their poor preservation may be due to the usage of very thin flans, a general minting policy pursued by the Late Sasanian kings (Frye 1962, 234). On the other hand, it may be a taphonomic problem related to the bad climatic conditions and erosion to which finds in the upper archaeological layers are generally exposed. Hence we must accept that numismatic evidence cannot be employed for the interpretation of historic events during this period. Consequently the relation between money circulation and military activities remains diffuse.

Conclusions

The synopsis and evaluation of the available sources has produced a reflection of political and social developments at the oasis and city of Merv. Naturally the information we gained is not always homogeneous and balanced. Some aspects are better illustrated than others and many still need further evidence to be explored. Yet the historical role of the city seems well defined.

From the outset Merv was a province of Sasanian Iran. During the fourth century it may have had a share in the government of or even formed an administrative unit with the Kushano–Sasanian territories. At the beginning of the 5th century new neighbours, the Hephthalites from the East, arrived. In the following decades they succeeded in establishing a powerful empire that interfered frequently with Sasanian state affairs. Their role in Sasanian politics was ambiguous, and more than once the Hephtalites actively decided the royal succession with their military support (Thierry 1993, 115–116). When the king did not show enough gratitude they attacked his provinces, which usually ended in warfare. During the first confrontation with the Hephthalites under Bahram V Merv appears as an important strategic base, from where the king tried to raise enough resources to satisfy his neighbours through financial means. This is reflected in the impact of his coinage on later Central Asian issues. His coins may have also been used to pay his own army units, though it remains unexplained why he did not release lower denominations, and of his army's presence at Merv nothing is reflected in the numismatic evidence.

To Bahram's successors Merv obviously seemed unfit to serve as a military base and the fact that coin evidence from Merv for this period is irregular and includes overstruck issues indicates that Merv was situated within the war zone and temporarily out of control (Zeimal 1996, 246). Peroz's army is attested in the city by the large amount of coins issued at Amul, Tabaristan.

During the 6th century the situation calmed down. Names of officials on the ostraca found in the city show Merv as part of the Sasanian provincial administration. If the epigraphic evidence brought forward by Gignoux may be regarded as proof for the military reforms ascribed to Khusro Anushirvan, we might see Merv advanced to one of the major Sasanian administrative, cultural and military centres with a highly cosmopolitan population and all major religious movements of the time present in the city. Apart from the Christian community, which was now headed by a Metropolitan of considerable ecclesiastical power, Buddhism made its mark in the urban landscape with a monumental sanctuary inside the city walls. In this context a few words need to be said about Judaism, which has not been mentioned so far. Judaism spread to eastern Iran and Central Asia probably in connection with commercial activities and (to a lesser extent) deportations (EncIr VII). During excavations of the sixth-century necropolis west of Merv four ossuaries were found with Jewish names in Hebrew inscriptions (Ershov 1959, 160f). Such sparse evidence is unable to provide information about the size, status or development of the Jewish community at Merv during these centuries, although by post-Sasanian times the community must have been of considerable importance, since Tabari records about the 8th century that one-third of the city's population was Jewish (Fiey 1979, 83).

With the beginning of the 7th century the Hephthalite problem was finally settled, but the decay of the empire soon began, which was literally sealed at Merv with the murder of its last king, Yazdgard III. The provinces and subjects of the empire had become estranged from their king and deliberately changed their masters. At first there was probably little change in the city's life. A few post-Sasanian coins prove that Merv was still governed by a Persian: they still bear Middle-Persian legends (Loginov and Nikitin 1993d, 313f).

ARCHAEOLOGICAL SETTING

Excavations of the International Merv Project

With the resumption of archaeological fieldwork at Merv by the International Merv Project (IMP), a comprehensive new research programme was set up to investigate and record the remains of the long-term history of urban settlement at the site. One of the objectives was to assess the occupational sequence in the different parts of the city through selective excavations (Herrmann *et al* 1993, 39). Following a reconnaissance survey which included aerial photographs, surface artefact survey and resistivity, single areas were chosen for excavation according to the accessibility of archaeological remains from specific chronological periods (Herrmann *et al* 1993, 48–50; 1994, 59–61; 1995, 37–40).

Methodology and excavation techniques were designed to establish the depositional history and guarantee a quantified recovery of the different categories of finds, such as artefacts, bones and plant material. The actual excavations were conducted by hand, usually with a trowel, and recorded in single contexts with a description and tentative interpretation of deposits. Stratigraphic relationships were documented in the form of a Harris Matrix (Herrmann *et al* 1995, 34). Certain contexts were dry-sieved in order to retrieve specific classes of objects, including small animal bones and coins (Herrmann *et al* 1994, 67; 1999, 10). Additional soil samples for flotation were taken throughout the excavations as part of the archaeobotanical project (Herrmann *et al* 1994, 71). Archaeological finds from these samples were kept for further analysis by the relevant specialists.

The present study will concentrate on two from a number of different trenches opened by the IMP. These are Area 1 in Erk Kala (MEK1) and Area 5 in Gyaur Kala (MGK5) (Figure 2.2). Both excavations were designed to explore single well-defined structures representative of discrete chronological periods, which were located close to the surface (Herrmann *et al* 1996, 4).

Erk Kala, Area 1 (MEK1)

MEK1 (Figure 2.3) on the eastern side of Erk Kala was chosen with special regard to the concentration of previous fieldwork on the central and western part of the citadel (Herrmann *et al* 1993, 50). In four seasons, from 1992 to 1995, a sequence of rooms was revealed over an area of 13.60 × 16m. Built-in features of the rooms including sufas (benches), hearths and permanent storage vessels pointed to a domestic function of the structure (Herrmann *et al* 1995, 34). Since external walls were not determined completely, the excavated structures represent only part of the building. Several phases of consecutive occupation could be distinguished, each comprising a number of rearrangements and alterations within the architectural plan (Herrmann *et al* 1995, 34ff). Locally minted copper-alloy coins from the reign of Khusro I (AD 531–579) onward date the structure to Late Sasanian times.

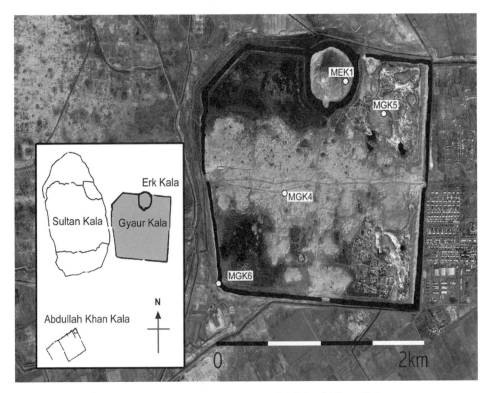

Figure 2.2: Plan with the locations of the IMP excavations in Erk Kala and Gyaur Kala.

STRATIGRAPHY

Due to the location of MEK1 in close proximity to the defensive wall of the citadel, the uppermost deposits were affected by erosion from rainwater (Herrmann *et al* 1993, 50), which created a slope running westward to the lower unoccupied area of Erk Kala. As a consequence, the uppermost layers were partly removed and deposits were destroyed more towards the west side of the trench resulting in a truncation of the stratigraphic sequence on this side (Herrmann *et al* 1993, 50; 1995, 34).

A single contemporary phase of use for all the rooms could therefore be established only for the earliest level (Herrmann *et al* 1996, 11). Most of the rooms were interlinked by doorways in this phase, providing a passage through the whole structure (Herrmann *et al* 1996, 12, fig 9). In subsequent phases the layout of the building changed and room structures were modified by alterations of access, blocking or opening of doorways and the construction or reinforcement of walls (Herrmann *et al* 1996, 9–10). Floor levels gradually rose and rooms were eventually arranged into discrete units with separate access (Herrmann *et al* 1995, 36). At this point the deposits in the western half of MEK1 were terminated by erosion, limiting later occupational levels to the eastern part of the trench. During the following period two rooms were constructed on top of the previous structures in this part of the building (Herrmann *et al* 1993, 51). The uppermost level excavated here is characterised by small hearths suggesting a post-occupational use of the area (Herrmann *et*

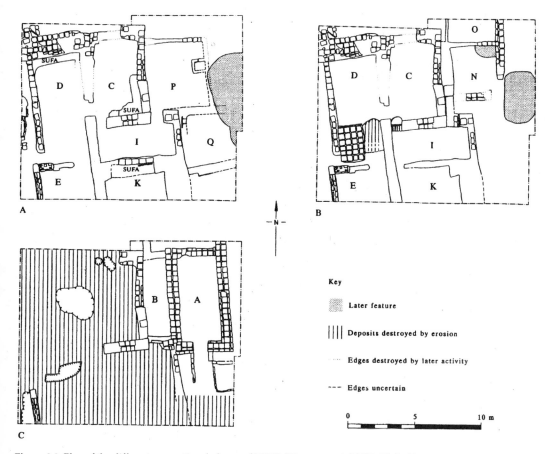

Figure 2.3: Plan of the different occupational phases of MEK1 (Herrmann *et al* 1995, 35, fig 2).

al 1993, 52). Some of the occupational phases are associated with pits that interfere with previous structures pointing to a largely flexible arrangement of spaces during the lifetime of the building. Not all pits were identified as rubbish deposits: they apparently served different purposes (Herrmann *et al* 1995, 34).

The sequence of occupational phases exemplifies the organic development of domestic mudbrick architecture at Merv, one of the characteristics of this building material. Minor maintenance activities conducted on a regular basis included the renovation and levelling up of floors which naturally affected built-in features, such as sufas and hearths. Each room displayed a series of floor levels, some rooms containing up to six (Herrmann *et al* 1993, 51; 1995, 34–36). More substantial refurbishment led to the reorganisation of rooms within the structure, their blocking off or, in single instances, temporary abandonment (Herrmann *et al* 1993, 50; 1995, 36). This suggests that the principal construction unit with this form of architecture was the room, which could be easily modified and adapted in a fairly pragmatic manner without necessarily affecting the life or function of the whole structure. Similar features in the development of domestic architecture are still visible in present-day northeastern Iran, where structures were frequently rearranged including changes in the function of single rooms (Horne 1983, 19; 1994, 129–131).

Gyaur Kala, Area 5 (MGK5)

Excavations in the northeast quarter of the town started in 1994 and continued over five seasons, being completed in 1999. Architectural remains identified on aerial photographs were classified as Middle Sasanian by the surface artefact survey (Herrmann *et al* 1995, 37). Initially a substantial area (4,400m²) was surveyed using resistivity to verify the evidence gained from aerial reconnaissance (Herrmann *et al* 1995, 37). The surface scraping of parts of this area (75 × 25m maximum extension) revealed the architectural plan of what appeared to be a domestic quarter consisting of small houses along narrow alleys (Herrmann *et al* 1995, 37–40). A number of test areas were subsequently explored in depth to assess the archaeology of the different structures and their interrelationships (Herrmann *et al* 1996, 5). Finally one building, structure C, and the adjacent streets in the northwest part of Area 5, were chosen for excavation (Figure 2.4). Deposits here indicated a less disturbed stratigraphic environment and promised to produce a larger body of more contemporary material (Herrmann *et al* 1996, 8). In comparison to other structures in Area 5 it was noticed that the bricks of structure C were of poor quality and contained a large amount of sand (Herrmann *et al* 1995, 40). Like MEK1 in Erk Kala, structure C was excavated until a single coherent phase of construction was established. Installations and built-in features similar

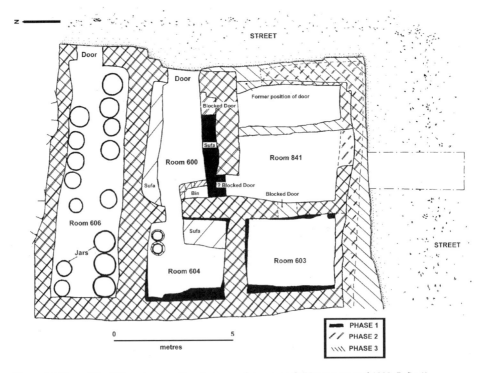

Figure 2.4: Plan of the different occupational phases of structure C (Herrmann *et al* 1999, 5, fig 1).

to those of MEK1, such as hearths and rubbish bins, attest to a domestic function. Changes in the arrangement of the rooms and passage through the building reflect an organic development similar to MEK1 (Herrmann *et al* 1998, 55). In addition to the rooms, sections of adjacent alleyways were opened to the south and east, to assess the stratigraphic correlation between the interior of the structure and contemporary street deposits (Herrmann *et al* 1998, 55f). Contexts excavated in the alleyways also facilitated a comparison between the material found within the structure and outside, since it is generally assumed that accidentally lost objects are more likely to be left in the streets, whereas they would have been retrieved inside the rooms (Herrmann *et al* 1998, 56). Most important in this respect are small denomination coins from street deposits, as they provide a more reliable source of dating than the material deliberately reused for construction activities (Herrmann *et al* 1998, 56).

STRATIGRAPHY

Structure C is situated at the western edge of a single flat-topped mound. Weathering and erosion affected the sloping western part of the structure more, where the uppermost deposits were destroyed with increasing force down the slope (Herrmann *et al* 1995, 40). Near-surface contexts excavated inside the better preserved eastern part of the structure seemed related to make-up layers for a later phase, the remains of which had been completely removed (Herrmann *et al* 1996, 8). Throughout the occupational phases structure C showed two architecturally distinct areas, a storeroom to the north and a group of residential rooms characterised by sufas and fire installations to the south (Herrmann *et al* 1999, 2). The storeroom remained unchanged over the entire lifetime of structure C except for the necessary rise of floor levels and single storage vessels occasionally exchanged or added (Herrmann *et al* 1999, 2f). More radical changes took place over time in the southern residential part of the building. Like MEK1, all rooms were interconnected at first, though a stricter division is noticeable between the southern and northern residential rooms in the following phases (Herrmann *et al* 1999, 2). Over the consecutive occupational periods walls were levelled and rebuilt, doorways blocked or opened and eventually a small courtyard established in the southern part of the building (Herrmann *et al* 1997, 5). Two bread ovens were excavated within a separate area in the southeast corner, which characterise the latest preserved phase of occupation. The layout of the structure, though, was essentially maintained throughout its lifetime. In connection with the street sections it was proved that the rise of floor levels within the structure was an attempt to compensate for the relatively quick accumulation of deposits in the street, following the maintenance of pavements to protect house walls from the accumulation of household refuse (Herrmann *et al* 1998, 56). This measure primarily affected the rooms open to the street, while floor levels of inner parts of the structure were not necessarily adapted simultaneously (Herrmann *et al* 1998, 55). The storeroom was at any time only accessible from the street (Herrmann *et al* 1999, 2). More than a dozen large storage jars found in this room could be associated with a single phase (Herrmann *et al* 1999, 3). Since this capacity appears out of proportion with regard to the relatively modest four-room layout of structure C, the storeroom may have been shared by several households. Apart from the storeroom, which has no equivalent in MEK1, both structures in Erk and Gyaur Kala display a similar scheme in the layout of the rooms and the organic development of the structures throughout the consecutive occupational phases.

Archaeological deposits

In accordance with the stratigraphy of both Area 1 and structure C, practically all the excavated deposits were created through artificial means, by maintenance and construction activities. Numerous contexts constitute floor and make-up layers or infillings of features (hearths, storage jars) and rooms. Another group is distinguished by constructional contexts, including sufas and walls. Most of these deposits have been artificially mixed, as the material derives from heterogeneous sources. Mudbricks are often tempered with older discarded pottery, creating a cycle of reuse, which intermingles material from various chronological periods. This process may still be observed in the Merv oasis today and in modern Iranian villages constructed of mudbrick architecture (Horne 1994, 129–130). Contexts that require a substantial amount of building material, such as infillings, make-up layers or walls, are likely to contain a higher quantity of re-deposited material. Floor levels or deposits immediately above the floor surface, which appear chronologically more reliable, on the other hand, are difficult to separate from make-up layers in this mudbrick environment. Often floor levels simply represent the compacted surface of a make-up layer without special plastering. Rubbish deposits were rare, although refuse was often re-deposited as part of make-up layers. Distinct domestic rubbish pits outside the structure were found only in MEK1 (Herrmann *et al* 1993, 52; 1995, 36).

Few deposits have been recovered from the excavations in Area 1 and structure C that represent first-instance discarded material, which could be classified as primary (cf Carver 1985, 353, 356; Schiffer 1987, 111–114). Most material was re-deposited at least once during site formation processes. Infills and make-up layers are frequently described as 'bricky' or containing 'mudbrick fragments' or 'demolition debris'. It is likely that material from demolished walls was reused for construction work of the subsequent phase in the same structure. As a consequence the ceramic assemblages retrieved from these deposits are expected to be archaeologically inhomogeneous, since they contain material of diverse post-depositional history (cf Orton and Tyers 1990, 96). The problem seems therefore not so much to distinguish between residual and contemporary, but rather to assess various degrees of residuality.

Pottery processing and recording methods

The systematic recording of the ceramic material formed an important part in the planning of the excavations. As with most objectives of internationally operating projects, the processing technique had to be carefully balanced between scientific obligations, practical feasibility and economical resource management.

A basic guideline for the processing and recording of the pottery was established beforehand by Simpson and its application continued throughout the project (Herrmann *et al* 1993, 52). All pottery fragments from a context were processed (Figure 2.5). From the beginning of the project emphasis was laid on the quantification of the material through sherd count and weight. Fragments were recorded in three groups: (a) sherds with both surfaces preserved; (b) sherds with one surface or less; (c) diagnostic sherds, which comprised rim and base fragments, handles and decorated or surface-treated body sherds. From the first two groups only sherd size, count and weight were recorded. Diagnostic sherds were given separate find numbers and processed in more detail. Fragments of the same context were joined as far as possible and recorded as 'sherd families' (Orton and

Figure 2.5: One of the contexts prepared for processing as described above. Plain body sherds are compiled according to size and state of preservation.

Tyers 1990, 105). Diameters and percentages of rim and base fragments were measured on a rim chart. The thickness of handles was noted with two measurements. Further classification considered form, decoration or surface treatment and traces of use or wear. Joins between contexts were noted on the record sheets as well. The small numbers of coarse ware fabrics were treated as a separate group. Many fragments were blackened, suggesting that the vessels had been used for cooking.

Fabric

Ceramic fabrics were sampled and coded during the first season using a pair of pliers and a 10x magnifying lens (Herrmann *et al* 1993, 52; see also Appendix 1). Subsequently all diagnostics were compared to the set of reference fabrics by creating a fresh break with pliers. A combined classification system based on petrographic types and colourings of sherds, as a result of various firing conditions, was adopted accounting for the obvious distinctions between common and coarse wares as well as possible chronologically sensitive colour variations as described in the Russian literature on previous Soviet excavations (Rutkovskaya 1962, 68). Plain wares are all made from the same petrographic fabric and only distinguished through colourings. One of the plain ware types is characterised by a red slip or wash on the surface. Three different coarse ware types could be identified according to inclusions and temper. Inclusions comprise vitrified clay or 'slag', calcite and grog and coarse organic material. A programme of petrographic analyses designed to compare plain and cooking wares from the Parthian to Islamic periods was conducted at the Scientific Department of the British Museum and is referred to below.

Form

In an environment of little change through time in ceramic fabrics and decoration techniques, form gains extra weight in pottery analysis. Form, on the other hand, is a variable difficult to determine, since it is rather a matter of individual perception. As the typological classification was established and used by one person, the bias has at least remained constant. The approach to the variable 'form' in this study is a pragmatic one without further pretensions. All definitions and groupings are regarded as temporary and should assist the process of analysis.

Ceramic assemblages at Merv are very fragmented with the exception of singular complete or semi-complete vessels. As a result only few forms of the ceramic repertoire are known and the often small rim or base sherds give no clear indication of the form of the whole vessel. An important part of the ceramic processing was therefore the reconstruction of vessel profiles, if possible. Once a shape is completely understood, it is much easier to recognise even small parts of it. Through the reconstruction and retrieval of semi-complete forms, it became more transparent how the single vessel types were defined within the repertoire. The great variety of shapes present in each context and their fragmented state made a standardised reference system difficult to define. Typological systems previously established by the YuTAKE suffered apparently from the same problem, although tentative combination of rim and base shapes are regularly suggested in their illustrations (Rutkovskaya 1962, 65, fig 8). Their discussion of pottery typology gives detailed verbal descriptions, but no systematic catalogue. Illustrations are often simplified and seem to be chosen at random without specific relation to the text (cf Rutkovskaya 1962, 44–107). While useful for the comparison of single vessel forms, this could not provide a reference typology for recording the pottery. An independent system was therefore established.

In the early seasons of the project the main aim was to gain a thorough overview of the spectrum of shapes. Recording sheets contained no information on shapes. These were effectively processed by the illustrator, who drew a large proportion of rim fragments from the contexts. Soon, however, sketches were added to the record on a regular basis. Newly discovered or better preserved forms continued to be drawn. When a ceramic database was finally started by the author in 1997, each shape received a code and a reference catalogue was gradually compiled (cf Appendix 2). 'Each shape' is, of course, not a very accurate description, but the general tendency was to be as detailed as possible, since unreasonable groupings could always be reversed. Principal criteria for the differentiation between reference shapes were morphological characteristics and diameter or size. The catalogue is seen as a preliminary tool to facilitate the recording of shapes and is constantly being revised and supplemented. It was set up in an unstructured form, each group of diagnostics being represented by a code followed by a continuous number, such as R1, R2 . . . for rims, BA1, BA2 and so on for bases. Additional refinement was achieved by the introduction of similar shapes. If a fragment appeared not identical to an existing shape, but yet not different enough to form an independent reference, an 's' was put before the code, expressing 'similar to'. What at first seemed to cause further confusion proved to be a helpful means during the analysis, since some of the 'similar' shapes turned out to be independent shapes and were subsequently separated, while others seemed incoherent and were deleted from the analysis to avoid distortion (cf Chapter 4). The preliminary shape catalogue is currently updated to be incorporated into a comprehensive fabric and form reference collection and handbook.

General problems

As indicated above, circumstances and archaeological reality make a deviation from the ideal usually inevitable. The pottery processing at Merv was restricted by two factors: lack of storage and discontinuity of team members.

Local conditions would not allow for a permanent storage facility or deposit and only a small proportion of the material could be exported as a study collection to the British Museum. Effort was therefore put into a quick and efficient manner of recording to keep pace with the volume of material produced by the ongoing excavations. Each season, however, an unavoidable backlog of a few sacks had accumulated. With the friendly support of local collaborators these could be stored privately over the year, where they seemed reasonably safe, except for environmental agents (eg mice) causing an intermingling of some contexts.

The second restraint lay in personnel resources. During the first seasons the pottery was processed by a group of different people with varying experience in the subject, inevitably leading to inconsistencies (cf Herrmann *et al* 1993, 52; 1994, 36, 41). This particularly concerned the sketches of pottery shapes, which vary greatly in detail and style, making later identifications sometimes ambivalent or impossible. Further variation regarded the size limit, when a fragment became too small to provide reliable information on diameter or shape. Since 1995 the Sasanian ceramic material was continuously processed by the author, but even then the fabric typing was excluded due to lack of time and usually done by Simpson towards the end of the season. Problems caused by this practice included misreading numbers and loss of material following the storage of backlog.

The material

Published descriptions of pottery from the Sasanian period are conventional and no systematic terminology has yet been defined. The descriptions given in this study follow a basic use classification (Rice 1987, 215–217) similar to those used implicitly in most publications with minor changes depending on different scholarly traditions (Rutkovskaya 1962; Venco Ricciardi 1970; Whitcomb 1985). In order to avoid confusion the formal differentiation is kept rather broad, relating to principal forms or morphological features, such as bowls, jars or jugs. Cross-references were made, where specific terms have been created in the archaeological literature. For the moment, however, a general outline will suffice to characterise the material.

The pottery assemblages are dominated by a variety of plain wares (Figure 2.6). These are wheel thrown except for very large vessels (height > 1m) and share a common repertoire of surface treatment and decoration contributing to the impression of uniformity. Vessel forms are mostly indicated by rim sherds, since only a limited number of semi-complete specimens and reconstructable profiles has been found in the excavations. A few forms can be distinctly identified according to their function as storage jars, lids or lamps, usually characterised by traces of soot along the rim, while the remainder falls into broader categories, such as bowls or jars. Rim fragments display great variation ranging from simple vertical to elaborately finished types. Some of the rim shapes are too indistinct to be attributed to specific vessel types, particularly when they occur in small fragments.

Handles follow a fairly standardised scheme. Most prominent are handles reaching from immediately below the neck–shoulder junction to the lower shoulder of the vessel,

Figure 2.6: Pottery assemblage from context no 560, MGK5.

which vary considerably in size. Another group of handles stretches from the neck to the maximum diameter of the vessel. Horizontally attached twisted handles occur less frequently. Specific handle shapes appear diagnostic for certain vessel types, such as the wavy handle attachments, which are found only on a particular bowl shape.

Base sherds are restricted in their variety and, with a few exceptions, relatively indistinct. Some perforated base fragments have been found, suggesting a special function: some were clearly secondary.

A large proportion of the pottery shows surface treatment. Sometimes this includes finishing techniques covering large parts or the complete body of the vessel. These comprise coatings, burnishing and chattering. Singular fragments are covered by a red slip, which is applied to both surfaces and generally associated with open shapes. Fragments of closed shapes sometimes have a very thin red slip coating on the exterior (Plate 3(a) between pp 26 and 27). Burnishing seems to be more common among the pottery from Merv. Burnish marks mostly run vertically along the body of small to medium-sized closed vessels but is also a characteristic feature of the grey ware. In exceptional cases a grid pattern is burnished on to the interior of rim fragments (Plate 3(b)). The vast majority of surface-treated sherds display a fluted effect apparently produced by chattering (Plate 1). This treatment is usually applied to the whole upper part of the body.

Other decorative techniques include incising, combing, impressing and application. Incisions occur as horizontal straight or wavy lines. Combed decoration only appears in wavy patterns (Plate 2). Lower body parts are sometimes embellished with a row of short vertical grooves produced by chattering. Impressions often subdivide horizontal ribs around necks and neck–shoulder junctions, or form decorative bands around shoulders.

They mostly resemble impressions of fingernails, but also take the shape of punctuations or stitches (Plate 2). Frequently, impressions of thumbs are found on lower handle attachments. Applications comprise flat discs, which are sometimes decorated by stamps, and distinct handle knobs. Each of these decorations occurs singly: more often, though, a combination of various techniques and motives is used. Yet the placement on the vessel body follows strict rules and is mainly concentrated on the upper part of vessels. Incisions and combed decoration are usually applied on the neck and shoulder of closed shapes and around the rim of open vessel forms. Chattering, one exception to the rule, is also found near the vessel base. Impressions embellish the neck and shoulder except for thumb impressions, which are only found on lower handle attachments. Flat discs are either mounted on the top of the handle or around the shoulder. Handle knobs are used for lids and sometimes in analogy to metal vessels as a stopper on strap handles.

Firing conditions can produce a decorative effect, such as the bichrome colouring of the external surface (fabric B4) caused by stacking vessels upside down on top of each other in the kiln (Plate 4).

Inscribed sherds represent a special group of pottery. Usually parts of words or a group of words are preserved, but occasionally drawings are found. Some of them have clearly been used in a fragmented state and can be called ostraca. Fluted sherds are often chosen for inscribing. Sometimes the writing carefully follows the horizontal lines of incisions or ribs, indicating that the fragment was probably part of an inscribed vessel rather than an ostracon (Plate 5). Inscriptions show a number of different languages, including Parthian, Middle Persian, Arabic and Sogdian.

Figure 2.7: Rim sherds from context no 948, MGK5.

A genuinely different group of pottery are coarse wares. Coarse wares are handmade and, as stated above, show a range of different petrographic fabrics. Rare decoration is confined to coarse diagonal scratches or wavy incisions. Cooking wares seem to relate to a specific range of shapes, which even varies from fabric to fabric. Coarse wares form a regular but minor component of pottery assemblages.

Sherds within an assemblage often look very heterogeneous as to their state of wear. Very abraded fragments are found together with fresh-looking broken parts of a vessel. Some pieces are stained or covered by organic deposits, while others appear clean (Figure 2.7).

Occasionally fragments of very different surface appearance found in one context belong to the same vessel and sometimes even abraded sherds join together into a semi-complete shape. This variation in the appearance of pottery fragments points to different taphonomic processes to which the individual parts of an assemblage were exposed.

– PART II –

ANALYSIS

— 3 —

CHRONOLOGICAL ANALYSIS

THE CONVENTIONAL APPROACH

WHY A STATISTICAL APPROACH?

As indicated by the review of previous research undertaken in the oasis, the understanding of the ceramic tradition of Sasanian Merv is poor. No reliable chronological sequence has been established on which to base the classification of new material. Moreover, regional differences, as indicated by some reports based on Sasanian pottery from other regions (Venco Ricciardi 1970, 430) and the lack of archaeologically comparable evidence from neighbouring areas, in terms of excavation and recording techniques, oppose the attempt to utilise analogies from other sites as chronological indicators. Purely typological and qualitative studies of ceramic material from the Sasanian period have been restrained in their chronological assessment, partly due to the lack of overt changes in ceramic technology and basic vessel forms throughout the immediately adjacent periods, partly because the analytical methods were not suitable to respond to the problems posed by multi-period sites. Much research on statistical applications has been devoted to these problems, and we hope to overcome some of the uncertainties by using appropriate techniques. In this sense statistical analysis should be understood as a supplementary tool that facilitates the handling of large and complex data sets and should not be mistaken as a replacement of conventional archaeological methods. The ceramics from the recent excavations at Merv are so far the only fully quantified corpus of Sasanian pottery in terms of proportions of vessel types. We believe that a statistical evaluation of this corpus contributes an objective perspective to the study of Sasanian pottery.

PROBLEMS AND OBJECTIVES

Contaminated assemblages and the often intricate stratigraphy have remained a major challenge to the construction of a reliable chronological sequence in the field of urban archaeology. The problem of choosing suitable evidence for dating affected all levels of chronological interpretation from the assessment of single structures to comprehensive studies involving seriation techniques. As a consequence a number of different selection mechanisms have evolved. Frequently archaeologists decided to concentrate on data, which are understood to come from 'well-stratified' contexts, that is from discrete structures, such as rubbish pits, or stratigraphically sealed contexts, below paved floors and so on (cf Boucharlat 1987, 201–202; Huff 1978, 130). Over the past decades a more systematic

43

approach has been pursued, trying to interpret archaeological contexts from the perspective of site formation processes (Carver 1985; Schiffer 1987). In order to facilitate the interpretation of archaeological evidence, a classification system for contexts has been developed (Schiffer 1987, 58ff). This was taken up in the discussion of urban seriation techniques, and Carver suggested a principal division between contexts of 'primary' and 'secondary status', depending on whether they are contaminated and contain material that entered the context after its deposition or had been retrieved from already existing deposits. This re-deposited material is termed 'residual' in the archaeological literature (Carver 1985, 353–356). Carver recommended basing pottery seriation on contexts of 'primary' status to avoid complications with residual material, which is likely to affect the stratigraphically constrained order of assemblages (Carver 1985, 358–359; cf Orton *et al* 1993, 192).

Residuality is certainly a major problem with the ceramic assemblages at Merv. In view of the stratigraphic sequence in both areas, however, a classification and a priori exclusion of contexts on grounds of assumed residuality seems impracticable. While very few deposits would actually match the criteria of a 'primary' context, the majority might still contain primary components, which would be lost to further considerations. The identification of residual material is undoubtedly a necessary requirement for this study, yet we prefer to assess residuality in the course of the analysis rather than to exclude it beforehand.

Pottery assemblages generally show a great variety in shapes, and shapes again vary in fabric, resulting in a rather confusing impression of difference and similarity at the same time. Significant patterns are therefore likely to be expressed in the proportion of certain vessel types within assemblages. A chronological sequence should be traceable through the comparison of assemblages with each other.

The statistical analysis is based on two different methods: a conventional approach to assemblage comparison (this chapter) and the more advanced applications used in the computer package 'Pie-slice' (Chapter 4). As this program is still relatively little known outside British Roman and medieval archaeology, the conventional approach first provides a useful point of departure to outline the theoretical problems and to evaluate the different methodologies. Both approaches share the principal objective to establish variation within the data regarding the variables context, fabric and form. Depending on the nature of the data set, the observed variations may express differences in function, spatial distribution or chronology. It is therefore essential to understand how the three variables interact, in order to be able to interpret the occurring patterns correctly. If the archaeological situation is clear, interactions of variables might be apparent. A single period site is likely to show primarily variation of vessel forms across contexts, ie form-by-context interaction, reflecting different activities in different areas of the site, while chronological changes probably entail both variation of ware and form across the stratigraphic sequence, ie ware-by-context interaction and form-by-context interaction. In the case of a long-living urban settlement such as Merv, interactions between variables are generally more difficult to understand, as functional and chronological patterns are often obscured through the reuse of deposits. A comprehensive analysis of the variations and underlying interactions of variables is particularly important for the purpose of this study to identify correctly the chronologically significant factors.

Although principally identical for both types of analyses, the arrangements of the three variables differ slightly, depending on the structure and statistical facilities of each approach. All three variables, context, ware and form, can be examined at different levels of detail, ranging from single contexts to phases or excavation areas for the variable 'context', or from individual shapes to broad functional categories for the variable 'form'. The different arrangements are discussed separately for each type of analysis.

In order to establish possible interactions, the variables are combined in tables either by two (eg ware-by-context (two-way table)), or by three (eg ware-by-context and form (three-way table)). The three basic tables analysing all two-way interactions between variables are 'context-by-ware', 'context-by-form' and 'form-by-ware'. As these tables contain the sum of all values recorded for each of the combinations; they are called *marginal tables* (Orton and Tyers 1993, 8). In a three-way table the rows represent the combinations of the first two variables, while the columns account for the third variable (cf Table 3.4(a)). This extended table facilitates an assessment of interactions with a view to all three variables. Both tables will be used in the following analyses.

The basic quantitative measure of the pottery are *eves*, estimated vessel equivalents. Discussions on reliable methods of classifying and measuring pottery have long occupied a prominent place in ceramic studies (Orton *et al* 1993; Rice 1987, 290–293). Comparisons of different types of measure for pottery demonstrated that estimated vessel equivalents are the only non-biased measure for quantitative analyses (Orton *et al* 1993, 168–171). Only recently, however, were *eves* introduced in studies concerned with Near Eastern pottery (Kennet 2004; Roodenberg and Thissen 2001). There are various possibilities of obtaining *eves* from ceramic fragments; most commonly, however, diagnostic parts of the vessel, such as rims, bases or handles, are used to assess the proportion of the preserved fragment in relation to the complete form (Orton *et al* 1993, 172). In this study the *eves* are derived from the percentage values of rim sherds (*rim-eves*). All fragments in a context belonging to the same rim are noted as one record (*rim sherd family*; cf Chapter 2).

The values in the cells of the two-way and three-way tables are calculated from these *eves* values for each combination of variables. It should be noted, however, that the final data format differs for each approach. Variations are then assessed by comparing the values for the different combinations. This is facilitated by mathematical calculations designed to express a measure of variation and to remove the impact of size differences for the individual groups of variables and their combinations, which would impair an immediate comparison. In the process variations are measured in deviations from a model which reflects the assumption of no interactions, also called independence of variables (Baxter 1994, 112–113). These deviations are called residual values or simply residuals (Baxter 1994, 113). Observed values of variables ('O') are compared against expected values ('E'), which represent a hypothetical even distribution across the table (Baxter 1994, 112). The higher the residual value of a group, the greater its deviation from the hypothesis of no association (Baxter 1994, 113).

THE DATA SET

Before the analysis can begin, assemblages have to be tested for their general comparability. This initial process of data selection applies to both types of analysis and follows general statistical guidelines as described below.

In total, 318 assemblages were recorded in the field, 211 in MEK1 and 107 in MGK5. Most of the pottery records from these contexts were put on a database (Microsoft Access), which is continually updated with data from current surveys and excavations at Merv.*

* The database is part of the project archive at the Institute of Archaeology, UCL.

In order to guarantee the validity of the analysis, it is important to select records of those contexts that are comparable with each other and representative for the pottery population. Several criteria have been established to ensure an appropriate selection procedure. These criteria refer to (a) recovery techniques, (b) average fragment weight (also known as average sherd size), and (c) the size of contexts.

(a) Different recovery techniques were developed to target specific categories of objects and consequently led to a bias in the recovery rate (Orton *et al* 1993, 46–47). Contexts which are sieved will in general produce a larger amount of small fragments than those excavated by trowel. In order to avoid distortions, only hand-recovered contexts are taken into consideration here.

(b) Average fragment size, sherd weight divided by sherd count, is considered a measure sensitive to site formation processes (Orton *et al* 1993, 179; Schiffer 1987, 267–269). A context dominated by very small fragments is generally assumed to be residual, whereas very large and heavy sherds are likely to reflect a special archaeological situation or function of vessels, such as a context dominated by storage jar fragments and so on, not informative for the overall pottery population. Since the measure of average fragment weight/size is related to the formation processes of the archaeological deposits, it has to be assessed separately for each excavation. Figure 3.1 shows the average fragment size for MEK1 and MGK5 in two histograms. A general comparison between the trenches shows that the average fragment size for MGK5 peaks with slightly larger sherds, while the proportion of smaller fragments is greater in MEK1. Both histograms clearly indicate the range of the most common mean fragment weights for each trench, facilitating an appropriate selection of representative contexts. Leaving aside the smallest sherds, contexts with an average fragment weight between 5 and 44 grams for MEK1 and between 5 and 39 grams for MGK 5 were chosen for analysis.

(c) Context size is of relevance to ensure that assemblages are comparable in terms of the range of pottery types. Contexts with a very small number of diagnostic fragments are not suitable for comparison, since they are unlikely to contain enough information on interactions between the single variables and might confuse statistical data reduction (Orton *et al* 1993, 175). It is of course difficult to assess the quantitative size of a context, but as a general rule we considered 20 to be the minimum number of diagnostics required for the analysis. This seems a sufficient size to guarantee a significant amount of pottery per assemblage.

Following this selection process, 127 contexts were chosen from the database altogether, 39 from MEK1 and 88 from MGK5. Out of all the diagnostics recorded for these contexts only those providing a measure of proportion may be used for the quantitative analysis. With regard to the Merv data, these are rim and base fragments. In view of the limited range of base shapes, the analysis was ultimately restricted to rim shapes, since these appeared to be chronologically most sensitive. The data set finally extracted from the primary table comprised 2169 records (ie *rim sherd families*).

In the conventional approach the pottery assemblages are compared in a series of tables, which express two-way interactions between variables, such as the variation of ware-by-context or form-by-context. A table including all three variables will finally be analysed to compare the two-way interactions.

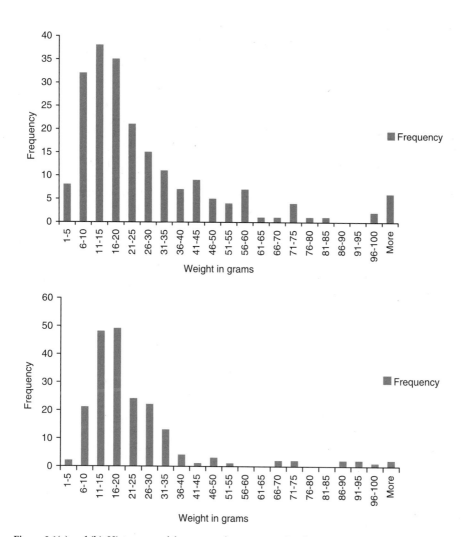

Figure 3.1(a) and (b): Histograms of the average fragment weight of MEK1 and MGK5 assemblages.

THE VARIABLES

The stratigraphic unit 'context' is initially grouped by trench, i.e. all contexts of one excavation area are regarded as one unit. In view of the lack of a coherent phasing for both excavation areas, the next possible stratigraphic unit would be the single context (see below).

'Ware' is first examined by petrographically determined groups. Subsequently the firing patterns distinguished within the group of fine wares are analysed in more detail.

With regard to the fragmentary state of the material, the variable 'form', recorded as shape codes, is arranged in basic groups, ranging from small to large open forms and small to large closed forms. A more specific identification seems unfeasible for parts of the data so far.

DISTRIBUTION OF WARES

Considering the difference in numbers of contexts for each excavation area, a variation in the amount of pottery for the two groups was to be expected. The inequality in size between the assemblage groups hampers an immediate comparison and all tables are therefore produced both in *eves* and percentage values.

The proportion of coarse ware fabrics in Table 3.1(a) is very small (5.3 per cent in total) in relation to the group of fine wares (74.5 per cent). Important in this context is also the high amount of unidentified material (20.2 per cent). While certainly regrettable, this does not lead to any bias against a specific fabric group, since the problem is related to the misreading of numbers or loss of material in storage (cf Chapter 2) and should not have any effect on the relative distribution of the groups shown in Table 3.1. The distribution of wares across MEK1 and MGK5 seems roughly equal, except for the calcite- and slag-tempered coarse wares (fabrics D and C). A more explicit way to visualise the variations in the data set is through its residuals (Table 3.1(b)). For the calculation of residuals Table 3.1 was reconfigured leaving aside the group of unidentified fabrics, as these would not contribute to our understanding of fabric variation between MEK1 and MGK5. Calculations are based on the *eves* values. The formulae used here are taken from Baxter (1994, 112–113): Expected values E = Row total × Column total/Overall total; residual values $r_{ij} = (O_{ij} - E_{ij})/E_{ij}^{1/2}$.

As expected, calcite- and slag-tempered wares show the greatest deviation (Table 3.1a). The low values of residuals are linked to the generally low values in the data table (Table 3.1). Although the degree of variation is illustrated by the residuals, it remains difficult to

Table 3.1(a) Proportional distribution of wares by excavation area.

Distribution of wares	Fabric group	MEK1 (eves)	%	MGK5 (eves)	%	Total (eves)	%
	Unidentified	(17.33)	33.2	(30.19)	16.5	(47.52)	20.2
	Calcite-tempered (D)	(0.57)	1.1	(0.33)	0.2	(0.90)	0.4
	Fine ware	(33.61)	64.3	(141.48)	77.3	(175.09)	74.5
	Grog-tempered (E)	(0.65)	1.2	(2.73)	1.5	(3.38)	1.4
	Slag-tempered (C)	(0.12)	0.2	(8.18)	4.5	(8.30)	3.5
Total		(52.28)	100	(182.91)	100	(235.19)	100

Table 3.1(b) Distribution of wares. Residuals.

Firing group	E	G
Calcite-tempered (D)	+0.97	−0.47
Fine ware	+0.18	−0.08
Grog-tempered (E)	+0.03	−0.01
Slag-tempered (C)	−1.15	+0.55

assess how significant these variations are with regard to the whole data set specifically, since in this case they occur with the smallest groups of ware. A formal significance test, known as the chi-squared test, is statistically possible (Baxter 1994, 113). In this process the contribution of each row in the table (ie in our case each fabric group) is assessed in relation to the overall variation of the data set (Baxter 1994, 112–113). The chi-square statistic, however, is conducted on discrete data (ie counts) (Orton and Tyers 1990, 87). Neither *eves* nor percentage data are suitable for such calculations and might lead to a distortion regarding the scale of variations (Orton and Tyers 1990, 87–88). Another problem concerns the sparsity of the table resulting in low expected values for some groups of variables. This would impair a significance test, since these groups might show spuriously high contributions to the overall variation (Baxter 1994, 113).

As a consequence, the analysis has to remain on a descriptive level, as illustrated in Tables 3.1 and 3.1a. We may conclude that the two excavation areas show a broadly similar distribution of petrographically defined wares with the potentially significant exception of the slag-tempered coarse ware fabric C, which contributes more to the data of MGK5 than to MEK1.

Fine wares: Distribution of firing patterns

Five groups prevail among the fine wares (Table 3.2(a)), including A, B2, B3, G1 and G2. The largest of these, G1 (27.3 per cent), shows very little variation between the two trenches (cf residuals). Groups A (21.2 per cent) and G2 (20.1 per cent), however, suggest some difference in distribution. Group A is considerably more abundant in MEK1, where it accounts for more than one-third of all fine wares (39.1 per cent), compared with less than one-fifth in MGK5 (16.9 per cent). Group G2, by contrast, is the second largest in MGK5 (22.7 per cent), whereas it is of minor importance in MEK1 (9.3 per cent) (cf Table 3.2(b)). Fabric groups B2 (9.9 per cent) and B3 (10.9 per cent) show a similarly diverse distribution pattern with B2 stronger in MEK1 and B3 more popular in MGK5. The strongest variation, however, occurs with fabric group A (see residuals, Table 3.2(a)). Neither the petrographically defined wares nor the fine ware groups are exclusive to any one excavation area. Three of the minor fabric groups, B1, I1 and K, will not be considered further here, as they

Table 3.2(a) Distribution of firing patterns by excavation area.

Distribution of firing patterns	Groups	MEK1		MGK5		Total	
		(eves)	%	*(eves)*	%	*(eves)*	%
	A	*(13.15)*	39.1	*(23.97)*	16.9	*(37.12)*	21.2
	B1	*(0.41)*	1.2	*(1.15)*	0.8	*(1.56)*	0.9
	B2	*(5.52)*	16.4	*(11.72)*	8.3	*(17.24)*	9.9
	B3	*(1.16)*	3.5	*(17.85)*	12.6	*(19.01)*	10.9
	B4	*(0.84)*	2.5	*(5.08)*	3.6	*(5.92)*	3.4
	G1	*(8.89)*	26.5	*(38.91)*	27.5	*(47.80)*	27.3
	G2	*(3.14)*	9.3	*(32.13)*	22.7	*(35.27)*	20.1
	I1	*(0.27)*	0.8	*(6.62)*	4.7	*(6.89)*	3.9
	I2	*(0.06)*	0.2	*(2.79)*	2.0	*(2.85)*	1.6
	K	*(0.17)*	0.5	*(1.26)*	0.9	*(1.43)*	0.8
Total		*(33.61)*	100	*(141.48)*	100	*(175.09)*	100

Table 3.2(b) Distribution of firing patterns. Residuals.

Firing groups	E	G
A	+2.25	−1.09
B1	+0.20	−0.90
B2	+1.21	−0.59
B3	−1.30	+0.63
B4	−0.28	+0.13
G1	−0.09	+0.04
G2	−1.39	+0.67
I1	−0.91	+0.32
I2	−0.66	+0.32
K	−0.19	+0.09

are unlikely to contribute to our understanding of fabric distributions. Groups B1 and K are very small in size and fabric K has been found to conflate distinct groups of slip ware (cf Chapter 4). Fabric group I1 represents misfired vessels.

Fine wares: Distribution of form

Key: SOF: small open form (dia < 12 cm); MOF: medium open form (12 cm < dia < 26 cm); LOF: large open form (dia > 26 cm); SCF: small closed form (H < 15 cm); MCF: medium closed form (15 cm < H < 35 cm); LCF: large closed forms (H > 35 cm); LID: Lid; XF: unidentified form.

Table 3.3(a) shows that, with the exception of medium open forms, the assemblages consist largely of closed vessel forms. There is, however, variation in the distribution of the single form groups across the two excavation areas. Medium open forms and small closed forms feature more prominently in MGK5. Small closed forms show the greatest difference in distribution (see residuals, Table 3.3(b)). Medium and large closed forms, on the other hand, constitute a sizeable proportion (68 per cent) of the pottery from MEK1. The variation between the excavation areas within the group of medium closed vessels is less strong, though (Table 3.3(b)).

Table 3.3(a) Distribution of forms by excavation area.

Distribution of form Classification	MEK1		MGK5		Total	
	(eves)	%	(eves)	%	(eves)	%
SOF	(1.10)	3.3	(1.70)	1.2	(2.80)	**1.6**
MOF	(3.84)	11.4	(36.11)	25.5	(39.95)	**22.8**
LOF	(1.40)	4.2	(5.53)	3.9	(6.93)	**3.9**
SCF	(1.33)	4.0	(28.32)	20.0	(29.65)	**16.9**
MCF	(13.81)	41.1	(43.21)	30.5	(57.02)	**32.6**
LCF	(9.06)	26.9	(21.71)	15.4	(30.77)	**17.6**
LID	(0.39)	1.1	(1.12)	0.8	(1.51)	**0.9**
XF	(2.68)	8.0	(3.78)	2.7	(6.46)	**3.7**
Total	**(33.61)**	**100**	**(141.48)**	**100**	**(175.09)**	**100**

Table 3.3(b) Distribution of forms by excavation area. Residuals.

Classification	E	G
SOF	+0.83	−0.39
MOF	−1.29	+0.61
LOF	+0.11	−0.05
SCF	−1.76	+0.84
MCF	+1.04	−0.49
LCF	+1.44	−0.68
LID	+0.21	−0.10

Distribution of context-by-form-by-firing group

Finally, the distribution of form by firing group is studied with regard to the different excavation areas. In contrast to the previous tables, variations are now expressed in a three-way table context-by-form-by-firing group (Table 3.4(a)).

As the two different excavation areas are now combined in the rows of the table, percentage values are no longer suitable to offset the differences in size between the assemblages, and the interpretation of this table will therefore focus on its residual values (Table 3.4(b)).

Key: Values noted with '. . .' are too small to be expressed as a decimal fraction.

Table 3.4 shows the context-by-form combinations of Table 3.3 now as rows, while the firing groups appear as columns. The dominant context-by-form combinations are for

Table 3.4(a) Distribution of context-by-form-by-firing group.

Context/form	Fabric A	Fabric B2	Fabric B3	Fabric B4	Fabric G1	Fabric G2	Fabric I2	Total (eves)
MGK5/SOF	0	0.08	0.16	0.31	0.23	0.68	0.08	*1.54*
MEK1/SOF	0.40	0.29	0.15	0	0	0.26	0	*1.10*
MGK5/MOF	1.66	4.55	5.93	4.11	6.55	6.57	2.44	*31.81*
MEK1/MOF	0.89	0.69	0.13	0.48	0.91	0.61	0.03	*3.74*
MGK5/LOF	1.41	0.47	0.71	0	1.52	1.10	0	*5.21*
MEK1/LOF	0.56	0.46	0	0	0.12	0.23	0	*1.37*
MGK5/SCF	6.39	0.98	2.43	0	9.79	8.19	0	*27.78*
MEK1/SCF	0.36	0.50	0.02	0.27	0.18	0	0	*1.33*
MGK5/MCF	8.83	3.58	5.56	0.03	13.14	10.23	0.16	*41.53*
MEK1/MCF	6.21	1.43	0.54	0.09	3.88	1.32	0.03	*13.50*
MGK5/LCF	5.6	1.17	2.05	0	7.22	4.04	0	*20.08*
MEK1/LCF	3.41	1.71	0.27	0	2.83	0.43	0	*8.65*
MGK5/LID	0.08	0.05	0.08	0.19	0.09	0.55	0	*1.04*
MEK1/LID	0.13	0.18	0.05	0	0	0.03	0	*0.39*
MGK5/XF	0	0.84	0.93	0.44	0.37	0.77	0.11	*3.46*
MEK1/XF	1.19	0.26	0	0	0.97	0.26	0	*2.68*
Total (eves)	*37.12*	*17.24*	*19.01*	*5.92*	*47.80*	*35.27*	*2.85*	*165.21*

Table 3.4(b) Distribution of context-by-form-by-firing group. Residuals.

Context/form	Fabric A	Fabric B2	Fabric B3	Fabric B4	Fabric G1	Fabric G2	Fabric I2
MGK5/SOF	−0.58	−0.19	−0.03	+1.23	−0.32	+0.60	+0.33
MEK1/SOF	+0.28	+0.53	+0.07	−0.18	−0.56	+0.04	−0.13
MGK5/MOF	−2.06	+0.73	+1.21	+3.19	−0.89	−0.10	+2.55
MEK1/MOF	+0.05	+0.50	−0.45	+1.08	−0.17	−0.21	−0.13
MGK5/LOF	+0.21	−0.07	+0.15	−0.39	. . .	−0.01	−0.29
MEK1/LOF	+0.45	+0.86	−0.39	−0.20	−0.44	−0.11	−0.15
MGK5/SCF	+0.04	−1.09	−0.40	−0.92	+0.58	+0.90	−0.69
MEK1/SCF	+0.10	+0.99	−0.36	+1.15	−0.33	−0.53	−0.14
MGK5/MCF	−0.17	−0.30	+0.38	−1.09	+0.29	+0.43	−0.65
MEK1/MCF	+1.81	+0.05	−0.80	−0.50	−0.03	−0.92	−0.41
MGK5/LCF	+0.05	−0.60	−0.15	−0.78	+0.55	−0.13	−0.58
MEK1/LCF	+1.00	+0.88	−0.71	−0.51	+0.19	−1.04	−0.38
MGK5/LID	−0.31	−0.16	−0.11	+0.90	−0.38	+0.69	−0.13
MEK1/LID	+0.14	+0.71	+0.05	−0.10	−0.33	−0.18	. . .

MGK5 medium open forms and small to large closed forms and for MEK1 medium and large closed forms and, to a lesser extent, medium open forms (Table 3.4). Medium open and small closed forms in MGK5 and medium and large closed forms in MEK1 show the greatest variation, while patterns for medium and large closed forms from MGK5 and medium open forms from MEK1 are less strong by comparison (Table 3.4a). Some of the two-way interactions established in the previous tables are still recognisable. Fabric A is particularly strong with medium and large closed vessel forms from MEK1 (Table 3.4a). Both groups individually were associated with MEK1 (Tables 3.2a and 3.3a). Fabric G2, by contrast, is popular with small closed vessel forms from MGK5 (Table 3.4a). Fabric G2 and small closed vessel forms were also well represented in MGK5 as individual groups (Tables 3.2a and 3.3a). The same applies to fabric B3 and medium open forms from MGK5 (Table 3.4a). Fabric B3 was more popular in MGK5, as were medium open forms (Tables 3.2a and 3.3a). Although fabric B3 shows high *eves* values for medium closed forms (Table 3.4), little variation is noted for this category with regard to the whole data set (Table 3.4a). Apart from these established variations, some new patterns emerge. Fabric B2, while predominantly occurring with form combinations from MEK1, seems also popular with medium open forms from MGK5 (Table 3.4a). Fabric B4, on the other hand, is relatively strong with medium open forms from MEK1 (Table 3.4a), although both, fabric and form group, are generally more associated with MGK5 (Tables 3.2a and 3.3a). This points to a fabric-by-form interaction in addition to the context-by-fabric and context-by-form interactions noted in the variation regarding the distribution of fabrics and forms across the two excavation areas. Other fabric groups also show clear preferences for certain vessel forms, including B3 and I2 which are both dominated by open forms (Table 3.4a), but at the same time this pattern fits with the context distribution previously observed (Tables 3.2a and 3.3a). Fabric I2 represents a very small group with a distinct pattern that might reflect a specific, chronologically sensitive, pottery style. In the case of fabric B4, the high residual values for closed vessel forms appear spurious, as *eves* values for closed forms occur only with MEK1, where they are very low (Table 3.4). In addition, this fabric seems generally more characteristic for open forms. It is interesting to note that fabric G1 again shows relatively little variation indicating a tendency towards MGK5 and closed vessel forms, but this is not very strong (Table 3.4a). The three-way table reflects more realistically the complexity of the data set. Viewed as a whole, however, it is more difficult to examine the interdependencies of the variables.

THE CONVENTIONAL APPROACH: AN ASSESSMENT

In the following an attempt is made to interpret the observed variations in distribution patterns chronologically. In this respect petrographically defined wares pose particular problems, since the coarse ware groups are very small by comparison (Tables 3.1 and 3.1a) and variations may be functional as well as chronological. Fine wares and among these specifically the firing groups are more likely to provide chronological distinctions.

With regard to form distribution, the main emphasis is put on the four dominant groups, including medium open and all closed vessel forms. Considering the numismatically testified earlier date of MGK5 (Chapter 2), we may assume that any form/fabric combinations specifically linked to these assemblages are likely to pre-date forms and fabrics prevailing in MEK1.

MGK5 assemblages by comparison show a high proportion of firing groups G2 and B3, and of medium open and small closed vessel forms. Firing group G2 is strongly represented by small closed vessel forms. Firing group B3 has a high proportion of medium open vessel forms in MGK5 assemblages. This suggests a correlation between the form and fabric distribution in these particular cases. Medium open and small closed forms in firing group G2 and B3 are therefore likely to be chronologically earlier than material predominantly linked to MEK1.

MEK1 assemblages are dominated by firing groups A and B2, and by medium and large closed forms. Group A often occurs with medium and large closed forms. Firing group B2 shows a greater amount of large closed forms in MEK1. As far as other form groups are concerned, however, B2 displays a diverse pattern with a large proportion of medium open forms in MGK5 assemblages. This may suggest that firing group B2 consists to a considerable extent of earlier pottery forms, which occur in MEK1 assemblages as residual material. Firing group G1, finally, is more popular with closed vessels, but does not display great variation across the excavation areas. There seems to be a larger proportion of G1 vessels in MGK5, but the fabric also contributes much to the MEK1 assemblages (Table 3.2). The minor firing groups, B4 and I2, also fit this rough chronological sketch, as both occur largely in medium open forms with preponderance in MGK5 assemblages.

From the perspective of gradual chronological change, there seems to be an increase in the size of closed forms, accompanied by a decrease in the use of open vessels. The minor form groups of small and large open vessels, though more popular in MEK1 assemblages, do not compensate for the strong decrease in medium open forms. Parallel to this development a change apparently occurs in firing patterns from B3, G2 and G1 towards A, which, in technical terms, corresponds to a gradual increase in firing temperature.

This broad chronological outline aside, problems remain with the interpretation at a more detailed level, specifically with the attribution of single vessel types and fabric groups. It is important in this respect to emphasise again that all analysed assemblages are of secondary status (Carver 1985, 356). Variations are therefore likely to reflect not only the actual chronological development, but also differences in site formation processes.

The system of grouping variables is so far determined by its practical feasibility and coherence throughout the data set. Many of these groups appear to be too coarse to facilitate a distinction between residual and contemporary pottery and most probably still comprise chronologically diverse material. This applies equally to form and fabric groups. As far as the form groups are concerned, it is difficult to refine the categories. The high degree of fragmentation of the pottery made the attribution of a sizeable proportion (c 15 per cent) to any specific form category, such as jar or jug, flagon or amphora, impossible. Even these vessel categories, though, were used over considerable periods of time with changes limited to stylistic variations. In order to be able to distinguish more reliably between residual and more contemporary pottery types, it is necessary to examine the individual shapes. The sparsity of the data set already noticeable in Table 3.4 makes it almost impossible to recognise any significant distribution patterns at such a detailed level. The same is true for the stratigraphic units, which are currently grouped by excavation area. On the level of single contexts, however, the values of variables would be too low.

With regard to the fabrics, they already represent separate ware or firing groups. However, it is not clear how chronologically determinant the single firing groups are and what period of time each group would cover. Firing group G1 is particularly problematic in this respect, as it is strongly represented in both excavation areas, suggesting some chronological overlap in the material. The numismatic evidence, however, indicates a potential time gap between the occupation levels of MGK5 and MEK1. Without an evaluation of the significance of variations and a more refined level of analysis for the variables 'context' and 'form' it is difficult to gain a better insight into the chronological relationship of the ceramic material from both areas.

— 4 —

CHRONOLOGICAL ANALYSIS USING 'PIE-SLICE'

PROGRAMME AND ANALYTICAL METHODS

'Pie-slice' is a computer package for quantitative assemblage comparison, which was developed at the Institute of Archaeology UCL (Orton and Tyers 1993).* The program was conceived specifically with a view to the problems of multi-period urban sites comprising a number of complementary statistical tools, which provide a comprehensive analysis of the data. The package addresses the problems outlined in the first part of the analysis, including the statistical restriction through the data format, the grouping of variables and the sparsity of the data set.

For some time, quantitative assemblage comparisons have been restrained by the lack of a statistically appropriate measure or format of the data (Orton and Tyers 1990, 87). Pottery measured in *eves* is recorded as fractional data. The relevant analytical statistics, however, are based on discrete data, ie counts. In the initial preparatory stage of the analysis, Pie-slice transforms the data through a series of calculations into counts, which due to their derivative nature are called 'pseudo-counts' (Orton and Tyers 1993, 5). These counts express the proportions of the different types of pottery present in each assemblage and the contribution the single types and assemblages make with regard to the complete data set (Orton and Tyers 1990, 89–91, 104). The data are currently in a format which enables us to compare assemblages in terms of proportions of pottery types present and to assess the significance of observed variations (Baxter 1994, 110–112; Orton and Tyers 1990, 91).

The subsequent assemblage comparison is conducted using quasi-log-linear and correspondence analysis. Over the past decade this combined approach of analytical and exploratory methods has gained preference in the statistical literature on seriation techniques (Baxter 1994, 138; Orton and Tyers 1993, 194).

Quasi-log-linear analysis is a model-based technique, which highlights interactions between variables, for pottery – usually context, fabric and form – reflecting the structure of the data set (Bishop *et al* 1975, 311–312; Orton and Tyers 1990, 91–96). These interactions are visually expressed by correspondence analysis, which also provides detailed information on the single components of the plot (Orton and Tyers 1993, 13–15). Correspondence

---

* The computer package 'Pie-slice' is currently available through Clive Orton, Institute of Archaeology, University College London.

analysis has received widespread application as a seriation technique, due to the immediately recognisable 'horseshoe' shape of chronological patterns in the plot (Baxter 1994, 119f.; Orton *et al* 1993, 192).

A detailed account of the mathematics and theories underlying the analysis was published by Orton and Tyers (1990, 1993). The single steps are here more generally explained with regard to the archaeological background. After the pseudo-count transformation the data are first examined by quasi-log-linear analysis. The models used in this procedure reflect the possible forms of interaction and interdependencies between the three variables. They are predetermined and follow a hierarchy of increasing complexity intended to simulate various archaeological scenarios relating to chronological, functional or spatial variations (Orton and Tyers 1990, 91–92). The data set is compared to each model using a goodness-of-fit test (Orton and Tyers 1990, 92). At the end of this mathematical process the best fitting model is presented as a guideline for further interpretation (Orton and Tyers 1990, 95).

One of the major difficulties of this study, as demonstrated in the conventional analysis, is the sparsity of the data set. As this frequently occurs with archaeological data, Pie-slice was adapted specifically to address this problem by offering facilities for data reduction, a mechanism to reduce the number of groups of variables by merging or deleting them, both manually and as an automated function (Orton and Tyers 1990, 98, 102). This allows for the input of personal archaeological expertise, while the mathematical process ensures the coherent handling even of very large and complex data sets. A further advantage of the manual data reduction is that specific configurations are saved separately without changing the original data set, which facilitates an experimental approach testing various different grouping strategies. The manual data reduction is optional and, if exercised, precedes the computerised function, which is an integrated part of the program to prepare the data for the quasi-log-linear analysis and follows strict mathematical rules. This function is called simultaneous reduction of dimension (*srd*) and searches the different marginal tables of the data set for small cells, cells with low values, to be either merged or, if this is not possible, deleted (Orton and Tyers 1990, 99). The three basic marginal tables are fabric-by-form, form-by-context and context-by-fabric (Orton and Tyers 1993, 6). In the reduction process these two-way marginal tables are extended to account for the respective third variable (eg fabric-by-form and context) (Orton and Tyers 1990, 99). As each of the three tables has a different set of values, emphasising interactions of different variables, each is reduced in a separate process. Starting from the two-way table, rows and columns are examined regarding the occurrence of combinations between the two variables. Within each variable, only groups that display a similar profile are merged. Groups with small cells, which display rare combinations in the data set below a certain set value, are not left on their own, but are considered to be either merged with a larger group or, if they are distinct from all others, deleted (Orton and Tyers 1990, 99). The remaining two-way combinations of the table are then used to build another two-way table with the third variable. In this second stage only the third variable is considered for reduction (Orton and Tyers 1990, 99). The resulting table is called 'doubly reduced' and provides the basis for the quasi-log-linear analysis (Orton and Tyers 1990, 99). According to the three doubly reduced tables, three hypotheses are tested: IIA – independence of fabric-by-form and context, IIB – independence of form-by-context and fabric, IIC – independence of context-by-fabric and form (Orton and Tyers 1990, 99). The analysis finally provides three different models for the three hypotheses, which should help in understanding the archaeological situation reflected by the data set. Apart from this aspect of analytical guidance, the quasi-log-linear models also provide an important control mechanism regarding the validity and soundness of the possible conclusions. If only the most complex model (model M5) is accepted, the established modes of interaction between variables are deemed very intricate and it would be hard to find a conclusive archaeological explanation (Orton and Tyers 1990, 95). In fact none of the configurations producing such models have been used in this study. There is also the possibility that the program might reject a data set as unsuitable for analysis, if none of the suggested models are accepted (Orton and Tyers 1990, 100).

Following the quasi-log-linear analysis and complementary to it, the reduced marginal tables are examined by correspondence analysis (Orton and Tyers 1990, 101–102). The correspondence analysis illustrates the contributions of the single groups of variables and expresses their variations by means of distance in a plot (Baxter 1994, 110–112). Additional information is given on the overall variation of the data set and how much of it is captured in the respective plot. This enables us to identify the most important groups and the most significant variations and focus on their interpretation. The groups shown in the correspondence analysis plot are those obtained from the statistical reduction and provide further insight into possible chronological interrelations of assemblages.

With its combination of statistical applications and personal input, Pie-slice offers a highly flexible and transparent approach with a maximum of control over the analytical process. The special provisions regarding the sparsity and lack of homogeneity, the co-occurrence of residual and contemporary elements of the data make the program particularly suitable for the analysis of the ceramic assemblages from Merv.

EXPLORING THE SEQUENCE OF MEK1 AND MGK5

The original analysis (Puschnigg 2000) was restricted to material excavated up until 1997, which comprised the whole of MEK1 assemblages and pottery of the first three seasons from MGK5. Although incomplete, this first study laid the foundation for our understanding of the relationship between the two excavation areas and shaped the strategies for the manual data reduction, and therefore provides the starting point for our account of the Pie-slice analysis.

Initial exploratory test runs demonstrated that the data set in its unmodified form was too large in terms of its variability, the calculations exceeded the computer facilities and the analysis was abandoned. Complementary methods had to be taken into consideration to gather information on typological aspects of the pottery shapes and interrelations between assemblages. We therefore undertook a qualitative seriation of the assemblages based on the presence/absence of vessel types. The seriation program 'seriate' was taken from the 'Iagraves' computer package (Duncan *et al* 1989). On the seriation diagram both areas – Gyaur and Erk Kala – appear in consecutive order (Figure 4.1). Within each trench, however, the sequence of contexts does not correspond with the stratigraphic matrices. Single contexts, which belong to late phases on the matrices, seem to appear much 'earlier', higher up, in the diagram. A cross-check against a file of general statistical calculations produced by the Pie-slice package during the data transformation showed a low mean measure of the pottery fragments from these contexts indicating a high degree of residuality (Orton and Tyers 1990, 96f). After manual readjustment of the seriation diagram some of the principal features became clearer (Figure 4.2). While the shape of the diagonal indicates a continuous sequence without interruptions (Carver 1985, 360f), the two excavation areas seem

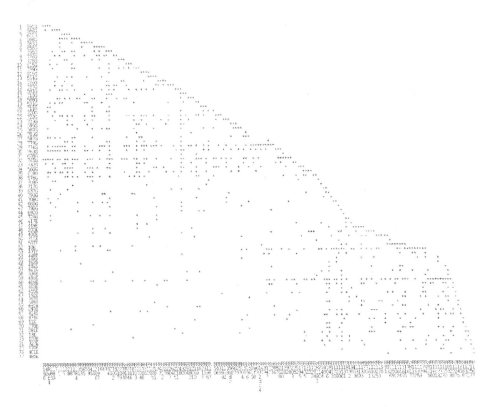

Figure 4.1: Seriation diagram for MEK1 and MGK5 using the 'Iagraves' computer package.

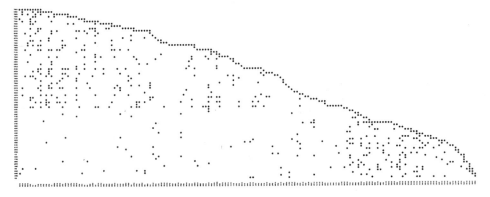

Figure 4.2: Manually readjusted seriation diagram using MS Excel.

strangely disconnected with a diffuse intermediate zone of rather sparse assemblages (Figure 4.2). Although the qualitative seriation cannot fully explain the relation between both areas, it clearly demonstrated that it is more intricate than first anticipated. The data structure within each area has been sufficiently articulated to resume the quantitative analysis.

Consequently the size of the data set was reduced manually by grouping values of variables based on archaeological criteria (Orton and Tyers 1990, 106). Any grouping, however, is derived from an interpretation of the role of the specific variables and must therefore follow strict and clearly defined guidelines. 'Pie-slice' with its comprehensive approach to assemblage comparison is designed for a variety of different research questions, including not only chronological, but also functional and spatial analyses (Orton and Tyers 1993). As this study focuses on the chronological aspect of the pottery, special care was taken to eliminate elements, which would obscure results and/or are likely to account for functional or spatial patterns (Orton and Tyers 1990, 107).

The variable 'context' (original number 86): Following the recording system applied in the excavations of MEK1 and MGK5, each context represents (as closely as possible) a single depositional event. Consequently each context may be regarded as an independent pottery assemblage (Orton and Tyers 1990: 107). As mentioned above, no coherent phasing has yet been established for the two buildings. The final phasing of contexts is also aggravated by the organic character, in which the mudbrick structures developed, including multiple alterations in separate rooms that were not necessarily synchronised (Herrmann *et al* 1996, 11). As a consequence the single contexts remained unmodified at first.

The variable 'ware' (original number 14): The fine ware types were defined with respect to their potential as chronological indicators. In order to observe changes of fabric through time, no groupings were suggested for the fine wares. The petrographically distinct coarse wares might show functional as well as chronological variation and were therefore omitted from the analysis. Also omitted were the fabrics 'K', which proved to be an ill-defined type conflating at least two different red-slipped wares, fabric 'I1', the misfired pottery, and 'X', the code for unidentified fabrics.

The variable 'form' (original number 483): Variation in form is often attributed to differences in function rather than in chronology. The secondary nature of the deposits at Merv, however, certainly obscures, if not eliminates, any functional patterns, increasing the significance of the variable 'form' as a chronological indicator.

The initial count of shape codes comprises rims and bases. Early on in the test analysis, it became clear that the base shapes would lead to a bias, as fragments on the whole were more complete, thus dominating the results, while they showed far less variability and change over time. The 83 codes representing base shapes and their 'similars' were consequently deleted, and the analysis focused on rim fragments, initially 1488.

Rims show by far the greatest variability, including a range of forms that occur only once or twice across the whole stratigraphic sequence. One of the most difficult issues in this study was to devise appropriate strategies for the rigorous sifting of shapes and sensible grouping of the key pottery types. Selection criteria were sought to be transparent and independent from previous classifications.

Two classes of shape codes were first considered for merging: codes that differed only in decoration and those labelled with 's' for similar shapes.

Alphanumeric suffices were added to the shape codes to describe patterns of decoration, such as 'dc2' (decoration 2) for a wavy incised line. Individual suffices were combined as necessary to express the relevant decorative patterns (eg a rim decorated with one straight incised line and an incised wavy line below was recorded as R*1l dc2) (Rim – 1 line – decoration 2). This system guaranteed a precise recording of decorative features, which might be characteristic of certain vessel types or indicate chronological development. In view of the sparsity of the data set, however, these distinctions proved to be too detailed, and all codes referring to variations of the same shape (eg R13dc3, R13dc2dc4) were joined. This reduced the amount of shape codes by 40.

In a further step, shape codes and their 'similars' were examined. If the records for a 'similar' code were consistent with the original shape code in diameter and range of fabric types, their values were merged. 'Similar' codes that differed from the original shape, but appeared to be coherent, were acknowledged as independent shapes. If the records of a 'similar' shape were inconsistent, the code was deleted.

In this process the values of 85 'similar' codes were joined with their original shapes. Five 'similar' shapes were left as independent codes, and ten were deleted as inconsistent. In one case the shape code of a vessel rim was merged with the code assigned to the near-complete form of the same type (R25 and Ref2).

In the next phase of the manual data reduction sparse rim shapes were targeted. Statistical analyses focus on average ceramic populations and identify dominating patterns and trends. Rare pottery types do not contribute to the results, but may increase the variability of the data set and consequently obscure the main patterns. Consequently all rim shapes, which occurred only once or twice in the data set, were deleted. These comprised 93 codes.

Another 46 shape codes were omitted, partly because they might have confused the results, partly because they would not have contributed. The records of ten of these shape codes appeared to be inconsistent. A further 34 shapes were omitted, because they appeared too distinct to be joined, yet too sparse to contribute to the analysis on their own. Their total *eves* value was generally below 1.0 and they occurred on average four times in the data set.

Two shape codes represented large storage vessels of the kind that furnished the store-room in MGK5. They were deleted to avoid possible functional patterns in the data set. No other shapes were found to be problematic in this respect.

Three shape codes proved to be invalid and were eliminated from the data set.

The remaining 132 shapes were arranged as groups. First, the rim shapes were distinguished according to patterns of occurrence, as shown in the seriation diagrams (Figure 4.2), which led to three principal groups: (a) shapes that were found only in MEK1; (b) shapes that were found only in MGK5; (c) shapes that occurred in both areas.

Within these groups these rim shapes were considered for merging, which were similar in diameter, range of fabric types and stylistic features. Decisions on the groupings were influenced both by the nature of this study and personal experience with the material in the field. As excavations progressed, an increasing number of vessel profiles could be reconstructed. These well-defined shapes, which would appear more likely to be contemporary with the occupation of the structures, were consequently left as separate groups, whereas lesser known shapes were combined as groups of open or closed forms. It is this part of the manual data reduction which is obviously prone to subjectivity and bias, although this seems inevitable with regard to the great variability in the data. Future research may prompt changes in the arrangements of the groups. However, most of the elements joined to larger groups in this process had very small values and limited alterations are highly unlikely to affect the main patterns that emerged from the computer analysis. Finally, 56 groups were submitted for the analysis (Table 4.1).

Following the deletion and grouping of values, configuration 'A' was obtained, which consisted of 86 contexts, nine wares and 56 forms.

Table 4.1 Summary of the manual reduction of values of the variable 'form'.

The variable 'form'	
Original number of shapes	**483**
Base shapes	−83
Codes distinguishing decorations	−40
Similar shapes	−85
Rims and semi-complete forms	−1
Rare shapes	−93
Inconsistent, sparse shape codes	−44
Functionally biased shapes	−2
Invalid shape codes	−3
Remaining shape codes	**132**

Two of the original configurations (A and B) are discussed below. The values given for each variable represent the number of context, ware and form groups obtained through manual grouping before the computerised data reduction (*srd*) is conducted to merge or delete cells, which still contained values below an expected limit (see above, cf Orton and Tyers 1990, 98f).

(a) Configuration 'A' aims at the representation of Erk Kala, Area 1. Contexts and form groups are included unmodified. For the variable 'fabric' all coarse ware fabrics are deleted. Configuration A before the *srd* – reduction: Context 86, Ware 9, Form 56.

(b) Configuration 'B' focuses on Gyaur Kala, Area 5. All Erk Kala contexts are drawn together in one group. The variable 'form' remains unmodified. Coarse ware fabrics are omitted. Configuration B before the *srd* – reduction: Context 48, Ware 9, Form 56.

For each configuration the interactions between the variables are summarised in three marginal tables, representing the various combinations between 'context', 'ware' and 'form' (Orton and Tyers 1993, 8). The order of the marginal tables corresponds with the automatic order of the computer package. All marginal tables are displayed in full length, since they will be examined in detail. Contexts marked with the letter 'E' refer to Erk Kala, Area 1, those with 'G' to Gyaur Kala, Area 5. For the first marginal table explanations are given for the single tables and parts of the analysis to facilitate an understanding of the plot and interpretation. The numbers in brackets inserted in the discussions indicate the coordinates for the location of the groups on the plot.

Configuration A (pie-slice ouput plus comments in brackets)

Marginal table: context-by-ware

Data from file 'ctestb.pie', 2020 records (context 86, ware 14, form 483)

[The number of records given here is taken from the transformed table, where records of the same shape code and fabric within a single context are merged into one. The numbers given for each variable refer to the initial numbers counted, as the data set was transformed into pseudo-counts.]

Configuration: 'context-ware', marginal table: 'context x ware' (9 × 6)

[The numbers in brackets represent the numbers of groups formed during the *srd* reduction, simultaneous reduction of dimension.]

DATA MATRIX

[Table 4.2 shows the raw marginal table with the distribution of each fabric within the single groups of contexts after the *srd* reduction. Values here no longer represent *eves*, but *pseudo-counts* calculated from the *eves* values. The totals in the right column and bottom line indicate the contribution of each group to the overall amount (cf Orton and Tyers 1993, 10). The tilde ~ designates groups that were joined in the process of data reduction. Detailed information on the constituents of these groups is given in the *membership lists* (see below). Three of the fabrics, A, G1 and G2 and two large context groups, ~409E and ~765G, are the most dominant features of this data matrix.]

RESIDUALS

[Table 4.3 indicates the differences between the values of fabrics recorded and the values expected with a 'flat' distribution of fabrics across the site (cf Orton and Tyers 1993, 11).

Table 4.2 Data matrix.

		1 A	2 B2	3 B3	4 B4	5 G1	6 G2	7 Total
1	~588G	29.6	1.7	0.6	1.0	0.3	2.9	36.3
2	~414E	4.6	3.2	0.6	1.1	4.5	1.0	14.9
3	~403E	9.9	17.8	2.9	0.6	13.5	4.8	49.5
4	~409E	43.2	9.3	5.3	2.1	44.7	16.1	120.8
5	~774G	1.8	1.3	4.6	3.0	21.2	10.3	42.2
6	~576G	3.8	0.3	8.9	0.3	30.5	2.1	45.9
7	~765G	28.4	5.4	8.3	0.9	45.6	45.3	134.0
8	~582G	1.7	3.7	1.9	6.4	5.6	4.9	24.1
9	~722G	10.0	1.1	8.5	0.5	11.1	3.7	34.8
10	Total	133.0	43.8	41.5	16.0	177.0	91.1	502.5

Table 4.3 Residuals.

		1 A	2 B2	3 B3	4 B4	5 G1	6 G2
1	~588G	+20.0	−1.4	−2.4	−0.1	−2.5	−3.7
2	~414E	+0.7	+1.9	−0.7	+0.6	−0.8	−1.7
3	~403E	−3.2	+13.5	−1.2	−1.0	−3.9	−4.1
4	~409E	+11.2	−1.2	−4.7	−1.7	+2.2	−5.8
5	~774G	−9.4	−2.4	+1.1	+1.7	+6.3	+2.6
6	~576G	−8.4	−3.7	+5.1	−1.2	+14.4	−6.2
7	~765G	−7.1	−6.3	−2.8	−3.3	−1.6	+21.0
8	~582G	−4.7	+1.5	−0.1	+5.6	−2.9	+0.5
9	~722G	+0.7	−1.9	+5.6	−0.6	−1.2	−2.6

The formula used here for calculating residual values is: Observed values minus Expected values, 'O' – 'E'. Note that this is different from the formula used in Part 1. High values are recorded for the fabrics A, B2, G1 and G2 in the context groups ~588G, ~403E, ~576G and ~765G.]

MEMBERSHIP LISTS

The following list shows all the groups of variables with their constituents. The dominating component usually determines the name of the group (Orton and Tyers 1993, 20f.).

Configuration: 'context-ware', Variable: 'context'

~588G =	192E	193E	200E	311E	327E	336E	449E	588G	637G
~414E =	414E	720G							
~403E =	257E	403E	425E	455E	489E	493E	660G	708G	728G
~409E =	245E	406E	409E	431E	448E	566G	583G	595G	618G
	711G	723G	763G	766G					
~774G =	581G	774G							
~576G =	567G	576G	715G	726G	776G				
~765G =	427E	560G	732G	765G	779G				
~582G =	492E	531G	544G	582G	615G	793G			
~722G =	281E	692G	722G	798G					

Configuration: 'context-ware', Variable: 'ware'

A   B2   B3   B4   G1   G2

CORRESPONDENCE ANALYSIS

Decomposition of inertia by principal axes.   [The decomposition of the inertia helps with the interpretation of the correspondence analysis, which concentrates on the first two principal axes. Table 4.4 shows how much of the variability of the data set is captured by each of the axis (Perc). In the following column these values are displayed cumulatively. A reliable plot should capture at least 50 per cent of the total variability in the first two axes (cf Orton and Tyers 1993, 14). This particular plot captures 64.25 per cent.]

Table 4.4 Decomposition of inertia by principal axes.

Principal axis	Inertia	Perc	Cum	Histogram
1	0.190806	37.41	37.41	*********
2	0.136941	26.85	64.25	******
3	0.091880	18.01	82.27	****
4	0.070590	13.84	96.11	***
5	0.019863	3.89	100.00	
	0.510080			

Units and variables related to the first two principal axes.   [In Tables 4.5 and 4.6 detailed values are given for the single groups of variables. Most important for the interpretation are QLT, K= (1 or 2), COR and CTR. QLT, the quality of representation, shows how well

Table 4.5 Units related to the first two principal axes.

	Unit	QLT	MASS	INR	K = 1	COR	CTR	K = 2	COR	CTR
1	~588G	922	72	228	−1186	871	531	287	51	43
2	~414E	885	30	21	−269	204	11	−492	681	53
3	~403E	626	99	182	−240	61	30	−730	565	383
4	~409E	613	240	34	−186	485	44	96	128	16
5	~774G	898	84	60	573	895	144	−35	3	1
6	~576G	616	91	135	627	523	188	265	93	47
7	~765G	286	267	102	131	88	24	197	199	76
8	~582G	560	48	184	303	47	23	−1000	513	351
9	~722G	179	69	54	105	28	4	246	152	30

Table 4.6 Variables related to the first two principal axes.

	Var	QLT	MASS	INR	K = 1	COR	CTR	K = 2	COR	CTR
1	A	971	265	254	−656	880	597	211	91	86
2	B2	786	87	221	−321	80	47	−956	706	581
3	B3	397	83	93	451	357	88	152	40	14
4	B4	421	32	193	284	26	13	−1107	395	285
5	G1	763	352	117	348	717	223	89	47	20
6	G2	125	181	123	180	94	31	104	31	14

each group is represented in the plot on a scale from 0–1000. K gives the co-ordinates of each group on the plot, K=1 for the first and K=2 for the second axis. COR indicates how well each group is correlated with the axes and CTR refers to the overall contribution of the groups to each axis, each again ranging from 0–1000 (Orton and Tyers 1993, 14).]

Key: QLT – quality of representation; MASS – mass of the point; INR – inertia in full space; COR – relative contribution; CTR – absolute contribution; all quantities are ×1000.

Along the first principal axis of the plot in Figure 4.3 a strong contrast is shown between context group '588G' (−1186) and the groups '576G' (627) and '774G' (573) on the opposite side. Fabric type 'A' (−656) is set in contrast to 'G1' (348) and 'B3' (451). The data matrix indicates some links between the contributing context groups and fabrics, although these associations appear much clearer in the table of residuals (Table 4.3) than the raw data. The second axis contrasts the context groups 403E (−730) and 582G (−1000) with the groups represented along the first axis. Both, however, are set apart from each other. Correspondingly, fabrics B2 (−956) and B4 (−1107) are differentiated along this second axis and separated from the other fabrics. We note that both fabrics are assumed to be chronologically significant. No clear chronological pattern emerges from the grouping of contexts, though. Most groups show a mixture between Erk and Gyaur Kala assemblages, yet certain tendencies are visible (cf membership lists above): on the first axis 588G shows many Erk Kala contexts, whereas 576G on the opposite end contains only Gyaur Kala assemblages. On the second axis 403E, associated with fabric B2 (cf Table 4.2), consists mainly of Erk Kala deposits, while 582G is dominated by Gyaur Kala. Fabric B4, which is related to 582G (cf Table 4.2), seems a relatively small, though very distinct, fabric.

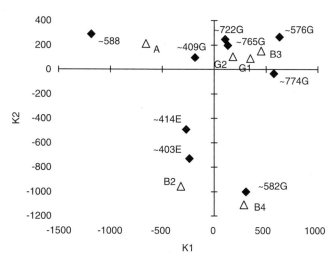

Figure 4.3: Configuration A: Correspondence analysis plot for the marginal table 'context-by-ware'. ♦ = Contexts; Δ = Fabrics.

Marginal table: context-by-form

Data from file 'ctestb.pie', 2020 records (context 86, ware 14, form 483)

Configuration: 'context-form', marginal table: 'context × form' (11 × 10).

Table 4.7 Data matrix.

		1 ~R181	2 ~R20	3 ~R116	4 ~R34	5 ~R25	6 ~R30	7 ~R185	8 ~sR1	9 ~R106	10 ~RRef4	11 Total
1	~406E	0.0	0.0	9.0	0.0	0.3	0.3	0.0	1.9	0.6	0.0	12.0
2	~409E	0.0	0.0	4.2	0.2	0.0	0.2	1.7	1.6	15.7	0.7	24.2
3	~560G	0.3	2.1	0.0	7.9	6.7	4.6	0.0	0.9	0.1	5.5	28.1
4	~595G	0.4	5.8	0.0	0.9	0.0	2.1	0.7	4.3	0.0	5.1	19.3
5	~588G	0.8	0.2	0.0	3.6	0.0	4.0	0.4	0.8	0.9	3.3	14.0
6	~763G	0.9	1.9	0.0	4.6	12.1	5.0	6.9	9.1	0.7	20.8	61.9
7	~765G	0.4	0.5	0.0	5.3	41.0	49.7	2.4	8.2	0.5	15.3	123.5
8	774G	9.2	0.0	0.4	1.8	8.6	0.9	2.1	6.2	0.0	6.3	35.5
9	~779G	0.0	0.0	0.0	12.4	1.2	1.0	0.0	1.6	0.0	1.6	17.7
10	~576G	0.9	0.0	0.0	0.0	4.4	3.3	0.2	1.5	0.2	4.4	14.8
11	~715G	0.0	2.4	0.0	0.8	12.1	0.0	0.0	0.6	0.0	0.2	16.1
12	Total	12.9	12.9	13.6	37.6	86.3	71.0	14.4	36.6	18.8	63.1	367.1

Table 4.8 Residuals.

		1 ~R181	2 ~R20	3 ~R116	4 ~R34	5 ~R25	6 ~R30	7 ~R185	8 ~sR1	9 ~R106	10 ~RRef4
1	~406E	−0.4	−0.4	+8.5	−1.2	−2.6	−2.1	−0.5	+0.7	+0.0	−2.1
2	~409E	−0.8	−0.9	+3.3	−2.3	−5.7	−4.5	+0.7	−0.8	+14.5	−3.5
3	~560G	−0.6	+1.1	−1.0	+5.1	+0.1	−0.8	−1.1	−1.9	−1.3	+0.7
4	~595G	−0.3	+5.1	−0.7	−1.1	−4.5	−1.7	−0.0	+2.4	−1.0	+1.7
5	~588G	+0.3	−0.3	−0.5	+2.2	−3.3	+1.3	−0.2	−0.6	+0.2	+0.9
6	~763G	−1.3	−0.3	−2.3	−1.7	−2.5	−7.0	+4.5	+2.9	−2.5	+10.2
7	~765G	−3.9	−3.8	−4.6	−7.3	+12.0	+25.8	−2.4	−4.1	−5.8	−6.0
8	774G	+7.9	−1.2	−0.9	−1.9	+0.3	−5.9	+0.7	+2.6	−1.8	+0.2
9	~779G	−0.6	−0.6	−0.7	+10.6	−3.0	−2.4	−0.7	−0.2	−0.9	−1.5
10	~576G	+0.3	−0.5	−0.5	−1.5	+0.9	+0.4	−0.4	−0.0	−0.5	+1.9
11	~715G	−0.6	+1.8	−0.6	−0.9	+8.3	−3.1	−0.6	−1.0	−0.8	−2.6

MEMBERSHIP LISTS

Configuration: 'context-form', Variable: 'context'

~406E =	10E	193E	336E	401E	406E
~409E =	192E	409E	474E	489E	
~560G =	560G	567G			
~595G =	531G	544G	595G		
~588G =	566G	588G	660G		
~763G =	581G	582G	615G	618G	637G	708G	728G	763G
~765G =	583G	722G	723G	726G	732G	765G
774G					
~779G =	766G	779G			
~576G =	576G	793G			
~715G =	608G	715G	815G		

Configuration: 'context-form', Variable: 'form'

~R181 =	R181	R182	sR181	sR182				
~R20 =	R18	R19	R20	sR18	sR20			
~R116 =	R115	R115dc7		R116	sR115	sR116	sR21	
~R34 =	R206	R27	R33	R332l1rb		R34	R341l	R35	sR206
	sR27	sR34	sR35					
~R25 =	R25	R38	R39	R42	R42N7dc5		R42dc4dc14		R42p
	Ref2	sR38	sR38dc14		sR39	sR39p			
~R30 =	R183	R189	R189dc3		R189dc3H		R198	R199	R30	R45
	R451l1rb		R451rb	R46	R461l	R461ldc4dc14		R461rb	sR183
	sR1832l		sR30	sR45					
~R185 =	R11	R147	R185	R186	R61	R63	sR11	sR147	sR185
	sR1851l		sR185dc16		sR186	sR189	sR61	sR63	sR87
~sR1 =	R1	R10	R12	R3	R4	R5	R6	R7	R84	R85
	R9	sR1	sR12	sR1dc9	sR3	sR4	sR5	sR6	sR7
	sR84	sR85	sR9						
~R106 =	R106	R107	R108	R128	R162	R168	R78	R79	R80	R81
	R91	R92	sR106	sR107	sR108	sR128	sR162	sR81	sR91
	sR92								
~RRef4 =	R100	R13	R132dc4		R13dc14		R13dc2	R13dc2dc4	
	R13dc3	R16	R17	R184	R184dc16		R188	R193	R2
	R204	R214	R28	R62	R67	R8	RRef4	Ref41rb	
	sR184	sR188	sR193	sR2	sR204	sR62	sR67	sRRef4	

CORRESPONDENCE ANALYSIS

Table 4.9 Decomposition of inertia by principal axes.

Principal axis	Inertia	Perc	Cum	Histogram
1	0.737828	38.44	38.44	*********
2	0.354392	18.46	56.90	****
3	0.261803	13.64	70.54	***
4	0.230315	12.00	82.54	**
5	0.168439	8.78	91.31	**
6	0.096290	5.02	96.33	*
7	0.059502	3.10	99.43	
8	0.008785	0.46	99.89	
9	0.002161	0.11	100.00	
	1.919514			

Table 4.10 Units related to the first two principal axes.

	Unit	QLT	MASS	INR	K = 1	COR	CTR	K = 2	COR	CTR
1	~406E	997	33	246	−2773	532	340	−2594	466	620
2	~409E	998	66	282	−2493	758	556	1402	240	366
3	~560G	221	77	22	348	221	13	14	0	0
4	~595G	25	52	72	255	25	5	−39	1	0
5	~588G	102	38	12	113	21	1	225	81	5
6	~763G	100	169	42	211	94	10	54	6	1
7	~765G	237	336	82	332	234	50	−38	3	1
8	774G	31	97	89	205	24	6	−112	7	3
9	~779G	30	48	99	339	29	7	73	1	1
10	~576G	203	40	7	267	203	4	−6	0	0
11	~715G	76	44	47	382	71	9	−99	5	1

Table 4.11 Variables related to the first two principal axes.

	Var	QLT	MASS	INR	K = 1	COR	CTR	K = 2	COR	CTR
1	~R181	16	35	82	249	14	3	−109	3	1
2	~R20	28	35	75	334	27	5	−39	0	0
3	~R116	997	37	267	−3023	661	458	−2157	337	486
4	~R34	49	102	121	325	46	15	83	3	2
5	~R25	258	235	59	347	248	38	−70	10	3
6	~R30	161	193	71	334	160	29	−29	1	0
7	~R185	93	39	19	−93	9	0	283	84	9
8	~sR1	69	100	15	−20	1	0	−140	68	5
9	~R106	996	51	259	−2503	645	434	1846	351	492
10	~RRef4	205	172	31	265	201	16	40	5	1

In the 'context-by-form' marginal table the two excavation areas are clearly separated from each other (Figure 4.4). Both principal axes of the plot are dominated by Erk Kala. The first axis expresses the difference of Erk Kala in relation to Gyaur Kala, while the second contrasts the two groups of Erk Kala contexts depicted on the plot '406E' (−2594) and '409E' (1402). Gyaur Kala itself does not receive enough space to show internal variations, as the

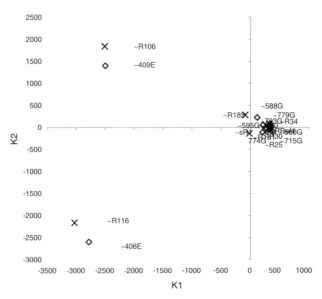

Figure 4.4: Configuration A: Correspondence analysis plot for the marginal table 'context-by-form'. ♦ = Contexts; × = Shapes.

contrast to Erk Kala and variations between Erk Kala context and shape groups dominate this plot. The strong differentiation within Erk Kala is also reflected by the variable 'form' with the groups 'R116' (–2157) and 'R106' (1846), each related to either of the antagonistic context groups (cf Tables 2.11 and 2.12).

An exact evaluation of the various shapes represented in the two groups is hampered by the high degree of fragmentation of the Erk Kala assemblages in particular. Hardly any semi-complete vessels or reconstructable profiles were found to provide additional evidence for the identification of Sasanian or residual shapes. In consequence we have to look for appropriate analogies (outside MEK1) to gain additional information. Two sources of material are available for comparison: the pottery excavated from MGK5 and published material from excavations around the oasis and at Merv. Although the chronological sequence for Merv so far is faulty, associations with specific levels can provide a rough idea about the residuality of certain types. This relates especially to sites of earlier periods, which were abandoned before Sasanian times.

Shape group 'R116' represents one manually formed group. No complete reference vessels are illustrated for any of the forms. Rim shapes of this type first occur at Merv in levels associated with coins from the 4th to the 6th centuries (Filanovich 1974, 63, fig 14). Since analogous shapes have been found only in the uppermost contexts of MGK5, we can assume that this rim type belongs to the later Sasanian pottery repertoire. 'R106' comprises four of the manual groupings. The dominating jar rims of 'R106' appear to be diagnostic for early sites in the Merv oasis. A range of analogous forms were found in the latest horizons of Yaz-Depe, called 'Yaz III', which is now commonly dated to the later Achaemenid period, when the area was part of the Persian Empire (Genito 1998, 89–91). A variety of comparable rim shapes has been found by the Italian-Turkmen-Russian mission on surveys and trial excavations in the northern part of the oasis (Cattani and Genito 1998, 75–87). Yaz III material is also known from the early occupational levels of Merv, from Erk and Gyaur Kala (Filanovich 1974, 24–36, figs 3 and 4; Usmanova 1992, 61–62, figs 7.5, 8, 13 and 8).

Context groups in their turn appear unrelated to their stratigraphic order in the correspondence analysis. Both groups, '406' and '409', comprise assemblages from various stratigraphic levels of the excavations at Area 1. The preoccupying aspect in the data structure of MEK1 appears to be the contrast between contexts with primarily Sasanian shapes and those dominated by residual material. It is remarkable that the residual elements found in Late Sasanian contexts are primarily linked to Achaemenid times, the assumed period of the foundation of the city. A slight variation is noticeable in the category of the deposits. Contexts producing Sasanian pottery shapes are primarily make-up layers within the structures, while the majority of contexts associated with residual shapes appear to be external deposits.

The context-by-form interactions show a more complex structure than previously, as visible from the decomposition of the inertia (Table 4.9). Despite the fact that a considerable amount of shapes regarded as diagnostic for the Late Sasanian period do not feature in the analysis, the plot captures a relatively high proportion of the overall variability (56 per cent).

Marginal table: ware-by-form

Data from file 'ctestb.pie', 2020 records (context 86, ware 14, form 483).
Configuration: 'ware-form', marginal table: 'ware x form' (6 × 8).

Table 4.12 Data matrix.

		1 ~R181	2 ~R116	3 ~R36	4 ~R17	5 ~sR1	6 ~R94	7 ~R30	8 ~R25	9 Total
1	A	0.6	44.7	5.9	1.2	3.2	3.0	44.7	32.8	136.2
2	B2	1.1	5.1	6.9	3.4	2.0	18.5	1.3	9.2	47.5
3	B3	0.8	0.2	9.9	10.6	4.1	1.3	5.3	13.5	45.7
4	B4	0.4	0.5	1.5	8.1	3.4	1.6	0.0	1.7	17.2
5	G1	14.8	41.2	8.9	4.4	6.1	4.8	19.4	77.4	177.0
6	G2	0.8	2.3	7.8	8.8	3.2	1.9	21.6	51.0	97.3
7	Total	18.5	94.1	40.8	36.6	22.0	31.1	92.4	185.5	521.0

Table 4.13 Residuals.

		1 ~R181	2 ~R116	3 ~R36	4 ~R17	5 ~sR1	6 ~R94	7 ~R30	8 ~R25
1	A	−4.2	+20.1	−4.8	−8.4	−2.5	−5.1	+20.6	−15.7
2	B2	−0.5	−3.5	+3.1	+0.1	+0.0	+15.6	−7.1	−7.8
3	B3	−0.8	−8.0	+6.3	+7.4	+2.2	−1.4	−2.8	−2.8
4	B4	−0.2	−2.6	+0.1	+6.9	+2.7	+0.6	−3.0	−4.5
5	G1	+8.5	+9.3	−5.0	−8.0	−1.4	−5.8	−12.0	+14.4
6	G2	−2.7	−15.3	+0.1	+2.0	−0.9	−3.9	+4.3	+16.3

MEMBERSHIP LISTS

Configuration: 'ware-form', Variable: 'ware'

A   B2   B3   B4   G1   G2

Configuration: 'ware-form', Variable: 'form'

~R181 =	R128	R168	R181	R182	R189	R189dc3		R189dc3H	
	sR128	sR181	sR182						
~R116 =	R100	R115	R115dc7	R116	R129	R13	R130	R132dc4	
	R136	R137	R13dc14	R13dc2	R13dc2dc4		R13dc3	R143	
	R144	R174	R175	R18	R19	R20	R28	R31	sR115
	sR116	sR129	sR130	sR144HA		sR18	sR20	sR21	sR31
~R36 =	R102	R103	R104	R147	R188	R193	R2	R204	R214	R29
	R32	R36	R373l	R61	R62	R67	R8	sR103	sR104
	sR147	sR188	sR193	sR2	sR204	sR32	sR32HA		sR36
	sR61	sR62	sR67						
~R17 =	R16	R17	R184	R184dc16	R3	R4	R5	R6	R7
	sR184	sR3	sR4	sR5	sR6	sR7			
~sR1 =	R1	R11	R185	R186	R63	R84	R85	sR1	sR11
	sR185	sR185ll		sR185dc16	sR186	sR189	sR1dc9	sR63
	sR84	sR85	sR87						
~R94 =	R106	R107	R108	R125	R140	R159	R44	R78	R79	R80
	R81	R93	R94	sR106	sR107	sR108	sR140	sR159	sR16
	sR44	sR81	sR94						
~R30 =	R101	R112	R113	R113dc2	R132	R133	R135	R160
	R161	R165	R198	R199	R30	R53	R55	R56	R57	R75
	R77	R77dc7	R83	R97	R971g	R98	R98p	sR112	sR113
	sR132	sR133	sR135	sR160	sR165	sR30	sR53	sR56	sR57
	sR75	sR75dc3		sR77	sR83	sR97			
~R25 =	R10	R12	R162	R183	R206	R25	R27	R33	R332l1rb
	R34	R341l	R35	R38	R39	R42	R42N7dc5		
	R42dc4dc14		R42p	R45	R451l1rb		R451rb	R46	R461l
	R461ldc4dc14		R461rb	R9	R91	R92	RRef4	Ref2	Ref41rb
	sR12	sR162	sR183	sR1832l		sR206	sR27	sR34	sR35
	sR38	sR38dc14		sR39	sR39p	sR45	sR9	sR91	sR92
	sRRef4								

CORRESPONDENCE ANALYSIS

Table 4.14 Decomposition of inertia by principal axes.

Principal axis	Inertia	Perc	Cum	Histogram
1	0.281758	46.48	46.48	***********
2	0.172064	28.38	74.86	*******
3	0.084119	13.88	88.74	***
4	0.055097	9.09	97.83	**
5	0.013173	2.17	100.00	
	0.606211			

Table 4.15 Units related to the first two principal axes.

	Unit	QLT	MASS	INR	K = 1	COR	CTR	K = 2	COR	CTR
1	A	622	261	179	487	573	220	−142	48	30
2	B2	994	91	316	−1030	505	344	−1013	489	544
3	B3	885	88	130	−672	504	141	584	381	174
4	B4	785	33	186	−1412	583	233	833	203	133
5	G1	286	340	103	226	280	62	−31	5	2
6	G2	382	187	87	−26	2	0	327	379	116

Table 4.16 Variables related to the first two principal axes.

	Var	QLT	MASS	INR	K = 1	COR	CTR	K = 2	COR	CTR
1	~R181	29	35	57	142	21	3	−87	8	2
2	~R116	721	181	138	499	536	160	−294	185	90
3	~R36	626	78	56	−514	608	74	89	18	4
4	~R17	931	70	221	−1071	601	286	795	331	258
5	~sR1	775	42	44	−581	531	51	394	244	38
6	~R94	992	60	304	−1187	456	299	−1285	535	573
7	~R30	503	177	105	422	496	112	49	7	3
8	~R25	230	356	74	115	106	17	125	125	32

On the first axis (Figure 4.5) the fabrics 'B2' (−1030) and 'B4' (−1412) are contrasted with fabric 'A' (487). This pattern is mirrored correspondingly by the variable 'form': shape group 'R94' (−1187) and 'R17' (−1071) appear in strong contrast to 'R116' (499). The data matrix indicates that shape groups 'R94' and 'R116' are closely linked with fabrics 'B2' and 'A', respectively. Shape group 'R17', however, is related to both fabric 'B3' and 'B4' in the data matrix (Table 4.12). Fabric 'B3' (−672) is of minor importance on this first axis, where it is principally set apart from fabric 'A'.

The second axis contrasts fabric 'B2' (−1013) with 'B3' (584) and 'B4' (833). Shape groups 'R94' (−1285) and 'R17' (795) follow this separation. Group 'R17' is plotted between the fabrics 'B3' and 'B4', which reflects its association with both fabrics (Tables 4.16 and 4.17). Both shape groups, 'R94' and 'R17', are relatively small, but obviously very distinct. We note that 'R94' comprises the shape codes, which were identified as residual in the 'context x form' marginal table. 'R17' comprises two manually formed units and gives a very homogeneous impression as a concise and well-defined group of bowl shapes. Shape group 'R116', which is related to fabric 'A' along the first axis, shows a range of shapes very popular in Erk and Gyaur Kala, including R116 itself.

Quasi-log-linear analysis

In the quasi-log-linear analysis the interactions between all three variables are tested against a set of mathematical models (Orton and Tyers 1993, 3). Model IIA is examining independence of ware-by-form and context, model IIB the independence of form-by-context and ware, and model IIC the independence of context-by-ware and form. The difference in the analytical procedure between the three models lies in the different order

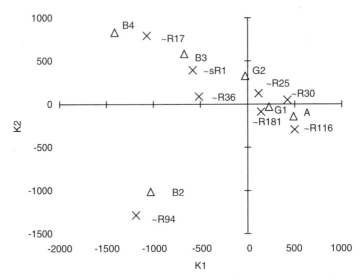

Figure 4.5: Configuration A: Correspondence analysis plot for the marginal table 'ware-by-form'. Δ = Fabrics; × = Shapes.

of merging the values of variables. In the case of model IIA, for example, the ware-by-form table is reduced first, before the variable context is included in the reduction process (Orton and Tyers 1990, 99). Results obtained for configuration A are given in Table 4.17.

Interpretation: The analysis (Table 4.17) shows all three-way interactions for models IIA and IIC, which is usually interpreted as an interplay of functional, chronological and geographical variability on the assumption that form accounts for function, fabric and form for chronology and fabric only for geographical differentiation (Orton and Tyers 1990, 95).

Model IIB, however, does not suggest any interactions for the variable 'ware'. This would imply that, considering the variation of form by context, the proportions of wares

Table 4.17 Summary of goodness-of-fit analysis.

	Result	*Models*	*Interactions*
IIA	Log-linear analysis	M4 M4	[12] ware × context interaction
			[23] ware × form interaction
			[13] form × context interaction
IIB	Log-linear analysis	M2B M2B	[13] form × context interaction
IIC	Log-linear analysis	M4 M4	[12] ware × context interaction
			[23] ware × form interaction
			[13] form × context interaction

(i.e. fabrics) do not change (Orton and Tyers 1990, 95). Based on the importance generally attributed to fabric changes in chronology, this model would indicate functional variation (Orton and Tyers 1990, 95). In order to understand the significance of the variables 'ware' and 'form' in this data set properly, we have to return to the correspondence analysis. The fabrics contributing primarily to the 'context-by-ware' and 'ware-by-form' marginal tables are fabrics 'A', 'B2' and 'B4', which are consistently set in contrast to each other. Three form groups are accordingly related to these: 'R116', 'R94' and 'R17' (cf Table 4.12). The context-by-form interaction shows a strong differentiation of form. Erk Kala is found on the opposite side of the plot to Gyaur Kala and within Erk Kala two contrasting groups were displayed (cf Figure 4.4). Erk Kala is through numismatic evidence associated with the Late Sasanian period, Gyaur Kala with the Middle Sasanian, and comparisons with material from the oasis have shown that the two antagonistic groups within Erk Kala represent Sasanian and residual pottery shapes respectively: the variable 'form' clearly indicates chronological variation. If the variable 'ware' would be of equal chronological significance, then certain forms should be bound to certain fabrics and the clear distinction between the excavation areas and residual contexts should be expressed in the context-by-ware interaction as well. This, however, is not reflected by the marginal tables. While distinct groups of forms are associated with specific fabrics, no clear separation is noticeable in the context-by-ware interaction marginal table. Most context groups formed through reduction are mixed, although tendencies are visible. Fabric 'B2' is more prominent in Erk Kala, whereas 'B4' seems confined to Gyaur Kala. This implies that chronologically important vessel types are defined by form rather than by ware. Fabric 'B2' accordingly comprises a group of various shapes, which do not fully coincide with the primarily residual shapes in the context-by-form marginal table. A look into the raw data shows that most forms occur in a variety of fabrics. Form is not strictly bound to fabric in this data set. The comparison between the context-by-ware and context-by-form marginal tables confirms this impression. Out of the context group associated with the residual material, only one context occurs in the group linked to fabric 'B2'. Most contexts of this group, on the other hand, do not contribute to the context-by-form marginal table.

In conclusion we can confirm that form seems chronologically more significant than ware. Ware shows tendencies in interaction with context and form, which can be interpreted as chronological, but these are not strong enough to feature on their own.

Configuration B

Configuration B was conceived to gain more information on the internal structure of Area 5, Gyaur Kala. The main modification is the joining of all Erk Kala contexts. We will follow again the order of the marginal tables in the discussion.

Marginal table: context-by-ware

Data from file 'ctestb.pie', 2020 records (context 86, ware 14, form 483)

Configuration: 'context-ware', marginal table: 'context-x-ware' (6 × 6).

ANALYSIS

Table 4.18 Data matrix.

		1 A	2 ~B2	3 B3	4 B4	5 G1	6 G2	7 Total
1	~409E	55.9	30.4	5.2	4.3	44.6	14.5	154.9
2	~774G	1.8	1.3	4.6	3.0	21.2	10.3	42.2
3	~576G	3.8	0.3	8.9	0.3	30.5	2.1	45.9
4	~765G	28.4	6.9	8.9	0.9	47.7	46.8	139.6
5	~582G	1.0	3.2	1.5	5.5	3.6	4.9	19.8
6	~763G	44.8	6.9	12.7	2.4	28.9	16.5	112.2
7	Total	135.7	48.9	41.8	16.5	176.5	95.2	514.6

Table 4.19 Residuals.

		1 A	2 ~B2	3 B3	4 B4	5 G1	6 G2
1	~409E	+15.0	+15.6	−7.3	−0.7	−8.5	−14.1
2	~774G	−9.3	−2.7	+1.2	+1.7	+6.7	+2.5
3	~576G	−8.3	−4.1	+5.2	−1.2	+14.8	−6.4
4	~765G	−8.4	−6.4	−2.4	−3.5	−0.2	+21.0
5	~582G	−4.2	+1.3	−0.1	+4.9	−3.2	+1.3
6	~763G	+15.2	−3.8	+3.6	−1.2	−9.6	−4.2

MEMBERSHIP LISTS

Configuration: 'context-ware', Variable: 'context'

~409E =	10E	11E	13E	166E	170E	192E	193E	200E	245E
	257E	270E	281E	311E	312E	327E	336E	338E	401E
	403E	406E	409E	414E	417E	425E	427E	431E	448E
	449E	455E	458E	460E	471E	474E	485E	489E	492E
	493E	507E	544E	660G					
~774G =	581G	774G							
~576G =	567G	576G	715G	726G	776G				
~765G =	560G	708G	728G	732G	765G	779G			
~582G =	531G	544G	582G	615G	793G				
~763G =	566G	583G	588G	595G	618G	637G	692G	711G	722G
	723G	763G	766G	798G					

Configuration: 'context-ware', Variable: 'ware'

A			
~B2	=	B1	B2
B3	B4	G1	G2

CORRESPONDENCE ANALYSIS

Table 4.20 Decomposition of inertia by principal axes.

Principal axis	Inertia	Perc	Cum	Histogram
1	0.138330	41.56	41.56	**********
2	0.102553	30.81	72.38	*******
3	0.066084	19.86	92.24	****
4	0.025683	7.72	99.95	*
5	0.000160	0.05	100.00	
	0.332810			

Table 4.21 Units related to the first two principal axes.

	Unit	QLT	MASS	INR	K = 1	COR	CTR	K = 2	COR	CTR
1	~409E	867	301	204	−442	867	425	−0	0	0
2	~774G	960	82	94	559	822	185	−229	138	42
3	~576G	590	89	213	613	473	242	304	116	80
4	~765G	320	271	148	234	301	107	58	19	9
5	~582G	980	38	259	82	3	2	−1480	977	821
6	~763G	372	218	83	−157	194	39	151	179	48

Table 4.22 Variables related to the first two principal axes.

	Var	QLT	MASS	INR	K = 1	COR	CTR	K = 2	COR	CTR
1	A	905	264	188	−429	776	351	175	129	79
2	~B2	827	95	162	−646	737	287	−226	90	47
3	B3	503	81	80	381	442	85	143	62	16
4	B4	940	32	259	51	1	1	−1591	939	790
5	G1	676	343	130	271	581	182	110	95	40
6	G2	265	185	180	266	217	94	−124	47	28

Along the first principal axis (Figure 4.6) a significant difference is expressed between the groups '409E' (−442) and '576G' (613). Fabrics 'A' (−429) with 'B2' (−646) and 'G1' (271) with 'B3' (381) reflect the contrast shown between the context groups '409E' and '576G'. Fabric 'A' in particular and fabric 'B2' are strongly represented in the assemblages of context group '409E' (cf Tables 4.18 and 4.19). All three groups are therefore closely positioned on the plot. Group '576G' by contrast seems linked to fabrics 'G1' and 'B3' (cf Tables 4.18 and 4.19). The second axis is completely preoccupied with the contrast of group '582G' (−1480) to all other context groups. Fabric 'B4' (−1591) appears equally distinct. On the first axis a separation is now visible between the two excavation areas Erk and Gyaur Kala. A certain preponderance of fabrics 'A' and 'B2' is noticeable in relation to Erk Kala, but the differentiation between the fabrics along this axis is not very strong. The main feature of this plot is the obviously huge difference between context group '582G' associated with fabric 'B4' and the remainder of the Gyaur Kala contexts and fabrics. Both '582G' and 'B4' represent the smallest group in either variable.

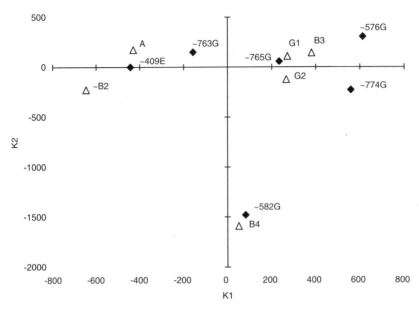

Figure 4.6: Configuration B: Correspondence analysis plot for the marginal table 'context-by-ware'. ♦ = Context, Δ = Fabric.

Marginal table: context-by-form

Data from file 'ctestb.pie', 2020 records (context 86, ware 14, form 483)
Configuration: 'context-form', marginal table: 'context x form' (10 × 11)

Table 4.23 Data matrix.

		1 ~R25	2 ~R181	3 ~R20	4 ~R34	5 ~R30	6 ~R45	7 ~R27	8 ~R185	9 ~sR1	10 ~R116	11 ~RRef 4	12 Total
1	~409E	1.5	1.3	0.2	0.4	1.2	0.0	1.2	2.9	4.4	122.3	1.3	136.8
2	560G	5.7	0.3	2.1	5.5	6.7	0.8	2.8	0.0	0.9	0.4	0.4	25.6
3	~595G	0.0	0.4	5.8	0.0	3.4	0.0	4.7	0.7	4.3	0.0	0.0	19.3
4	~588G	0.0	0.8	0.2	3.6	4.0	0.0	0.8	0.4	0.8	0.9	1.5	13.1
5	~763G	12.1	0.9	1.9	0.9	6.0	0.0	12.5	6.4	9.1	0.2	9.0	58.8
6	~765G	35.8	0.4	0.5	3.4	48.9	9.4	8.5	3.0	6.8	1.0	2.1	119.8
7	774G	8.1	9.2	0.0	0.5	1.4	0.0	6.3	2.1	6.2	0.4	1.3	35.5
8	~779G	1.2	0.0	0.0	9.2	1.0	0.0	4.8	0.0	1.6	1.2	0.0	18.9
9	~576G	2.0	0.9	0.0	0.0	5.8	1.6	1.7	0.2	1.5	0.6	1.0	15.2
10	~715G	11.4	0.0	2.4	0.8	0.6	0.0	0.2	0.0	0.6	0.0	0.0	16.1
11	**Total**	77.7	14.2	13.2	24.4	79.0	11.8	43.4	15.6	36.1	127.1	16.6	459.0

Table 4.24 Residuals.

		1 ~R25	2 ~R181	3 ~R20	4 ~R34	5 ~R30	6 ~R45	7 ~R27	8 ~R185	9 ~sR1	10 ~R116	11 ~RRef4
1	~409E	−21.7	−2.9	−3.7	−6.8	−22.4	−3.5	−11.8	−1.8	−6.3	+84.5	−3.6
2	560G	+1.3	−0.4	+1.3	+4.2	+2.3	+0.1	+0.4	−0.9	−1.2	−6.7	−0.5
3	~595G	−3.3	−0.2	+5.3	−1.0	+0.0	−0.5	+2.8	+0.1	+2.8	−5.3	−0.7
4	~588G	−2.2	+0.4	−0.1	+2.9	+1.8	−0.3	−0.4	−0.1	−0.2	−2.7	+1.0
5	~763G	+2.1	−0.9	+0.2	−2.2	−4.2	−1.5	+6.9	+4.4	+4.4	−16.1	+6.9
6	~765G	+15.5	−3.2	−2.9	−3.0	+28.3	+6.3	−2.8	−1.1	−2.6	−32.2	−2.3
7	774G	+2.1	+8.1	−1.0	−1.4	−4.7	−0.9	+2.9	+0.9	+3.4	−9.4	−0.0
8	~779G	−2.0	−0.6	−0.5	+8.2	−2.2	−0.5	+3.0	−0.6	+0.1	−4.0	−0.7
9	~576G	−0.6	+0.4	−0.4	−0.8	+3.2	+1.2	+0.3	−0.4	+0.3	−3.6	+0.4
10	~715G	+8.7	−0.5	+1.9	−0.1	−2.1	−0.4	−1.3	−0.5	−0.6	−4.5	−0.6

MEMBERSHIP LISTS

Configuration: 'context-form', Variable: 'context'

~409E =	10E	11E	13E	166E	170E	192E	193E	200E	245E
	257E	270E	281E	311E	312E	327E	336E	338E	401E
	403E	406E	409E	414E	417E	425E	427E	431E	448E
	449E	455E	458E	460E	471E	474E	485E	489E	492E
	493E	507E	544E						

560G
~595G =   531G   544G   595G
~588G =   588G   660G
~763G =   581G   582G   615G   618G   708G   728G   763G
~765G =   637G   722G   723G   732G   765G
774G
~779G =   766G   779G
~576G =   576G   793G
~715G =   608G   715G   815G

Configuration: 'context-form', Variable: 'form'

~R25 =   R25   Ref2
~R181 =   R181   R182   sR181   sR182
~R20 =   R18   R19   R20   sR18   sR20
~R34 =   R206   R33   R332l1rb   R34   R341l   R35   sR206   sR34
           sR35
~R30 =   R183   R189   R189dc3   R189dc3H   R198   R199   R28   R30
           R38   R39   R42   R42N7dc5   R42dc4dc14   R42p   sR183
           sR1832l   sR30   sR38   sR38dc14   sR39   sR39p
~R45 =   R45   R45l1rb   R451rb   R46   R461l   R461ldc4dc14   R461rb
           sR45
~R27 =   R16   R17   R184   R184dc16   R188   R193   R2   R204
           R214   R27   R62   R67   R8   sR184   sR188   sR193   sR2
           sR204   sR27   sR62   sR67
~R185 =   R11   R147   R185   R186   R61   R63   sR11   sR147   sR185
           sR1851l   sR185dc16   sR186   sR189   sR61   sR63   sR87
~sR1 =   R1   R10   R12   R3   R4   R5   R6   R7   R84   R85
           R9   sR1   sR12   sR1dc9   sR3   sR4   sR5   sR6   sR7
           sR84   sR85   sR9

~R116 =	R101	R102	R103	R104	R106	R107	R108	R112	R113	
	R113dc2		R115	R115dc7		R116	R125	R128	R132	
	R133	R135	R136	R137	R140	R143	R144	R150	R150dc3	
	R159	R160	R161	R162	R165	R168	R174	R175	R44	R52
	R75	R77	R77dc7	R78	R79	R80	R81	R83	R91	R92
	R93	R94	R97	R971g	R98	R98p	sR103	sR104	sR106	
	sR107	sR108	sR112	sR113	sR115	sR116	sR128	sR132	sR133	
	sR135	sR140	sR144HA		sR150	sR159	sR16	sR160	sR162	
	sR165	sR21	sR44	sR52	sR75	sR75dc3		sR77	sR81	
	sR83	sR91	sR92	sR94	sR97					
~RRef4 =	R100	R13	R132dc4		R13dc14		R13dc2		R13dc2dc4	
	R13dc3	RRef4	Ref41rb		sRRef4					

CORRESPONDENCE ANALYSIS

Table 4.25 Decomposition of inertia by principal axes.

Principal axis	Inertia	Perc	Cum	Histogram
1	0.819561	48.63	48.63	************
2	0.257435	15.27	63.90	***
3	0.240724	14.28	78.19	***
4	0.163351	9.69	87.88	**
5	0.103659	6.15	94.03	*
6	0.081136	4.81	98.84	*
7	0.016053	0.95	99.80	
8	0.002906	0.17	99.97	
9	0.000536	0.03	100.00	
	1.685361			

Table 4.26 Units related to the first two principal axes.

	Unit	QLT	MASS	INR	K = 1	COR	CTR	K = 2	COR	CTR
1	~409E	1000	298	340	1386	999	699	−44	1	2
2	560G	410	56	33	−629	401	27	97	10	2
3	~595G	242	42	92	−593	96	18	732	146	87
4	~588G	237	28	28	−443	120	7	438	117	21
5	~763G	421	128	85	−542	261	46	423	160	89
6	~765G	982	261	135	−655	492	137	−653	489	432
7	774G	363	77	107	−499	106	23	774	256	180
8	~779G	284	41	104	−468	51	11	999	233	159
9	~576G	532	33	17	−549	345	12	−405	187	21
10	~715G	182	35	59	−688	168	20	−200	14	5

The first axis (Figure 4.7) is entirely occupied by the difference between Erk and Gyaur Kala. Erk Kala with its amalgamated assemblages '409E' (1386) makes the main contribution to this axis and is accompanied by shape group 'R116' (1453), which unites all the shapes related primarily to MEK1. Gyaur Kala is represented by context group '765G' (−655), the strongest of the Gyaur Kala groups (cf Table 4.23). None of the shape groups of Gyaur Kala is contributing to the first axis. Along the second axis, '765G'

Table 4.27 Variables related to the first two principal axes.

	Var	QLT	MASS	INR	K = 1	COR	CTR	K = 2	COR	CTR
1	~R25	596	169	89	−640	465	85	−340	131	76
2	~R181	256	31	86	−376	30	5	1033	226	128
3	~R20	165	29	89	−634	77	14	678	88	51
4	~R34	216	53	135	−556	72	20	786	144	127
5	~R30	852	172	97	−649	444	89	−622	408	259
6	~R45	844	26	32	−705	240	16	−1120	605	125
7	~R27	835	95	43	−562	411	36	571	424	120
8	~R185	214	34	18	−221	56	2	370	158	18
9	~sR1	643	79	25	−359	244	12	458	399	64
10	~R116	999	277	348	1453	997	713	−65	2	5
11	~RRef4	205	36	40	−435	102	8	438	103	27

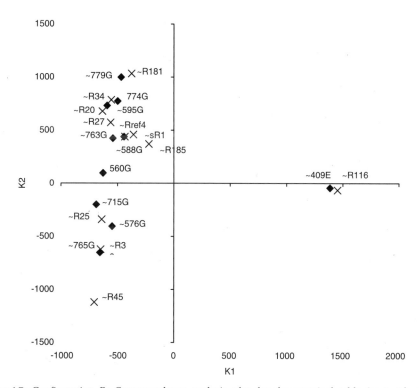

Figure 4.7: Configuration B: Correspondence analysis plot for the marginal table 'context-by-form'. ♦ = Context, × = Form.

(−653) is set in contrast to context groups '774G' (774) and '779G' (999). The shape groups reflect this divergence with 'R30' (−622) associated with '765' and a number of smaller groups, 'R181' (1033), 'R34' (786) and 'R27' (571), situated on the opposite side of the second axis.

With most of the shapes related to MGK 5 it is generally easier to identify contemporary material, since a number of complete vessels have been found and several of the vessel profiles were reconstructed from fragments. During pottery processing a certain differentiation was noticeable between rim shapes which often produced several conjoining fragments and those primarily occurring singly.

Group 'R30' is constituted by a number of very well-defined jar and bowl types, the complete vessel form of which is mostly known. Out of the three opposing groups, two, 'R181' and 'R34', are very small and have been subjectively perceived as insignificant. Their state of preservation varies from relatively small fragments to nearly complete rims. Body profiles are partly known; however, their pattern of occurrence is irregular and distinguishes them from the rim types regarded as most representative for Area 5. 'R181' comprises two bowl shapes that are known from previous excavations, where they were found in levels unrelated to the pottery types most prominent in Area 5 (Filanovich 1974, 76, fig 19). 'R34' represents a variety of jar rims. The complete vessel forms or possible patterns of decoration are unknown. Group 'R27' seems more comprehensive and, to some extent, unhomogeneous. Some of the shapes included in this group appear relatively well preserved, while others occur singly and resemble shapes associated with early occupational levels at Merv, following the Yaz III period (Filanovich 1974, 57, fig 10). All these observations suggest that the difference visible on the plot reflects again the contrast between contemporary and residual material. In comparison to the 'context × form' marginal table of configuration A, the internal differentiation of Area 5 does not appear to be fundamental. The contrast between Erk and Gyaur Kala is still dominating (cf Table 4.25) with the second axis contributing only a minor proportion to the overall variability. In configuration A both principal axes were occupied with the internal structure of Erk Kala. The context groups from Gyaur Kala do not show any specific patterns and no distinction is made between assemblages from inside the house and those from the adjacent streets.

Marginal table: ware-by-form

This table is identical to the corresponding marginal table from configuration A (cf Figure 4.5). The only difference to the first configuration is the amalgamation of all Erk Kala contexts. Since the modified variable 'context' does not contribute to the ware-by-form interaction, the results of configurations A and B are identical. We therefore confine our discussion to a brief summary of the main features of the ware-by-form marginal table.

Fabric 'A' appears in contrast to fabrics 'B2' and 'B4' on the first axis, which are both again differentiated along the second. All three fabrics have specific shape groups associated with them. 'R116' in relation with fabric 'A' represents a group of Sasanian material, whereas 'R94' associated with fabric 'B2' includes several shapes, characteristic for levels of the Yaz III or Achaemenid period, respectively. 'B4' with 'R17' is clearly separated from both of them. This constellation gains additional significance when considered together with the context-by-ware marginal table. In amalgamated form, the Erk Kala assemblages are shown between fabric 'A' and 'B2' (cf Figure 4.6). Although fabric 'B2' seems slightly removed from the Erk Kala group, it is undoubtedly associated with this excavation area. The main difference between fabric 'B4' and the remainder of Gyaur Kala now appears stronger than in configuration A (cf Figure 4.6). In the marginal table, ware-by-form fabric

'B4' is closely related to shape group 'R17', which contains some of the shapes included in 'R27', one of the three groups identified as residual. These particular rim types belong to vessel forms attributed to the Late and post-Achaemenid period (cf Katsuris and Buryakov 1963, 122). Consequently, 'B4' seems to represent a 'residual' fabric in MGK5 and shows parallels with fabric 'B2' and MEK1 in this respect. A 'Sasanian' fabric, on the other hand, is not clearly defined for Gyaur Kala. Fabric 'G1' is the strongest group in opposition to 'B4' but is not very well represented on the plot. In relation to the fabrics 'B2' and 'B4', fabrics 'A' and 'G' are plotted rather close to each other in the ware-by-form marginal table (cf Figure 4.5).

Quasi-log-linear analysis

A summary of goodness-of-fit analysis is given in Table 4.28.

Table 4.28 Summary of goodness-of-fit analysis.

	Result	Models	Interactions
IIA	Log-linear analysis	M3A M4	[23] ware-×-form interaction
			[13] form-×-context interaction
IIB	Log-linear analysis	M3A M3C	[13] form-×-context interaction
IIC	Log-linear analysis	M4 M4	[12] ware-×-context interaction
			[23] ware-×-form interaction
			[13] form-×-context interaction

INTERPRETATION

The analysis (Table 4.28) shows essentially a similar picture in comparison to configuration A. Through the amalgamation of the Erk Kala contexts, the variables 'fabric' and 'form' are set in clear relation to each other. Variations of 'fabric' seem largely dependent on variations of 'form', as expressed in model 3a (cf Orton and Tyers 1990, 95). Some of the fabrics are clearly associated with certain shape groups, such as 'B2' with 'R94', 'B4' with 'R17' and 'A' with 'R116'. The fabrics, which appear most significant for Gyaur Kala, apart from 'B4', 'G1' and 'B3', however, are not related to shape or context groups that contribute to the context-by-ware or ware-by-form interactions. In configuration A, a certain concordance is visible between the shape groups that dominate the context-by-form interactions and those characterising the ware-by-form marginal table. The situation is more diffuse in Gyaur Kala, where only minor components from one of the contributing groups of the context-by-form marginal table recur in correlation to the fabrics. This may explain the models accepted for IIB, independence of context-by-form and fabric, in the quasi-log-linear analysis: M3a, ware varies only in relation to form, and M3C, form varies in some of the contexts while ware varies in others (Orton and Tyers 1990, 95). Fabric 'B4' is the most distinct, but also the smallest group in Area 5. Analogous to fabric 'B2' in MEK1, 'B4' is bound to a restricted number of chronologically much earlier shapes and consequently noticeable only if a sufficient amount of residual material is present in the assemblage. Form is the chronologically more significant variable in Gyaur Kala.

ERK KALA, AREA 1 (MEK1)

Configurations A and B show that the variable 'form' is of greater significance than 'ware'. Both are also dominated by the contrast between MEK1 and MGK5, offering few hints on their internal structures. A number of distinct groups of contexts and shapes are captured in the plots, but it is difficult to assess them in relation to the remaining groups of their respective area. In order to gain more insight into the individual areas, the data sets were separated for further exploration.

As was already shown in configuration A, fewer of the MEK1 contexts and shape groups contributed to the analysis compared with MGK5. The attempt to conduct a *srd* reduction on the MEK1 data set failed and none of the quasi-log-linear models were accepted. This may not, however, reflect problems with the data structure proper, but may rather be linked to the inconsistencies and fragmentary state of the primary records. Although the excavations at MEK1 were finished before the analysis began, the data set remained incomplete through the lack of suitably recorded assemblages from the first two seasons and the sometimes insufficiently defined groupings. While the MEK1 data set therefore appears too sparse for individual analysis, this problem does not affect the basic results of configuration A. Our understanding of MEK1 at the moment, however, remains limited to one aspect of the data structure and a selected group of pottery assemblages.

GYAUR KALA, AREA 5 (MGK5)

The situation is different for MGK5: excavations here continued until 1999, though the initial analysis was restricted to data from the seasons 1995 to 1997. Before a separate data reduction was attempted for MGK5, material from the last two seasons, comprising 681 rim sherds, was included increasing the number of records from MGK5 to 1562. The distribution of average fragment sizes for contexts in MGK5 remained largely unchanged and the selection criterion of 5 to 39 gram average fragment weight was maintained. With regard to the three variables – context, ware and form – the new records were treated in the same way as the initial data set.

- *Context*: Another 41 contexts were added.
- *Ware*: No changes were made to the number of fabrics. The amendments lead merely to an increase in the values of the single fabrics.
- *Form*: Work with the additional material prompted minor changes to the number and arrangement of groups. A number of new pottery types were identified among the additional material and 27 new shape codes were assigned. Of these, 24 were deleted as rare or insignificant. The other three (3, 5 and 11 occurrences) were merged with existing groups or shape codes, of which two were deleted during the *srd* reduction. Only one new code was depicted in the plots, although it did not contribute to any of the principal axes.

More evidence for already known shapes was also gained in the process of data amendment, leading to slight modifications of the manual groupings in three cases: two rim shapes, R214 and R34, were split from their groups and left independent. The former represents a version of the well-known fishplate and was very well documented in the lower levels of MGK5. It seemed increasingly different from its former group consisting of very shallow bowls or lids, which are not so well defined. Rim code R34, a jar rim, proved to be much better preserved throughout the new assemblages than its fellow group members and was consequently left separate. One shape code, R199 (five occurrences), was found to belong to the same amphora-shaped jar type as R30 and both were therefore joined. This move is also consistent with the results of configuration B, where these shapes had been merged during the *srd* reduction (cf configuration B, membership list).

Exploring the new data set

In order to assess the impact of the amended material on the data structure, configuration B was restored and the analysis repeated with the now complete data set of MGK5. The correspondence analysis plots and quasi-log-linear models obtained are mostly coherent with the initial outcome, although some variation is noticeable with regard to the variable 'ware'.

The context-by-ware marginal table now focuses on the contrasts between the larger groups of fabrics A, B3, G1 and G2. Fabrics B2, B4 and I2, on the contrary, do not contribute significantly to any of the principal axes.

Results for the context-by-form marginal table are similar to configuration B. All MEK1 contexts and shapes appear in strong contrast to MGK5. On the whole, the complexity of this table increased (14 dimensions/axes) and the total inertia captured by the first two axes fell below 50 per cent (45.58 per cent).

Instead of previously 10, MGK5 is now represented by 14 shape groups. Some of the groups differentiated in the analysis have changed, although the overall picture remains the same. Of the large and somewhat heterogeneous group ~R27 only a small fraction, ~R17, has remained and is now merged with bowl shapes that were previously part of ~R185. R27 is now left separate and appears on the opposite side of the axis, although it does not contribute in this plot. Group ~R34 has also changed sides. The small group ~R181 remained unchanged and is together with ~RRef4 set in contrast to ~R46. Shape group ~R46 has changed its name from previously ~R45, since a higher proportion of the group is now constituted by rim fragments of R46. Group R30 does no longer contribute to this plot. While ~R181 and ~R17 clearly represent residual pottery forms, it is more difficult to identify the jar shapes of R34 and R46. Some more complete specimens of R34 indicate that this plain type of jar may well belong to the Sasanian period. The small and neckless jars of R46 are more difficult to assess. Their rich incised decoration may yet prove to be late Parthian or Sasanian in date. The difference between MEK1 and MGK5 remains the main pattern in this plot.

With regard to the ware-by-form marginal table, apart from the inclusion of fabric I2, no changes are noticeable in the relationship of the previous fabrics and forms.

Quasi-log-linear analysis

Table 4.29 Summary of goodness-of-fit analysis.

	Result	*Models*	*Interactions*
IIA	Log-linear analysis	M4 M4	[12] ware-×-context interaction [23] ware-×-form interaction [13] form-×-context interaction
IIB	Log-linear analysis	M3A M4	[23] ware-×-form interaction [13] form-×-context interaction
IIC	Log-linear analysis	M4 M4	[12] ware-×-context interaction [23] ware-×-form interaction [13] form-×-context interaction

INTERPRETATION

The results in Table 4.29 reflect the increased complexity in the data set, although the trend of the variable 'form' prevailing over 'fabric' remains unchanged for model IIB. In a further step, contexts and shape codes related to MEK1 were deleted, and the analysis concentrated on the internal structure of MGK5. The separate examination of this data set led to several consecutive configurations aimed at exploring the relationships of the most common groups of fabrics and shapes. Not all of these configurations are discussed in detail here, since some produced unreliable results (total inertia of the first two axes below 50 per cent), while others showed very complex models in the quasi-log-linear analysis (M5 – M5: all possible interactions), which appeared unsatisfactory for further interpretation.

In contrast to MEK1, the data set from MGK5 seemed perfectly suitable for individual analysis. The data structure of MGK5, though, remained very complex at first. All common ware fabrics, apart from B1, are now present in the analysis. B1, however, is a fabric linked primarily to storage vessels and is thus negligible in this study.

Patterns of the context-by-form interaction were characterised by distinct groups of single vessel types shown in strong contrast to the remainder of vessel shapes. These strong discrepancies seem to reflect very specific situations of site formation processes. After their individual assessments, the respective shape codes were gradually removed to reveal more relationships. Finally, configurations grew more balanced, capturing a sufficient proportion of the inertia, while most of the common fabrics and shape groups are represented in the plots.

Configuration C

Marginal table: context-by-ware

Data from file 'urim.pie', 1978 records (context 127, ware 14, form 411)

[The number of forms is now given without the base shapes and decorations.]

Configuration: 'context-ware', marginal table: 'context × ware' (7×7)

Table 4.30 Data matrix.

		1 A	2 B2	3 B3	4 B4	5 G1	6 G2	7 I2	8 Total
1	~722G	17.0	5.2	18.8	4.1	18.3	8.9	1.7	74.1
2	~774G	1.8	2.8	7.5	5.3	11.2	25.9	5.1	59.6
3	~732G	17.3	4.0	3.1	5.8	8.0	57.9	0.0	96.1
4	~765G	41.4	6.9	8.9	1.8	30.3	31.7	1.0	122.1
5	~576G	0.0	1.5	18.8	0.4	13.9	5.9	1.4	42.0
6	~530G	0.3	9.1	6.1	1.5	7.0	10.6	0.0	34.5
7	~948G	5.5	2.0	2.0	6.1	47.3	14.0	0.6	77.5
8	**Total**	83.4	31.5	65.3	25.0	136.0	154.9	9.9	505.9

Table 4.31 Residuals.

		1 A	2 B2	3 B3	4 B4	5 G1	6 G2	7 I2
1	~722G	+4.8	+0.6	+9.3	+0.4	−1.6	−13.7	+0.2
2	~774G	−8.0	−0.9	−0.2	+2.4	−4.8	+7.6	+4.0
3	~732G	+1.5	−2.0	−9.3	+1.1	−17.9	+28.5	−1.9
4	~765G	+21.2	−0.7	−6.8	−4.2	−2.5	−5.7	−1.4
5	~576G	−6.9	−1.1	+13.4	−1.6	+2.7	−6.9	+0.6
6	~530G	−5.4	+6.9	+1.7	−0.3	−2.3	−0.0	−0.7
7	~948G	−7.2	−2.8	−8.0	+2.3	+26.4	−9.8	−0.9

MEMBERSHIP LISTS

Configuration: 'context-ware', Variable: 'context'

~722G =	615G	618G	722G	796G	798G	813G	869G		
~774G =	1057G	774G	872G						
~732G =	531G	637G	732G	766G	779G	793G	801G	804G	815G
	825G	867G	879G						
~765G =	595G	711G	720G	723G	763G	765G	819G	863G	917G
	956G								
~576G =	1018G	1039G	576G	853G	874G	961G			
~530G =	1053G	530G	660G	728G	776G	818G	971G		
~948G =	560G	581G	708G	715G	726G	730G	803G	824G	948G
	973G								

Configuration: 'context-ware', Variable: 'ware'

A   B2   B3   B4   G1   G2   I2

ANALYSIS

CORRESPONDENCE ANALYSIS

Table 4.32 Decomposition of inertia by principal axes.

Principal axis	Inertia	Perc	Cum	Histogram
1	0.192338	38.36	38.36	*********
2	0.125820	25.09	63.45	******
3	0.103869	20.71	84.16	*****
4	0.052997	10.57	94.73	**
5	0.021441	4.28	99.01	*
6	0.004979	0.99	100.00	
	0.501444			

Table 4.33 Units related to the first two principal axes.

	Unit	QLT	MASS	INR	K = 1	COR	CTR	K = 2	COR	CTR
1	~722G	444	146	77	336	429	86	−61	14	4
2	~774G	335	118	106	−67	10	3	−383	325	137
3	~732G	919	190	196	−668	861	441	−173	58	45
4	~765G	443	241	119	−193	151	47	268	292	138
5	~576G	891	83	183	882	701	335	−459	190	139
6	~530G	264	68	115	153	28	8	−448	236	109
7	~948G	679	153	204	318	151	80	593	527	428

Table 4.34 Variables related to the first two principal axes.

	Var	QLT	MASS	INR	K = 1	COR	CTR	K = 2	COR	CTR
1	A	379	165	185	−332	196	95	321	183	135
2	B2	145	62	101	65	5	1	−337	140	56
3	B3	864	129	232	703	548	332	−533	316	292
4	B4	13	49	31	−64	13	1	−3	0	0
5	G1	870	269	193	379	399	201	412	471	362
6	G2	866	306	188	−475	733	359	−202	133	99
7	I2	261	19	71	341	64	12	−599	197	56

The first principal axis (Figure 4.8) contrasts context group ~732G (−668) with ~576G (882). Fabric G2 (−475) is differentiated from B3 (703) and G1 (379). Fabric G2 is strongly represented in context group ~732G, while group ~576G contains a sizeable proportion of fabric B3 (cf Table 4.30). The second axis expresses the difference between context group ~948G (593) and ~576G (−459). Context groups ~765G (268) and ~774G (−383) are also contrasted, although this distinction is secondary as these groups contribute less and have a relatively low quality of representation (443 and 335, respectively). Fabric G1 (412) is contrasted with B3 (−533) along this second axis. As with the first axis, the difference between fabrics is again analogous to that of context groups. Apart from the connection between context group ~576G and fabric B3, there is also a link between context group ~948G and fabric G1, which is an important contributor to ~948G (cf Table 4.30). Another

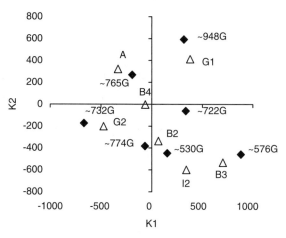

Figure 4.8: Configuration C: Correspondence analysis plot for the marginal table 'context-by-ware'. ♦ = Context, Δ = Ware.

fabric, A (321), is differentiated from fabric B3, although it seems less significant in this plot (cf Table 4.34).

In contrast to configuration B, fabrics G2 and B3 have gained in significance. Fabric G2, together with G1, represents the main groups in the MGK5 data set. Fabric B3 was previously plotted close to G1, but has gained significance as a group and, with the absence of the MEK1 data, now seems to provide an important counterpart. Fabric A was clearly dominant in the MEK1 contexts, but seems less defining for MGK5. None of the smaller fabric groups, B2, B4 or I2, are captured in the plot. The difference between B4 and the remaining groups so dominant in configuration B appears to be less characteristic now.

A comparison with configuration B in terms of context groups presents greater difficulties, as a substantial part of the contexts (MEK1) has disappeared, while many new ones have been added. Context group ~576G, the main contrast to the MEK1 group 409E, is still contributing. In configuration B, context group ~576G was positioned between fabrics G1 and B3; now the group has different constituents, apart from its main and name-giving context, and is linked primarily to fabric B3. Context groups ~765G and ~774G have already been present in configuration B, but did not contribute. The members of these groups have also changed.

Marginal table: context-by-form

Data from file 'urim.pie', 1978 records (context 127, ware 14, form 411)
Configuration: 'context-form', marginal table: 'context × form' (11 × 8)

Table 4.35 Data matrix.

		1 ~R13	2 ~R25	3 ~R183	4 ~R27	5 ~sR38	6 ~R30	7 ~R7	8 ~RRef4	9 Total
1	~595G	1.4	0.4	0.4	1.0	0.0	2.3	4.6	0.0	10.1
2	~779G	0.0	0.9	0.0	5.3	0.0	0.7	3.5	0.0	10.3
3	~576G	0.9	5.1	2.2	0.0	7.3	5.0	1.9	0.5	22.9
4	~763G	3.9	15.8	0.4	0.9	0.0	1.0	11.3	4.0	37.3
5	~819G	0.8	8.5	1.0	0.0	0.0	6.4	8.9	9.4	34.9
6	~917G	8.2	3.3	0.0	0.9	0.5	0.5	3.0	4.1	20.6
7	~618G	0.9	3.4	1.5	2.8	0.0	2.3	28.0	2.3	41.1
8	~774G	0.6	37.9	0.7	11.4	2.3	8.3	25.2	0.0	86.4
9	~1057G	0.3	1.6	0.2	0.0	0.0	22.8	16.2	0.0	41.0
10	~765G	0.2	47.8	6.4	0.7	1.7	13.4	6.8	1.1	78.2
11	~732G	0.9	18.2	7.5	7.4	6.1	40.5	8.9	2.6	92.1
12	**Total**	18.1	142.9	20.2	30.4	17.9	103.2	118.4	24.0	475.1

Table 4.36 Residuals.

		1 ~R13	2 ~R25	3 ~R183	4 ~R27	5 ~sR38	6 ~R30	7 ~R7	8 ~RRef4
1	~595G	+1.0	−2.6	−0.0	+0.4	−0.4	+0.1	+2.1	−0.5
2	~779G	−0.4	−2.3	−0.4	+4.7	−0.4	−1.6	+0.9	−0.5
3	~576G	−0.0	−1.8	+1.2	−1.5	+6.4	+0.1	−3.8	−0.6
4	~763G	+2.5	+4.6	−1.2	−1.5	−1.4	−7.1	+2.0	+2.1
5	~819G	−0.5	−2.0	−0.5	−2.2	−1.3	−1.2	+0.2	+7.6
6	~917G	+7.4	−2.9	−0.9	−0.4	−0.3	−4.0	−2.1	+3.1
7	~618G	−0.7	−9.0	−0.3	+0.2	−1.6	−6.6	+17.7	+0.2
8	~774G	−2.7	+11.9	−3.0	+5.9	−1.0	−10.4	+3.6	−4.4
9	~1057G	−1.2	−10.8	−1.6	−2.6	−1.5	+13.9	+6.0	−2.1
10	~765G	−2.8	+24.3	+3.1	−4.3	−1.2	−3.6	−12.7	−2.8
11	~732G	−2.6	−9.6	+3.6	+1.5	+2.6	+20.5	−14.0	−2.1

MEMBERSHIP LISTS

Configuration: 'context-form', Variable: 'context'

~595G =	595G	728G	766G				
~779G =	515G	779G					
~576G =	576G	608G	867G				
~763G =	1053G	763G	869G				
~819G =	591G	708G	720G	730G	793G	819G	872G
~917G =	583G	711G	804G	879G	917G		
~618G =	530G	531G	544G	586G	615G	618G	796G	949G
~774G =	560G	581G	726G	774G	813G	830G	853G	956G
~1057G =	1039G	1057G	660G	863G	910G	961G	
~765G =	715G	723G	765G	798G	815G	874G	971G
~732G =	722G	732G	801G	824G	948G	973G	

Configuration: 'context-form', Variable: 'form'

~R13 =	R100	R13							
~R25 =	R198	R25	Ref2	sR198					
~R183 =	R183	R212	sR183	sR212					
~R27 =	R27	sR27							
~sR38 =	R206	R38	R39	R42	sR206	sR38	sR39	sR42	
~R30 =	R188	R199	R30	R67	R8	sR188	sR30	sR67	
~R7 =	R11	R16	R17	R184	R185	R186	R3	R4	R5	R6
	R63	R7	sR10	sR11	sR184	sR185	sR186	sR189| sR3	sR4
	sR5	sR6	sR63	sR7	sR87				
~RRef4 =	RRef4	Ref4	sRRef4						

CORRESPONDENCE ANALYSIS

Table 4.37 Decomposition of inertia by principal axes.

Principal axis	Inertia	Perc	Cum	Histogram
1	0.278004	29.77	29.77	*******
2	0.205056	21.96	51.73	*****
3	0.185150	19.83	71.56	****
4	0.115656	12.39	83.95	***
5	0.078947	8.45	92.40	**
6	0.058732	6.29	98.69	*
7	0.012202	1.31	100.00	
	0.933747			

Table 4.38 Units related to the first two principal axes.

	Unit	QLT	MASS	INR	K = 1	COR	CTR	K = 2	COR	CTR
1	~595G	457	21	18	−438	246	15	−405	211	17
2	~779G	363	22	85	−95	2	1	−1149	361	140
3	~576G	433	48	121	572	140	57	830	293	162
4	~763G	774	78	42	−603	733	103	143	41	8
5	~819G	247	74	84	−488	224	63	156	23	9
6	~917G	856	43	195	−1704	691	452	833	165	147
7	~618G	737	87	99	−435	177	59	−775	561	253
8	~774G	177	182	62	42	5	1	−233	171	48
9	~1057G	294	86	97	307	89	29	−464	205	91
10	~765G	393	165	103	300	154	53	374	239	112
11	~732G	563	194	93	489	533	167	118	31	13

The first principal axis of the plot (Figure 4.9) contrasts context group ~917G (−1704) with ~732G (489) and, to a lesser extent ~576G (572). Context group ~763G (−603) occupies a place towards the centre of the plot differentiated from the other groups, ~917G, ~732G and ~576G. Analogous to this constellation, shape group ~R13 (−1739) is set in contrast to ~R30 (504) and ~sR38 (735), though this last group contributes more to the second axis. Shape group ~RRef4 (−1035) is distinguished from ~R13, but is clearly differentiated from ~R30. Both ~R13 and ~R30 are well represented in the contrasted context groups, ~917G and ~732G respectively (cf data matrix). The link of the third group, ~RRef4, to context group

Table 4.39 Variables related to the first two principal axes.

	Var	QLT	MASS	INR	K = 1	COR	CTR	K = 2	COR	CTR
1	~R13	784	38	194	−1739	637	415	838	148	131
2	~R25	198	301	130	95	22	10	267	176	104
3	~R183	620	42	32	511	375	40	414	245	35
4	~R27	278	64	115	4	0	0	−683	278	146
5	~sR38	423	38	129	735	170	73	898	253	148
6	~R30	403	217	147	504	403	199	−10	0	0
7	~R7	812	249	130	−278	159	69	−563	653	386
8	~RRef4	556	50	124	−1035	467	194	452	89	50

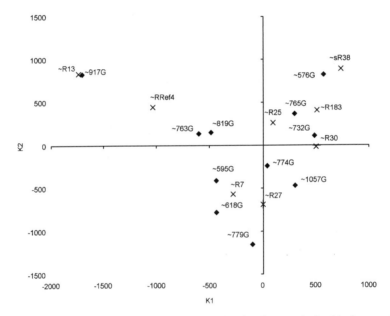

Figure 4.9: Configuration C: Correspondence analysis plot for the marginal table 'context-by-form'. ♦ = Context, × = Form.

~763G is less strong, though, and the rim shape ~Rref4 is also well represented in context group ~917G.

Along the second axis context and shape groups plotted in the upper half of the diagram are differentiated with those in the lower half. The contexts of ~618G (−775) and ~779G (−1149) are set against ~576G (830), ~917G (833) and, to a lesser degree, ~765G (374). Shape groups ~R7 (−563) and ~R27 (−683) are contrasted with ~sR38 (898), ~R13 (838) and, to a lesser extent, ~R25 (267).

Most of the groups present in the plot are now contributing to one of the axes, although the percentage of the total inertia captured is still relatively low with 51.73 per cent. On the whole the picture reflected in this plot shows three distinct groups of contexts and shapes in MGK5. In the left upper quarter scattered along a line towards the centre of the plot are the contributing groups ~R13, ~RRef4, ~917G, ~763G and ~819G. In the right upper quarter and touching the axis groups ~sR38, ~R25, ~R30, ~732G, ~576G, and ~765G form another cluster. The third scatter is finally constituted by groups ~R7, ~R27, ~618G, ~779G, ~595G, ~1057G and ~774G in the lower half of the plot.

While many of the contributing groups have changed or been modified in comparison to configuration B, some of the previous interactions have remained, namely the distinction between shape groups ~R7 and ~sR38. A number of shapes included in ~R7 were part of shape group ~R27 in configuration B, which was contrasted with shape group ~R30. Group ~sR38 was then part of ~R30. With the increased data and level of detail most elements of group ~R30 are now separated (~sR38, ~R183, ~R30), although they are still located close to each other, forming one group of scatters in the upper right quarter of the plot (Figure 4.9). A number of contributing contexts from configuration B is also present in this plot. Parts of context group ~732G were previously merged with ~765G. These are now separated, but again plotted in relative vicinity in the upper right corner of the diagram. The close links between shape group ~R30 and context group ~732G are unchanged. Another context group, ~779G in the lower half of the plot, was among the groups opposed to ~765G in configuration B. This differentiation has remained, although the second member of group ~779G has changed. Shape groups ~R13 and ~Rref4 were joined in configuration B, but did not contribute to either axis. The omission of MEK1 has provided space to display the strong contrast of ~R13 and ~Rref4 to the other groups, which appears to be the really new aspect of this marginal table. On the whole, however, the distinctions between the groups of contexts and forms are broadly consistent in both configurations B and C.

No obvious archaeological difference is noticeable between the context and shape groups in the upper half of the plot. The groups mainly consist of repair layers, infillings, make-up layers or floor deposits. There is no specific stratigraphic correlation between the contexts of any one group. Equally, no obvious mode of distinction is visible regarding the individual vessel types. Most of them can be fully reconstructed and some have been found as near-complete specimens.

In contrast, the contributing context groups of the lower half, ~618G and ~779G, contain a large amount of constructional deposits, walls, mudbrick surfaces and benches. Shape group ~R7, which is well represented in the assemblages of ~618G, consists of a number of bowl forms that usually occur as small fragments throughout the deposits of structure C. Rim sherds of the other group ~R27, a closed vessel type, are on average better preserved, although details of the body form or patterns of decoration are unknown. This group shows some correlation with ~779G and ~618G, albeit these links are not very strong. In configuration B elements of ~R7 were merged with ~R27. Both groups are still relatively close on this plot, although ~R27 is not that well represented (Table 4.39, quality of representation, QLT) and seems typologically distinct. The bowl shapes of ~R7 have close analogies with vessel forms found in the chronologically earlier deposits of MGK6, the defensive wall of Gyaur Kala (Herrmann *et al* 2000, 23–24, figs 17, 18). They are also associated with occupational levels of Gyaur Kala excavated by the YuTAKE (Usmanova 1963b, 195, fig 24, AOS 26, 30). While the general stratigraphic distribution of ~R7 shapes, their higher rate of fragmentation and predominance in constructional contexts seems to suggest that they are residual, a coherent evaluation of the closed vessel type of R27 is much more difficult and any further classification has to remain open at the moment. The conclusive picture for group ~R7/~618G provides the only readily interpretable pattern in this plot. Specifically the groups in the upper half of the diagram lack any clear distinction from an archaeological point of view. Some of the vessel types, such as the bowl shape of R183 or the jars of sR38, have not been individually identified in the YuTAKE reports, but all other shapes, including R30, R25, R13 and Rref4, were regarded as contemporary (cf Katsuris and Buryakov 1963, 145, fig 16).

With no control over the grouping of contexts, the diversity expressed in the plot primarily reflects differences in the composition of assemblages, which most probably derive from distinct formation processes. The relatively low degree of completeness of the individual vessel types and assemblages, however, suggests that the material retrieved to form the deposits of structure C was taken from already inhomogeneous contexts. This would have obscured any functional variation and it therefore seems likely that the recurrent distinctions between shape and context groups shown throughout the analysis ultimately reflect chronological differences. More reliable archaeological evidence is, however, needed to clarify this hypothesis.

Marginal table: ware-by-form

Data from file 'urim.pie', 1978 records (context 127, ware 14, form 411)

Configuration: 'ware-form', marginal table: 'ware × form' (6 × 6)

Table 4.40 Data matrix.

		1 ~R240	2 ~R17	3 ~R7	4 ~sR63	5 ~R183	6 ~R25	7 Total
1	B2	6.2	8.8	6.6	2.4	9.9	7.3	41.2
2	B3	1.4	14.5	15.3	6.7	2.8	30.6	71.4
3	B4	0.0	5.6	13.7	6.5	3.0	0.3	29.2
4	~G1	1.0	3.8	10.0	4.6	7.5	201.8	228.7
5	G2	0.8	6.0	16.6	4.1	14.6	116.1	158.2
6	I2	1.2	0.0	1.3	11.3	0.6	0.2	14.6
7	**Total**	10.6	38.7	63.4	35.6	38.4	356.5	543.3

Table 4.41 Residuals.

		1 ~R240	2 ~R17	3 ~R7	4 ~sR63	5 ~R183	6 ~R25
1	B2	+5.4	+5.8	+1.8	−0.3	+7.0	−19.8
2	B3	+0.0	+9.4	+7.0	+2.0	−2.3	−16.2
3	B4	−0.6	+3.5	+10.3	+4.6	+1.0	−18.8
4	~G1	−3.5	−12.5	−16.7	−10.4	−8.7	+51.8
5	G2	−2.3	−5.3	−1.9	−6.2	+3.4	+12.3
6	I2	+0.9	−1.0	−0.4	+10.3	−0.4	−9.3

MEMBERSHIP LISTS

Configuration: 'ware-form', Variable: 'ware'

```
B2    B3    B4
~G1    =    A    G1
G2    I2
```

Configuration: 'ware-form', Variable: 'form'

~R240 =	R106 sR64	R107	R108	R240	R64	sR106	sR107	sR108	sR240	
~R17 =	R16 sR67	R17	R184	R188	R67	R8	sR10	sR184	sR188	
~R7 =	R3	R4	R5	R6	R7	sR3	sR4	sR5	sR6	sR7
~sR63 =	R11 sR87	R185	R186	R63	sR11	sR185	sR186	sR189	sR63	
~R183 =	R10 sR193	R12 sR212	R183 sR62	R193 sR9	R212	R62	R9	sR12	sR183	
~R25 =	R100 R30 sR206	R13 R38 sR27	R198 R39 sR30	R199 R42 sR38	R2 RRef4 sR39	R204 Ref2 sR42	R206 Ref4 sRRef4	R25 sR198	R25l sR204	R27

CORRESPONDENCE ANALYSIS

Table 4.42 Decomposition of inertia by principal axes.

Principal axis	Inertia	Perc	Cum	Histogram
1	0.397964	59.04	59.04	**************
2	0.171987	25.52	84.56	******
3	0.084196	12.49	97.05	***
4	0.018721	2.78	99.83	
5	0.001135	0.17	100.00	
	0.674003			

Table 4.43 Units related to the first two principal axes.

	Unit	QLT	MASS	INR	K = 1	COR	CTR	K = 2	COR	CTR
1	B2	747	76	218	−856	378	140	846	369	316
2	B3	630	131	84	−460	489	70	247	141	47
3	B4	742	54	184	−1295	725	226	201	17	13
4	~G1	984	421	143	451	887	215	−150	98	55
5	G2	706	291	29	216	698	34	24	8	1
6	I2	971	27	341	−2164	545	315	−1912	426	569

Table 4.44 Variables related to the first two principal axes.

	Var	QLT	MASS	INR	K = 1	COR	CTR	K = 2	COR	CTR
1	~R240	466	20	121	−1183	336	69	733	129	61
2	~R17	884	71	131	−754	457	102	729	427	220
3	~R7	655	117	132	−625	514	115	326	140	72
4	~sR63	999	66	368	−1559	642	400	−1161	356	513
5	~R183	574	71	66	−351	196	22	489	378	98
6	~R25	997	656	183	422	948	293	−96	49	35

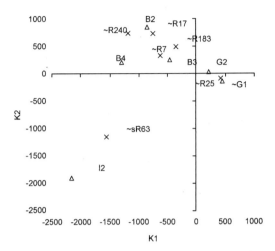

Figure 4.10: Configuration C: Correspondence analysis plot for the marginal table 'ware-by-form'. Δ = Ware, × = Form.

The first principal axis of the plot (Figure 4.10) differentiates between Fabrics I2 (−2164), B4 (−1295), ~G1 (451) and, to a lesser extent, B2 (−856). Shape group ~sR63 (−1559) is contrasted with ~R25 (422). Two further groups, ~R7 (−625) and ~R17 (−754), are also distinguished from the previous ones and positioned between the two contrasting shape groups along this first axis.

The second axis contrasts fabrics I2 (−1912) and B2 (846). This contrast is also reflected in the differentiation between shape group ~sR63 (−1161) and ~R17 (729). One look at the raw data reveals that the shapes of ~sR63 are closely linked to fabric I2, while ~R17 is also strongly represented with fabrics B3 and B4. Shape group ~R7 is also associated with fabric B4 (cf Table 4.41).

The main change to configuration B is certainly the dominating contrast of fabric I2 and shape group ~sR63 to the remaining fabric and form groups. After the removal of the MEK1 data and with the additional MGK5 material, the distinction of fabric B4 has lost in significance. The whole plot of configuration B now seems pushed into the upper part of the diagram. Fabric A, which has been one of the main fabrics in MEK1, appears to be less important and is merged with fabric G1, the main fabric of the MGK5 pottery types. This conjunction is interesting in terms of the visual classification system of wares, as similarities are noted between the two fabrics in the type series: some sherds are marginal A/G1 (see Appendix 1, p 176).

Shape groups ~sR63, ~R7 and ~R17, which are associated with fabrics I2, B4 and B2, are regarded as residual, while the constituents of shape group ~R25 are generally interpreted as more contemporary or Sasanian.

Quasi-log-linear analysis

Table 4.45 Summary of goodness-of-fit analysis.

	Result	*Models*	*Interactions*
IIA	Log-linear analysis	M4 M4	[12] ware-×-context interaction
			[23] ware-×-form interaction
			[13] form-×-context interaction
IIB	Log-linear analysis	M3A M4	[23] ware-×-form interaction
			[13] form-×-context interaction
IIC	Log-linear analysis	M4 M4	[12] ware-×-context interaction
			[23] ware-×-form interaction
			[13] form-×-context interaction

INTERPRETATION

The models suggested by the quasi-log-linear analysis (Table 4.45) seem slightly more complex than in configuration B. The variable 'fabric' has gained in significance and now shows some independence from 'form' in the analysis of model IIA (Independence of fabric-by-form and context, Orton and Tyers 1990, 99): fabric may vary from context to context independent of form, which itself may vary between contexts independent of fabric, but both may also interact with/on each other (Orton and Tyers 1990, 95). This is also supported by the marginal tables. The ware-by-form table does not immediately translate into the context-by-ware marginal table: contexts with a particularly high proportion of a specific fabric do not necessarily contain a high proportion of the shapes that are associated with this fabric in the ware-by-form marginal table. This discrepancy is linked to the fact that most shapes are not confined to any single fabric.

For model IIB (Independence of form-by-context and fabric, Orton and Tyers 1990, 99), however, form still remains the dominating variable as expressed in model M3A (Orton and Tyers 1990, 95). There is no interaction between wares and contexts independent of form. The picture is coherent with configuration B, though less extreme as far as the dominance of 'form' is concerned.

Nothing has changed in the models accepted for Model IIC (Independence of context-by-fabric and form, Orton and Tyers 1990, 99).

Both the context-by-form and fabric-by-form marginal tables of this configuration were dominated by the contrast of relatively small groups, ~R13, ~Rref4 and I2 with ~sR63, with the remaining data. These groups were subsequently excluded in order to explore further patterns of interaction. In this process more modifications became necessary as new results emerged. Shape group ~R2, context 803G and fabric B2 were deleted, after they had been identified as distinct groups, while fabrics A and G1 were merged following the grouping obtained in the fabric-by-form marginal table of configuration C.

Configuration D

Marginal table: context-by-ware

Data from file 'urim.pie', 1978 records (context 127, ware 14, form 411) (minus fabrics I2, B2 and minus context 803G)

Configuration: 'context-ware', marginal table: 'context × ware' (7 × 4)

Table 4.46 Data matrix.

		1 B3	2 B4	3 ~G1	4 G2	5 Total
1	~774G	5.2	6.5	22.2	39.8	73.6
2	~765G	6.3	2.8	42.7	25.7	77.5
3	~722G	17.3	0.0	27.8	8.8	53.9
4	~948G	0.4	6.8	25.2	6.3	38.7
5	~560G	2.8	0.0	28.9	3.6	35.2
6	~813G	13.9	0.4	4.1	3.3	21.8
7	~867G	3.1	1.6	2.0	29.0	35.6
8	**Total**	*48.9*	*18.1*	*152.8*	*116.5*	*336.2*

Table 4.47 Residuals.

		1 B3	2 B4	3 ~G1	4 G2
1	~774G	−5.5	+2.5	−11.2	+14.3
2	~765G	−5.0	−1.3	+7.5	−1.1
3	~722G	+9.5	−2.9	+3.3	−9.8
4	~948G	−5.3	+4.7	+7.7	−7.1
5	~560G	−2.4	−1.9	+12.9	−8.6
6	~813G	+10.8	−0.8	−5.8	−4.2
7	~867G	−2.1	−0.4	−14.2	+16.6

MEMBERSHIP LISTS

Configuration: 'context-ware', Variable: 'context'

~774G =	531G	732G	774G	793G	818G		
~765G =	595G	763G	765G	776G	863G	872G	
~722G =	1039G	530G	576G	618G	722G	796G	917G
~948G =	581G	726G	824G	869G	948G		
~560G =	560G	715G	723G	819G	956G		
~813G =	813G	874G	961G				
~867G =	1057G	801G	815G	867G	971G		

Configuration: 'context-ware', Variable: 'ware'

B3	B4			
~G1	=	A	G1	
G2				

CORRESPONDENCE ANALYSIS

Table 4.48 Decomposition of inertia by principal axes.

Principal axis	Inertia	Perc	Cum	Histogram
1	0.242265	50.50	50.50	***********
2	0.196381	40.94	91.44	**********
3	0.041066	8.56	100.00	**
	0.479711			

Table 4.49 Units related to the first two principal axes.

	Unit	QLT	MASS	INR	K = 1	COR	CTR	K = 2	COR	CTR
1	~774G	975	219	101	−457	944	188	−83	31	8
2	~765G	709	230	26	−17	5	0	197	704	46
3	~722G	983	160	124	567	870	213	−205	114	34
4	~948G	685	115	141	2	0	0	635	685	236
5	~560G	866	105	120	425	329	78	544	537	158
6	~813G	964	65	266	885	398	210	−1055	566	368
7	~867G	986	106	222	−842	707	311	−529	279	151

Table 4.50 Variables related to the first two principal axes.

	Var	QLT	MASS	INR	K = 1	COR	CTR	K = 2	COR	CTR
1	B3	992	146	372	758	469	345	−801	523	475
2	B4	341	54	112	−441	194	43	384	147	40
3	~G1	981	454	219	255	282	122	402	699	374
4	G2	985	346	297	−585	832	489	−251	153	111

The first principal axis of the plot (Figure 4.11) contrasts context groups ~867G (−842) and ~774G (−457) with ~722G (567) and ~813G (885). Fabric G2 (−585) is set against fabric B3 (758) along this axis. Fabric group ~G1 (255) is also differentiated from the others, although it contributes less to this axis.

Context group ~813G (−1055) is contrasted with ~948G (635) along the second axis. ~560G (544) and ~867G (−529) are also differentiated, although this distinction appears to be secondary, as they contribute less to this axis. Fabric B3 (−801) is set in contrast to fabric group ~G1 (402). Fabric G2 (−251) is also distinguished.

The picture now seems to be clearer than in configuration C. Through the elimination of the smaller fabric groups that were identified as mainly residual, B2 and I2, the context groups appear to be rearranged as a sequence. One context group ~765G is plotted slightly out of order towards the centre of the diagram. It does not contribute to either of the principal axes (Table 4.49). Fabric B4 is not very well represented on the plot and does not contribute either (Table 4.50). The sequence of contexts depicted on the plot once again does not follow any preliminary stratigraphic phasing, nor does it reflect differences in the types of contexts, or spatial distinctions. Any chronological interpretation therefore has to be derived through evidence from the other marginal tables in this configuration and the

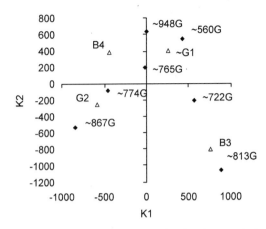

Figure 4.11: Configuration D: Correspondence analysis plot for the marginal table 'context-by-ware'. ♦ = Context, Δ = Ware.

former archaeological excavations. Fabric B3 is mainly associated with vessel forms that are regarded as residual through analogies with material from the excavations of the defensive wall, MGK6 (Herrmann *et al* 2000, 23, fig 17), including the bowl shapes of group ~R7 (cf configuration C, above). Many of the vessel types linked to the fabrics G1, now merged with A, and G2, by contrast, are interpreted as Sasanian, because of their generally better state of preservation and also their consistent stratigraphic distribution illustrated in the YuTAKE reports (cf Katsuris and Buryakov 1963, 145, fig 16). The separation between G1 and G2 has been consistent throughout the individual configurations, although variation in the respective form distribution seems to be limited. Any definitive conclusion regarding the two fabrics, therefore, has to await more reliable evidence.

Marginal table: context-by-form

Data from file 'urim.pie', 1978 records (context 127, ware 14, form 411) (minus context 803G and minus shape groups ~R13, ~Rref4, ~sR63, ~sR2, and ~R27)

Configuration: 'context-form', marginal table: 'context × form' (6 × 6)

Table 4.51 Data matrix.

		1 ~R25	2 ~R183	3 ~R30	4 ~sR38	5 ~R17	6 ~R7	7 Total
1	~530G	0.0	1.2	1.5	0.0	0.8	7.6	11.1
2	~576G	4.0	2.2	4.8	6.6	1.6	0.4	19.6
3	~618G	5.4	1.1	1.8	0.0	2.7	3.1	14.1
4	~765G	36.3	17.2	39.6	7.4	4.1	4.8	109.4
5	~774G	75.9	0.9	14.1	2.8	6.8	20.3	120.9
6	~1057G	3.6	0.0	31.6	0.4	3.1	9.6	48.2
7	**Total**	125.1	22.7	93.3	17.3	19.1	45.9	323.3

Table 4.52 Residuals.

		1 ~R25	2 ~R183	3 ~R30	4 ~sR38	5 ~R17	6 ~R7
1	~530G	−4.3	+0.4	−1.7	−0.6	+0.1	+6.1
2	~576G	−3.6	+0.8	−0.9	+5.6	+0.5	−2.4
3	~618G	−0.1	+0.1	−2.3	−0.8	+1.8	+1.1
4	~765G	−6.1	+9.5	+8.0	+1.6	−2.3	−10.8
5	~774G	+29.1	−7.6	−20.8	−3.7	−0.3	+3.2
6	~1057G	−15.1	−3.4	+17.7	−2.1	+0.2	+2.7

MEMBERSHIP LISTS

Configuration: 'context-form', Variable: 'context'

~530G =	530G	531G	793G						
~576G =	576G	867G							
~618G =	618G	796G	874G						
~765G =	722G	732G	765G	819G	948G				
~774G =	560G	581G	715G	723G	726G	763G	774G	798G	813G
	815G	853G	869G	872G	917G	956G	971G		
~1057G =	1039G	1057G	720G	779G	801G	824G	863G	961G	973G

Configuration: 'context-form', Variable: 'form'

~R25 =	R25	Ref2								
~R183 =	R183	R198	R212	sR183	sR198	sR212				
~R30 =	R199	R30	sR30							
~sR38 =	R206	R38	R39	R42	sR206	sR38	sR39	sR42		
~R17 =	R16	R17	R184	R188	R240	R64	R67	R8	sR184	
	sR188	sR240	sR64	sR67						
~R7 =	R3	R4	R5	R6	R7	sR3	sR4	sR5	sR6	sR7

CORRESPONDENCE ANALYSIS

Table 4.53 Decomposition of inertia by principal axes.

Principal axis	Inertia	Perc	Cum	Histogram
1	0.228169	42.26	42.26	**********
2	0.171440	31.75	74.00	*******
3	0.080459	14.90	88.90	***
4	0.046624	8.63	97.54	**
5	0.013288	2.46	100.00	
	0.539979			

Table 4.54 Units related to the first two principal axes.

	Unit	QLT	MASS	INR	K = 1	COR	CTR	K = 2	COR	CTR
1	~530G	481	34	169	167	11	4	1117	470	249
2	~576G	634	61	195	−616	219	101	−849	415	255
3	~618G	282	44	39	312	203	19	194	79	10
4	~765G	717	338	135	−322	482	154	−224	234	99
5	~774G	965	374	229	562	958	519	−48	7	5
6	~1057G	885	149	234	−558	368	204	662	517	381

Table 4.55 Variables related to the first two principal axes.

	Var	QLT	MASS	INR	K = 1	COR	CTR	K = 2	COR	CTR
1	~R25	925	387	213	472	750	378	−227	174	117
2	~R18 3	486	70	130	−537	288	89	−446	198	81
3	~R30	861	289	224	−552	725	385	239	136	96
4	~sR38	679	53	202	−625	191	91	−999	488	311
5	~R17	66	59	29	88	29	2	100	37	3
6	~R7	734	142	201	298	116	55	687	618	391

The first axis of the plot (Figure 4.12) differentiates between context groups ~774G (562) and ~1057 (−558). Context groups ~765G (−322) and ~576G (−616) are also captured on the plot in contrast to ~774G, although they contribute less. Shape group ~R30 (−552) is contrasted with ~R25 (472) along this axis.

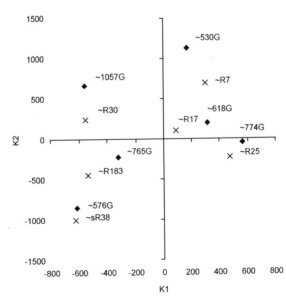

Figure 4.12: Configuration D: Correspondence analysis plot for the marginal table 'context-by-form'. ♦ = Context; × = Form.

The second axis differentiates context groups ~1057G (662), ~576G (–849) and ~530G (1117). Shape group ~R7 (687) is contrasted with ~sR38 (–999). Shape group ~R25 (–227) is also distinguished.

At first sight, the plot appears to be separated into two parts to either side of the vertical axis. The clear distinction between R30 and R25 is a new pattern, not shown in the previous configurations. Shape and context groups ~sR38 with ~576G and ~R7 with ~530G were already contrasted in the last configuration. Groups ~R17 and ~618G are not captured in this plot. Apart from the interactions expressed diagonally across the plot, there are also some distinctions along either side of the vertical axis between the context groups on the left (~1057G and ~576G) and the shape groups on the right side of the diagram (~R7 and ~R25). Thus four different groups are ultimately marked. As in configuration C, the distinctions most likely reflect differences in site formation processes. Shape group ~R7 is again very clearly associated with constructional contexts, ~530G representing largely a splinter group of ~618G. No obvious difference is noticeable between the context groups 774G, 1057G and 576G, which mostly comprise repair and levelling layers. There is also no immediately recognisable variation between the shape groups ~R25, ~R30 and ~sR38. All vessel types are thought to belong to the Sasanian period on grounds of their average completeness and, where possible, stratigraphic distribution. In the case of sR38 and R30 there are also similarities in decorative features (cf Part 3: Stylistic evaluation). The three shape groups are associated with the same fabrics and have continuously been merged in the ware-by-form marginal table (cf configurations C and D). Any interpretation therefore seems difficult at the moment and chronological implications may be relatively marginal in some instances. Shape group sR38 is the least complete of the three followed by R30 and R25. How these differences exactly relate to chronological variation remains tentative at the moment.

Marginal table: ware-by-form

Data from file 'urim.pie', 1978 records (context 127, ware 14, form 411) (minus fabrics I2, B2 and shape groups ~R13, ~Rref4, ~sR63, ~R2, and ~R27)

Configuration: 'ware-form', marginal table: 'ware × form' (4 × 4)

Table 4.56 Data matrix.

		1 ~R183	2 ~sR10	3 ~R7	4 ~R25	5 Total
1	B3	1.8	7.8	23.4	25.1	58.1
2	B4	3.0	0.4	18.8	0.0	22.3
3	~G1	4.0	3.6	11.3	155.0	173.8
4	G2	9.8	2.5	20.3	91.1	123.7
5	Total	18.7	14.4	73.8	271.1	378.0

Table 4.57 Residuals.

		1 ~R183	2 ~sR10	3 ~R7	4 ~R25
1	B3	−1.0	+5.6	+12.1	−16.6
2	B4	+1.9	−0.4	+14.5	−16.0
3	~G1	−4.6	−3.0	−22.7	+30.3
4	G2	+3.7	−2.2	−3.8	+2.4

MEMBERSHIP LISTS

Configuration: 'ware-form', Variable: 'ware'

```
B3      B4
~G1  =    A   G1
G2
```

Configuration: 'ware-form', Variable: 'form'

~R183 =	R183	R212	sR183	sR212					
~sR10 =	R188	R240	R64	R67	R8	sR10	sR188	sR240	sR64
	sR67								
~R7 =	R16	R17	R184	R3	R4	R5	R6	R7	sR184	sR3
	sR4	sR5	sR6	sR7					
~R25 =	R10	R12	R193	R198	R199	R206	R25	R30	R38	R39
	R42	R62	R9	Ref2	sR12	sR193	sR198	sR206	sR30
	sR38	sR39	sR42	sR62	sR9				

CORRESPONDENCE ANALYSIS

Table 4.58 Decomposition of inertia by principal axes.

Principal axis	Inertia	Perc	Cum	Histogram
1	0.299949	85.80	85.80	********************
2	0.044244	12.66	98.46	***
3	0.005393	1.54	100.00	
	0.349586			

Table 4.59 Units related to the first two principal axes.

	Unit	QLT	MASS	INR	K = 1	COR	CTR	K = 2	COR	CTR
1	B3	999	154	259	640	696	210	422	303	619
2	B4	996	59	513	1686	936	559	−428	60	244
3	~G1	976	460	199	−384	975	226	10	1	1
4	G2	720	327	29	−65	133	5	−136	587	136

Table 4.60 Variables related to the first two principal axes.

	Var	QLT	MASS	INR	K = 1	COR	CTR	K = 2	COR	CTR
1	~R183	834	49	64	403	360	27	−462	474	239
2	~sR10	979	38	128	531	240	36	934	739	749
3	~R7	997	195	581	1016	994	673	−53	3	12
4	~R25	999	717	227	−333	999	265	−3	0	0

The first principal axis of the plot (Figure 4.13) contrasts fabric B4 (1686) with fabric group ~G1 (−384). Correspondingly, shape group ~R7 (1016) is distinguished from ~R25 (−333). Fabric B3 (640) appears to be differentiated from both fabric B4 and ~G1 along this first axis. Group R25 is mainly linked to fabric group G1, whereas group R7 is represented in both fabric B3 and B4.

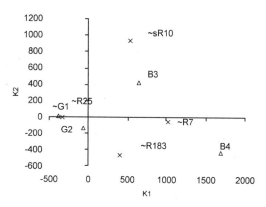

Figure 4.13: Configuration D: Correspondence analysis plot for the marginal table 'ware-by-form'. Δ = Ware; × = Form.

The second vertical axis contrasts fabric B3 (422) with fabric B4 (–428). Shape group ~sR10 (934) is contrasted with ~R183 (–462) along this axis. Fabric G2 (–136) contributes less than the other two. While shape group ~sR10 is linked primarily to fabric B3, R183 has a closer relationship with fabric G2 than fabric B4 (Tables 4.60 and 4.61).

This marginal table clearly focuses on the distinction between shape group R25 and R7 and their respective fabric associations. The difference between shape groups ~sR10 and R183 adds little to the overall pattern (Table 4.58).

Quasi-log-linear analysis

Table 4.61 Summary of goodness-of-fit analysis.

	Result	*Models*	*Interactions*
IIA	Log-linear analysis	M4 M4	[12] ware-×-context interaction
			[23] ware-×-form interaction
			[13] form-×-context interaction
IIB	Log-linear analysis	M3A M4	[23] ware-×-form interaction
			[13] form-×-context interaction
IIC	Log-linear analysis	M4 M4	[12] ware-×-context interaction
			[23] ware-×-form interaction
			[13] form-×-context interaction

INTERPRETATION

All models (Table 4.61) are identical to those of configuration C (cf Table 4.45). Nothing has changed in the proposed interactions for configuration D.

Conclusions

In this last configuration, finally, all three marginal tables present a complementary picture. The main interactions take place between the three fabric groups ~G1, G2 and B3, their associated shape groups and contexts. In the following paragraph the variables are discussed individually.

Context

At the level of the individual contexts few conclusive patterns emerge. This reinforces the impression that all assemblages are mixed and their groupings and associations may alter depending on the perspective of the analysis. As a consequence it is difficult to follow any specific context group through the different marginal tables, since group members change, even if the name of the group stays the same. Individual contexts clearly show consistent relationships with specific fabric or form groups. One such link is observed with the wall and mudbrick contexts in group ~618G (configuration C: context-by-form marginal table) and ~530G (configuration D: context-by-form marginal table) and shape group ~R7. As the pottery forms according to the classification underlying this study are not strictly bound to any single fabric, however, this correlation is not transferred into the context-by-ware marginal table. Still, the strong presence of an obviously residual pottery type in these constructional contexts provides valuable evidence for the assessment of site formation processes at Merv.

Ware

The variable 'ware' has clearly a more significant role in MGK5 than in MEK1. From the outset the individual fabrics were left unmodified and only one group was formed (G1 and A) in the last configuration, following preliminary results in configuration C. Fabric in its current definition with the focus on differences in firing conditions seems slightly arbitrary in the classification of pottery types. Certain tendencies, however, are visible in the context-by-ware marginal table, specifically in configuration D and, following an argumentative line based on the other two marginal tables, we may assume that fabric B3 is very popular with early or residual pottery shapes in MGK5. Smaller fabric groups, including B2, B4 and I2, have also been linked to shapes that were identified as pre-Sasanian. Fabrics A, G1 and G2 seem associated with later or contemporary Sasanian material. A more comprehensive evaluation of the variable 'fabric' is undertaken in the following section.

Form

Form has emerged as the overall dominant variable throughout the analysis. This is not surprising in itself, as form shows the greatest variability at Merv. In addition, form is the only variable for which a coherent system for manual interference was developed. The suggested shape groups are a first step towards a more coherent typology, but some of the groupings may ultimately prove to be inhomogeneous and will change in the future. However, the most significant shape groups in the analysis were well defined and often restricted to one vessel form, leaving little room for mistakes. Many of the interactions between vessel shapes were consistent, such as the contrast between the groups ~R7, ~R17 and ~R30, sR38. This pattern is also reflected in the ware-by-form marginal table. Without any control over the grouping of contexts, the single groups of shapes are too detailed and express many individual interactions that refer to specific situations of site formation processes rather than a coherent sequence. For the moment the chronological interpretation of the individual shape groups, therefore, rests on archaeological argumentation rather than statistics. The analysis, however, has highlighted the structure of the data set and has helped to identify the main pottery types and their relationships.

THE VARIABLE 'WARE' FROM A PETROGRAPHIC PERSPECTIVE

A preliminary petrographic analysis of the pottery was conducted by the Department of Conservation, Documentation and Science (then the Department of Scientific Research) at the British Museum† as part of the post-excavation research programme of the International Merv Project. A number of research topics were selected, focusing on the key problems of the specific periods covered by the archaeological fieldwork. For the pre-Islamic period the programme concentrated on an examination of the typological correlation of fabrics and a comparison between plain and coarse wares that were roughly attributed to Parthian and Sasanian times (Joyner 1999, 2). A selection of pottery fragments (overall 17) was chosen for thin-sectioning, including fabrics A, B3, G1, G2, I2, K and the coarse ware fabrics C, D, E. In total, five groups were distinguished petrographically, although the last one may be regarded as a subdivision of group 4 (Joyner 1999, 3, 6). The correlation between petrographic fabric types and those established in the preliminary type series is illustrated in Table 4.62.

Table 4.62 Correlation between petrographically defined fabric groups and fabrics from the type series, after Joyner (1999, 3).

Petrographic fabric group	Vessel type	Shape code	Fabric
Group 1: Slag-tempered fabric	Jar, cooking pot	R195, R50	C
Group 2: Calcite-tempered fabric	Cooking pot	BA 26	D
Group 3: Grog-tempered fabric	Ledge-handled cooking pot	H12	E
Group 4: Silty quartz and biotite mica fabric	Coarse red slipped jug	RRef4	K
	Grey bowl	R186	I2
	Cream jar	Ndc6dc4	G1
	Cream bowl/plate	R13dc3	A
	Red patterned burnished bowl	R183	G1
	Juglet	R25	B3
	Juglet	BA5	G1
	Bowl	R83	G2
Group 5: Fine red fabric	Fine red slipped bowl	Bsdc9	K

A clear distinction is visible between plain and coarse wares, which reflects a broadly functional division. There might also be a chronological aspect in relation to the three groups of coarse ware. Early Parthian levels of the defensive wall of Gyaur Kala (MGK6) have only produced fragments of coarse ware fabric E (cf Herrmann *et al* 2001, 26), while fabrics C and D seem to be linked to Sasanian deposits.

We have already mentioned that some of the fabrics registered in the type series were excluded from the analysis. Fabric I1 forms a group of misfired wares, while fabric K turned out to comprise two visibly different types of slip ware: one covering internal and

---

† I am very grateful to Dr Louise Joyner and to the Department of Conservation, Documentation and Science at the British Museum for their kind permission to use results of Joyner's unpublished report.

external surfaces, and a slightly rougher slip, which occurs only on the exterior of the vessel. Although petrographically similar, the fine version of slip ware was put in a separate group (Table 4.62; Joyner 1999, 3, 5f). Over the last seasons some diversity in the shape range displayed by the two slip wares was recognised, which may indicate chronological variation. Fine red slip occurs more often with open forms, while coarse slip seems popular with jars. The decision to leave aside fabric K proved consequently to be correct.

As shown in Table 4.62, fabrics A, B3, G1, G2 and I2 all belong to the same petrographic group, which confirms that the differentiation of plain wares relates to firing conditions only. Characteristic nuances in the appearance of the individual fabrics reflect fine variations in the kiln atmosphere and temperature, so that it is often difficult to follow a strict division between the groups, particularly with respect to fabrics A/G1 and G2/B2 (cf Appendix 1, p 176). Since the atmosphere inside the kiln during firing and cooling is almost inevitably variable (Rye 1981, 110, 119), many vessel types display a range of different shades. This explains why most of the shapes occur in a number of different fabrics. The majority of vessel forms, however, show a clear preference for one specific fabric. We may assume that vessel types were generally produced in one particular ware. Shapes which occur in a small quantity, however, may not be represented in their 'indigenous' fabric. In our definition of the term, fabric on its own is not a suitable chronological indicator when considered in isolation with individual fragments or vessels. Regarding the entirety of the pottery assemblages quantitatively, though, a general tendency is noticeable over time from fabric B2 towards B3, G and A, in chronological order (cf configuration B and C, marginal tables context-by-ware and ware-by-form). This complete fabric sequence is only noticeable when 'fabric' and 'form' interactions are examined together. A core sequence emerged from the context-by-ware marginal tables of configurations C and D. The relative position of fabrics A and B2, however, is only understood through configuration A, specifically the results and interpretation of the context-by-form and ware-by-form marginal tables. Only close examination of the shape groups formed during the *srd* reduction in relation to fabrics provided conclusive information. Most of the shapes related to fabric B2 are analogous to forms of the Yaz III horizon. Fabrics A occur with shapes of distinctly later periods, particularly Sasanian. With regard to fabrics A, G1 and G2, a certain diffusion between earlier and later is noticeable within the Sasanian time range (cf configurations A and D, marginal tables context-by-ware and ware-by-form), although G1 appears to be dominant in Area 5, while fabric A prevails in Area 1. Fabric G2 appears to be linked to Sasanian material of MGK5, while fabric B3 occurs predominantly with pre-Sasanian shapes.

Some of the colour effects are clearly intentional. Fabric I2 was fired in a deliberately reducing atmosphere and reflects a particular fashion, which usually provides a reliable chronological criterion. Grey ware is often mentioned in publications on YuTAKE excavations at Merv (Filanovich 1974, 49, 55; Rutkovskaya 1962, 55f) and seems equally popular in neighbouring areas in Iran and Bactria, where it is dated to the early Parthian period (Haerinck 1983, 190). In contrast to other fabrics, however, it never comprised the entire repertoire of shapes and as a residual component appears statistically less significant (cf configurations A, B and C). In the material from Area 1 and Area 5 fabric I2 occurs primarily in open shapes.

Fabric B4 was not included in the petrographic analysis mentioned above, but was examined earlier in a pilot project and found to be identical with fabrics A, B3, G1, G2 and

I2.‡ The characteristic light or white upper part of the vessels derives from stacking the bowls on top of each other in the kiln, where the sheltered lower part of the vessel is not directly exposed to the surrounding temperature. As a result, fabric B4 is mainly restricted to open vessel forms. This effect may have occurred accidentally at first, but appears to have subsequently developed into a fashion characteristic for a specific period, probably in succession to the final phases of Yaz III (cf Rutkovskaya 1962, 44–45).

SITE FORMATION PROCESSES AND RELATIVE CHRONOLOGY

In the following section results and inferences from the statistical analysis are considered in the light of site formation processes, which are essential to the understanding of the chronological correlations between Erk Kala and Gyaur Kala.

As far as the basic data structure is concerned, Area 1 in Erk Kala and Area 5 in Gyaur Kala appear analogous: for each trench representative groups exemplify the contrast between residual and more contemporary material. Both expressions, 'residual' as well as 'more contemporary', are used in a rather general sense here, since the various groups of pottery shapes are certainly difficult to define within the framework of technical archaeological vocabulary. Terminological discussions focus mainly on the classification of deposits as a whole rather than on a further differentiation of already contaminated contexts (Carver 1985, 353, 356; Schiffer 1987, 58f, 111–114). Most of the definitions therefore appear unsuitable to classify the groups of variables discussed here. These groups are created gradually in the course of the analysis as a result of archaeological considerations on the one hand and statistical calculations on the other. While the first was based largely on morphological criteria and the presence/absence of pottery types, the latter searches for statistically similar patterns of interactions. As a consequence the groupings are not representative for event histories or theoretically well-determined categories of deposits. They are, however, significant for various stages of material reuse, which are often found simultaneously in the same context. Thus, the terms 'residual' and 'more contemporary' should broadly characterise the relative chronological distance (measured in cycles of redeposition) to the actual occupation levels of the buildings. Each of the groups may in itself still comprise material of heterogeneous depositional history, which can vary chronologically to some extent.

A slight distinction is noticeable in this respect between the two excavation areas: in Gyaur Kala the more contemporary groups of pottery shapes include vessels which had already been discarded but were incorporated into the deposit in a fairly well-preserved or semi-complete state. With respect to the high preservation of these vessel types in general, we may assume a rather low frequency of re-deposition (cf Orton and Tyers 1990, 86; Schiffer 1987, 276). Some of them possibly even constitute 'primary' components, such as R25, and were discarded among the mixture of various refuse material at the time of deposition of the contexts. In view of the continuity and regularity of the processes of material reuse within mudbrick architecture illustrated by ethno-archaeological studies for Iran (cf Horne 1994, 129–131, 140f), we may regard the more contemporary material to be chronologically close to, in some cases even identical with, the time of refurbishment activities and occupation of the structure. Vessel shapes of the equivalent group in Area 1

‡ The pilot project included ten samples of pre-Islamic pottery and was completed by Ann Feuerbach at the Institute of Archaeology, University College London.

appear, overall, to be less well preserved. However, since the average fragment size for Erk Kala is generally smaller, it is doubtful whether we can assume a proportionally greater chronological distance to the occupation levels for this group of pottery types. Certainly the 'more contemporary' material of Area 1 indicates a higher frequency of depositional events than the corresponding group in Area 5. Only very few semi-complete vessels were recovered from Area 1 in general. Whether this partly reflects archaeological chance or a different concept of material reuse for both areas remains unclear. The fact that one of the contexts associated with the more contemporary group in Area 1 is a mudbrick wall indicates that at least in the later construction phases of the building, this group of pottery shapes was residual. However, in comparison to the remaining vessel types, they still appear to represent the generally best preserved ceramic shapes.

Pottery shapes of the purely residual groups are generally less complete, pointing to a considerably higher frequency of re-deposition. Some of the groups give a heterogeneous impression (cf group ~R106 in configuration A and group ~R27 in configuration B), which may reflect an advanced stage in the cycle of material reuse, where already contaminated deposits from previously abandoned buildings are again reclaimed as construction material (cf Schiffer 1987, 111–114).

The context groups, finally, associated with the various pottery shapes again do not stand for different categories of deposits, but reflect a distinction between deposits with a significant amount of roughly contemporary material and those dominated by repeatedly reused material, which has also been termed 'reclaimed refuse' in the literature (Schiffer 1987, 111ff).

As far as the correlation between the two excavation areas is concerned, they both appear totally separate and diverse. All pottery groups representing the two excavation areas are distinct. Contemporary as well as residual material is differentiated. For the more contemporary material, this divergence also implies chronological differences between the occupational phases of the structures. In this context it is important to note that a few of the vessel types diagnostic for the more contemporary pottery in MGK5 recur as small and rare fragments in MEKI, where they form an insignificant part of the residual material. This provides an archaeological basis for the relative chronological correlation between the estimated periods of occupation of both areas aside of and independent from the numismatic evidence which was presented above.

The residual groups, though themselves partly mixed, are yet again diverse, which indicates chronological variations between the deposits or material reused for construction and maintenance of the buildings and surrounding external surfaces or pavements. To judge from analogies within the site and the oasis, the residual material from MEKI is slightly older than that from MGK5. Area 1 produced a significant amount of pottery dating as far back as the Yaz III period (Late to post-Achaemenid), whereas the earliest pottery from Area 5 seems to belong to Later Hellenistic or Early Parthian times. This corresponds roughly with the alleged foundation periods of those areas of the city (Bader et al 1998a, 160f; 1998b, 187; Genito 1998, 91). The chronological correlation between residual material and early periods of occupation in both areas suggests that, at least for the buildings in Area 1 and Area 5, material was reclaimed from sources in relatively close vicinity to the building sites. A large pit outside the structure in Erk Kala, which seems closely related to residual shapes, has been interpreted as a 'quarry pit for bricks' (cf context records IMP Archive, context no 472). Any assumptions on reclamation processes within the city in general are purely tentative at the moment, since the evidence provided by the IMP excavations is restricted to very small areas within a large urban settlement, and the patterns visible in Area 1 and Area 5 may not be representative for the whole city. However, we may assume that the supply of building materials was organised in a pragmatic manner and would have been taken from sources nearby, specifically with regard to the high city walls around the citadel in Erk Kala. Regarding the level of organisation, it seems unlikely that reclamation processes would have been outside public responsibility as far as the citadel is concerned.

In its various attempts and modifications the chronological assessment has once again illustrated the problematic nature and complexity of a meaningful evaluation of the ceramic evidence from a multi-period urban site. Through the methodological precision and strictness required for a statistical approach, the structure and archaeological characteristics of the data set could be understood and handled accordingly. The individual treatment of the excavation areas subsequently opened up their internal structure and interrelations. An antagonistic grouping representative for specific stages in the processes of site formation seems generally characteristic of the ceramic material of both excavation areas. In a detailed analysis of the sequence and correlation of the depositional events, a basic chronology could be established, placing MGK5 and MEKI in consecutive order.

Both areas form two chronologically discrete units and would probably appear as two separate phases in a parabolic sequence if the seriation had covered a longer period of time. The perspective taken in this analysis, however, proved to be almost microscopic, which emphasised the differences between the areas rather than their chronological interrelation. From a statistical perspective we cannot judge the chronological distance between both trenches in terms of absolute dates. The careful evaluation of the numismatic evidence from both areas (Chapter 5), however, helps in understanding the absolute chronological position of the trenches.

Statistical calculations focus principally on the most significant interactions and only illustrate a restricted part of the overall information gained from the data set. An immanent disadvantage is the relative insensitivity towards quantitatively smaller groups. A considerable number of vessel types and contexts were consequently not represented in the plots calculated above. This problem seems worse in Erk Kala for two reasons:

(a) Pottery assemblages in Erk Kala generally show a higher degree of brokenness, and a greater variability of shapes.

(b) The differences in style and detail of pottery processing over the first field seasons made an exact identification of fragments often impossible. Many shapes may have been misinterpreted by the author, which would have led to confusion during statistical calculations and the subsequent deletion of shape groups, fabrics or contexts.

— 5 —

CHRONOLOGICAL ANALYSIS

ABSOLUTE DATES

Coins have always been regarded as reliable means to assess the absolute date range of a site, yet problems related to the interpretation of numismatic evidence are often under-estimated. The specific problems inherent in the interpretation of coin evidence are given brief consideration here from a numismatic and archaeological perspective, before evaluating the data for MEK1 and MGK5. Copper-alloy coins form a regular part of the archaeological assemblages at Merv, especially from Parthian levels onwards (Filanovich 1974; Herrmann *et al* 1993–1999). From the IMP excavations in MEKI and MGK5 alone, 263 stratified coins are recorded (IMP archive). Although a few coins attest to an international background, including Roman, Byzantine, Sogdian and also Sasanian specimens from different regions, most issues are attributed to the local mint, which goes back to Parthian times (Hobbs 1995; Loginov and Nikitin 1993a, 225f).

NUMISMATIC PERSPECTIVE

The series of Sasanian coins from Merv found during excavations at the site spans the Early to Late Sasanian periods. Most rulers from Ardashir I (AD 224–240) to Khusro II (AD 590–628) are represented with at least one, sometimes even several different issues, although certain irregularities occur and the coin sequence is not complete (Loginov and Nikitin 1993a, 230). Even within the issues strong fluctuations are noticeable with respect to the quantity of coins recorded for each king. This may partly reflect differences in the duration of individual reigns (Loginov and Nikitin 1993b, 248). However, various other factors seem involved here, which cannot be fully assessed due to the lack of necessary evidence. Over decades of numismatic research on the Sasanian period a basic sequence of coin issues has been established, following the identification of the individual crowns of the kings (Alram 1986; Göbl 1971). Greater difficulties occur in evaluating the entire monetary system, since our knowledge is restricted to a limited amount of coin issues from relatively few mints. Basic patterns of the economic and financial system of the Sasanian state are traceable, although its internal structures and payment modalities on all different levels of political, administrative and military organisation remain obscure, including the frequency and circulation of issues. Generally, lower copper-alloy denominations are believed to have served primarily the local market (Alram 1986, 12; Göbl 1971, 27). Irregularities in the release of coin issues at Merv may therefore reflect a reaction to changes in the local market, in this case the oasis of Merv (Loginov and Nikitin 1993a, 230). Frequently an increase in coin issues has been related to military activities of the Sasanians (Loginov and Nikitin 1993a–c). Locally at Merv the mere presence of an army unit would have resulted in an expansion of copper-alloy denominations in use.

Further complications occur for the Early Sasanian period, as issues of a local ruler are minted at Merv parallel with those of the Sasanian king of kings (Loginov and Nikitin 1993a, 229). Nothing is known as yet on the exact correlation between these issues. Since this specific problem is restricted to the 3rd century, the chronological assessment of the IMP trenches is not affected.

More significant for the evaluation of the coins from MEK1 and MGK5 are: (a) the fluctuation in quantity of coins for each issue, since the original size of an emission immediately affects its survival rate and small coin issues are less likely to appear in the archaeological record; (b) the unknown period of circulation. At the present level of numismatic research, it is impossible to estimate how long the copper-alloy coins of one specific issue retained their monetary value and could be used for payments. This is particularly problematic for issues of large size from long-ruling kings, whose successors often reigned for a much shorter period and may not have struck low denomination coins in a quantity that immediately would have replaced previous issues on the local market.

ARCHAEOLOGICAL PERSPECTIVE

In addition to these numismatic factors, taphonomic processes might influence the structure of the recorded data. The survival rate of coin issues is not only related to the quantity of coins originally in circulation, but also depends on their physical properties. Towards the later Sasanian period, coins are generally minted from larger and thinner flans, which are less likely to survive processes of weathering and erosion. Thus only a small number of coins from Khusro II could be identified from excavations (Loginov and Nikitin 1993c, 275).

Another problem lies in the small size of the coins, which facilitates their 'migration' through stratigraphic layers. Single coins might easily be dislocated through animal disturbance or other taphonomic processes and enter originally not associated contexts. Only careful archaeological observation can help to prevent erroneous interpretation in this case.

Finally, the reuse mechanisms observed for the pottery in MEKI and MGK5 apply equally to the low copper-alloy denominations, since, once lost, they would not have been automatically retrieved. As objects of low value, they underwent the same cycles of reclamation and re-depositional activities as the ceramic material. As a result Parthian coins are often found in later contexts together with Sasanian issues (Figures 2.15–2.16 and 2.18–2.20). Depending on the distribution of coins within contexts, these 'residual' coins can provide misleading chronological evidence, and the different types of archaeological deposits need to be taken into account in order to assess the *terminus post quem* provided by the latest coin correctly.

Previous YuTAKE excavations at Merv based their absolute chronology on coins that were classified by Masson (Filanovich 1974; Katsuris and Buryakov 1963, 152). These preliminary attributions seemingly supported early dates for many of the structures excavated, which also corresponded well with the theoretical preconceptions (cf Chapter 1, pp 12–13). In recent years Loginov and Nikitin undertook a reassessment of the numismatic evidence and corrected several earlier identifications, so that a later date for most of these trenches is now evident (Loginov and Nikitin 1993b, 251). The coins found during the IMP excavations in MEKI and MGK5 were identified by Loginov, Nikitin and Smirnova (Herrmann *et al* 1994–1999).

GYAUR-KALA, AREA 5 (MGK5)

The total number of coins registered from this excavation between 1995 and 1998 is 138, 28 of which were too poorly preserved for identification. Since 1996 excavations were extended into the narrow alleys east and south of structure C, to provide evidence for a comparison between external and internal contexts. This should also clarify the chronological position of structure C, since coins found within street contexts were assumed to be casually lost, while those recovered from internal floor and make-up layers were probably re-deposited and were more likely to be residual (Herrmann *et al* 1998, 56). A comparison between the coin finds from different types of deposits is undertaken here briefly, to verify this assumption.

Three context groups are distinguished: (a) room deposits, all non-constructional contexts excavated inside the rooms of structure C; (b) street deposits, contexts excavated in the adjacent alleys to the east and south of structure C, and (c) constructional deposits, i.e. deposits consisting primarily of mudbrick. The date range given here for each ruler follows Loginov and Nikitin (1993a–c). Cleaning layers have been omitted from the assessment. Unidentified coins were also excluded, since they are only mentioned as totals in the coin lists (IMP archive).

Group 1: Room deposits (46 coins)

The coin issues from deposits inside structure C cover a long chronological sequence with a large proportion of 3rd- and 4th-century coins (Figure 5.1, Table 5.1). All 5th-century coins

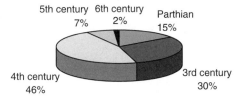

5th century 7% 6th century 2% Parthian 15% 4th century 46% 3rd century 30%

Figure 5.1: MGK5, coin distribution in room deposits.

Table 5.1 MGK5, coin distribution in room deposits.

Parthian*		7
Ardashir I	AD 220–240	2
Shapur I	AD 240–273	10
Varahran II	AD 276–293	2
Shapur II	AD 309–379	20
Varahran IV	AD 388–399	1
Yazdgard I**	AD 399–420	2
Anonymous	5th century	1
Khusro I	AD 531–579	1

* The majority of Parthian coins consist of third-century issues.
** Counted as fifth-century rules.

found in room deposits derive from post-occupational contexts (context nos 517, 523, 536, 544, cf context sheets, IMP Archive). This leaves a rather curious pattern for the occupational deposits of structure C, with an increasing number of coins from Parthian times up to the 4th century, followed by a gap for the 5th century and only one single coin from the Late Sasanian period (Khusro I, context no 576 in room 603). Although context 576 is not the uppermost layer in this room, there is a possibility that the coin was moved by post-depositional processes and a single 6th-century coin is not sufficient to provide a valid *terminus post quem* for the structure. More information is obtained from the second group of contexts.

Group 2: Street deposits (23 coins)

Late Sasanian coins generally constitute a larger proportion in the street deposits than inside structure C (Figure 5.2, Table 5.2). Three of the late issues were retrieved from context nos 547, 640/1 and 856 which correspond to levels of room deposits that only contained coins of the 4th century and earlier. The stratigraphic correlation of the single sequences of contexts from the rooms and the street sections is still at an early stage and the final matrix is not yet complete. One room and its adjacent street deposits are illustrated here with the preliminary matrix, to exemplify the distribution pattern of coins in MGK5 (Figure 5.3). Despite the generally low number of 5th-century issues, a tendency is noticeable that the coins from street deposits reflect a greater variety of more contemporary issues than those in room deposits. Coin issues from Shapur II (AD 309–379) are strongly represented in both room and street contexts. In this respect it is useful to examine the constructional contexts of structure C.

Figure 5.2: MGK5, coin distribution in street deposits.

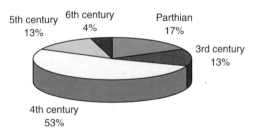

Table 5.2 MGK5, coin distribution in street deposits.

Parthian		4
Shapur I	AD 240–273	2
Merv king*	AD 240–260	1
Shapur II	AD 309–379	10
Shapur III	AD 383–388	1
Varahran IV	AD 388–399	1
Yazdgard I	AD 399–420	1
Peroz	AD 457–484	1
Kavad I	AD** 484–531	1
Khusro I	AD 531–579	1

* Refers to the issue of a local ruler under Shapur I (Loginov and Nikitin 1993c, 279).
** Kavad's reign was interrupted twice (AD 484, 488–497, 499–531).

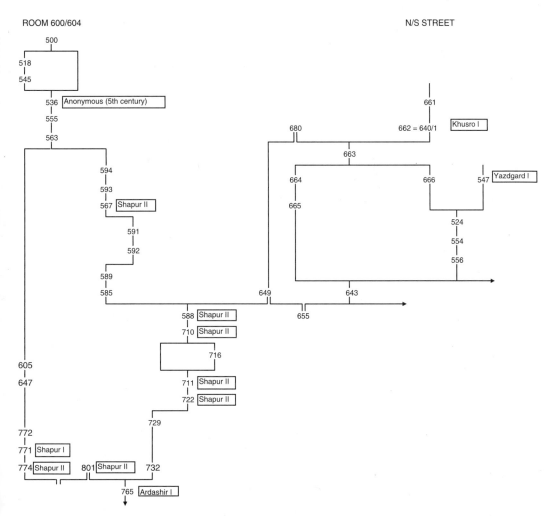

Figure 5.3: Preliminary Harris Matrix of MGK5, Room 600/604 and the adjacent street deposits (IMP arch-ive). Parthian (early 3rd century), Ardashir I (AD 220–240), Shapur I (AD 240–273), Shapur II (AD 309–379), Yazdgard I (AD 399–420), Anonymous (5th century), Khusro I (AD 531–579).

Group 3: Constructional deposits (seven coins)

In comparison to the previous groups, constructional deposits are few in number and accordingly produced a smaller amount of coins (Table 5.3). However, they indicate an interesting pattern of coin distribution. The proportion of Parthian issues has grown in relation to the room and street deposits, while 3rd- and 4th-century coins are represented equally by two specimens each (Figure 5.4). Later coins are missing from the constructional deposits. According to their archaeological classification, the coins of this third group are primarily residual; yet issues of Shapur II are already present with two coins. Moreover,

Figure 5.4: MGK5, coin distribution in constructional deposits.

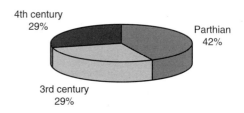

4th century
29%

Parthian
42%

3rd century
29%

Table 5.3 MGK5, coin distribution in constructional deposits.

Parthian		3
Shapur I	AD 240–273	1
Merv king	AD 240–260	1
Shapur II	AD 309–379	2

both specimens (found in context nos 801 and 952) are tentatively attributed to issues (type 3 and type 5, IMP archive) which belong to the later period of Shapur's reign (Loginov and Nikitin 1993b, 250f). On the whole, coins from Shapur II constitute the overwhelming part of the issues from structure C and the adjacent alleys.

While this is to some extent explicable by the unusually long reign of this king (AD 309–379), it also raises the question of money circulation: some of Shapur's issues may have remained in circulation for several decades under his successors. In this case some of the coins from Shapur II would have been residual, whereas others were contemporary.

Considering the numismatic evidence for MGK5 in total, a period starting no earlier than the very end of the 4th up to the later 5th century may be suggested as a tentative chronological frame for the occupational levels of structure C. Roughly the same date range would apply to the more contemporary group of pottery shapes from MGK5. No further differentiation of single phases of occupation is possible at present and the post-occupational contexts are not represented with ceramic material, since none of them qualify for the statistical analysis.

ERK-KALA, AREA 1 (MEK1)

For the assessment of MEK1 we have no supplementary evidence in the form of domestic and street contexts. The only possible division between different context types is non-constructional or constructional deposits. A total of 147 coins were found in Erk-Kala, MEK1 between 1992 and 1995. 58 of these were either not identified or of ambiguous attribution (cf coin lists, IMP archive). A comparison of coin evidence from the two groups of contexts is undertaken below. Cleaning layers are again excluded from the assessment.

Group 1: Non-constructional deposits (64 coins)

The coin issues from deposits of this first group basically reflect a prolongation of the sequence recorded for MGK5 (Figure 5.5, Table 5.4). All early issues are present in addition

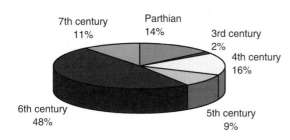

Figure 5.5: MEK1, coin distribution in non-constructional deposits.

Table 5.4 MEK1, coin distribution in non-constructional deposits.

Parthian		9
Shapur I	AD 240–273	1
Shapur II	AD 309–379	6
Shapur III	AD 383–388	1
Varahran IV	AD 388–399	3
Yazdgard II	AD 438–457	1
Peroz	AD 457–484	3
Anonymous	5th century	1
Kavad I	AD 484–531	1
Khusro I	AD 531–579	29
Hormizd IV	AD 579–590	1
Sogdian	6th century	1
Khusro II	AD 590–628	2
Late/Post Sasanian	7th century	5

to the later 6th- and 7th-century coins. Issues of Khusro I (AD 531–579) constitute the largest proportion and the pattern for coins from this king appears to be similar to those of Shapur II in MGK5. Evidence for the 5th century is still sparse, suggesting that the overall quantity of coins minted in this period was substantially smaller than during the 4th and 6th centuries respectively. 7th-century coins are recorded from the upper layers of MEK1 associated with the occupational activities truncated by erosion (cf IMP archive; see also Figure 5.7).

Group 2: Constructional deposits (ten coins)

Group 2 shows a distribution pattern similar to the first group for the period up to the 6th century (Figure 5.6, Table 5.5). Issues of Khusro I again form the largest part within the

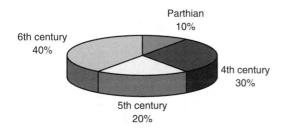

Figure 5.6: MEK1, coin distribution in constructional deposits.

ANALYSIS

Table 5.5 MEK1, coin distribution in constructional deposits.

Parthian		1
Shapur II	AD 309–379	2
Shapur III	AD 383–388	1
Yazdgard I	AD 399–420	1
Yazdgard II	AD 438–457	1
Khusro I	AD 531–579	4

constructional contexts. Most significant is the absence of 7th-century coins from these deposits. A summary of the correlation between coin finds and stratigraphic sequence is illustrated here by the matrix of context groups, which represent certain phases of occupational activities (Figure 5.7). Next to each group the identification of the latest coin is given. The sequence demonstrates that Khusro I issues are found practically throughout the sequence and, as shown above, in all types of deposits. Coins from the 7th century occur within the later occupational phases of MEK1 associated with rooms A and E (cf Figure 1.5). In conclusion, a period from the end of the 6th century to probably Post-Sasanian times may be suggested as the period of occupation for MEK1. In contrast to the pottery from structure C, the more contemporary group of vessel types found in MEK1 appears to be chronologically earlier than the actual occupation activities. This is also supported by the fact that fragments of the more contemporary group occur in constructional contexts of the later occupational phases. It therefore seems justified to assess

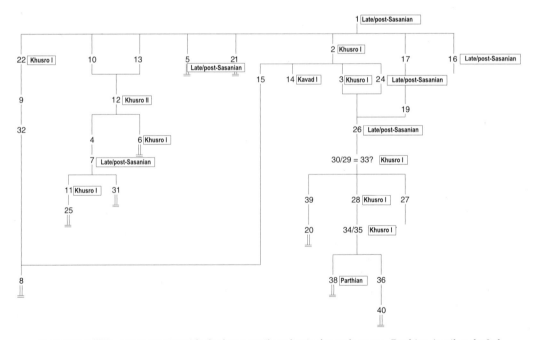

Figure 5.7: MEK1, group matrix with the latest attributed coin for each group. Parthian (until early 3rd century), Kavad I (AD 484, 488–497, 499–531), Khusro I (AD 531–579), Khusro II (AD 590–628), Late/post-Sasanian (7th century).

118

the date range of this group of pottery as the 6th century, probably the earlier rather than the later phases of this century.

CONCLUSION

Despite the problematic nature of evaluating numismatic evidence in the context of mud-brick architecture, certain tendencies may be seen throughout the stratigraphic sequence. Coin distribution in both structures, MEK1 as well as MGK5, has shown once again how much mechanisms of reuse and residuality affect different categories of objects. While the date range given for each trench appears relatively broad, it is currently impossible to pin down single phases of occupation more precisely. This applies equally to independent scientific dating methods for pottery, including Thermoluminescence, since error spans, specifically with regard to contaminated deposits, are still too wide to help resolve the fine chronological questions of the first centuries AD. At the moment we have to rely on the broad chronological framework outlined above.

(a) Gyaur-Kala, MGK5: The period of occupation starts from the end of the 4th century at the earliest through the 5th century.

(b) Erk-Kala, MEK1: The occupational phases cover a period from the end of the 6th century through post Sasanian/Early Islamic times.

According to this suggested date range a gap occurs for most of the 6th century in the occupation of the two areas. However, this seems less significant for the sequence of pottery production, since the Sasanian shapes associated with MEK1 are not exactly contemporary with the occupational activities of this structure (cf Chapter 4, p 108). Following

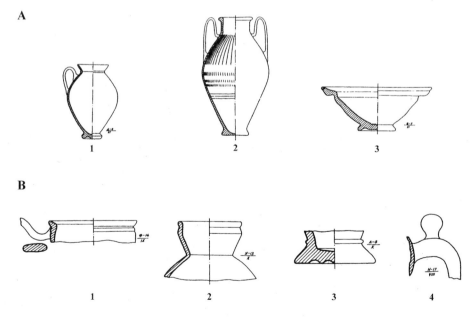

Figure 5.8: Schematic illustration of the two consecutive phases in YuTAKE Trench 6, the 'Millers' Quarter'.

the assumption that the more contemporary group of pottery from MEK1 belongs to the 6th century, the two phases of ceramic production appear to be approximately consecutive without a distinct interruption. Consequently no significant stage of development within the ceramic sequence will have been missed. This seems to be confirmed by the pottery assemblages from the uppermost contexts excavated in the alleys east and south of structure C, which contained fragments of vessel types, such as R116 and R130, characteristic of the material from MEK1 (context nos 660, 873, 939, IMP archive). As the uppermost level of occupation in MGK5 is truncated, however, this argument seems difficult to prove and a few occurrences of diagnostic shapes are not suitable as an unambiguous chronological indicator.

Evidence from the former YuTAKE excavations of Trench 6, the 'Millers' Quarter, showed a similar sequence of ceramic shapes (Figure 5.8), supporting the assumption that the assemblages from MGK5 and MEK1 respectively represent consecutive stages in the pottery design at Merv.

— PART III —

STYLISTIC EVALUATION

— 6 —

POTTERY FROM EARLY AND MIDDLE SASANIAN TIMES

OBJECTIVES AND METHODS

The pottery analysis so far has concentrated on problems of developing a differentiated method of dating ceramic material in an attempt to produce a more reliable chronology for the pottery from Sasanian contexts at Merv. Reusing previous chronological sequences or stylistic preconceptions would have anticipated any original analysis. Through an independent statistical approach the risk of such circular arguments was minimised. As a result, three pottery groups were distinguished, which are representative of different phases in the development of ceramic design at Sasanian Merv. Following the identification of Sasanian pottery types, we are now able to focus on stylistic aspects which will complete the analysis. The discussion will focus mainly on the groups highlighted in the correspondence analyses, but not exclusively. Forms not featuring on the computer plots were included if they are independently attributed to the same chronological phase. For the Later Sasanian material from Erk Kala in particular this seems indispensable, since the statistically determined contemporary material has been restricted to one vessel form only. Many of the annotations made for the 'more contemporary' groups in the discussion of site formation processes are equally valid for the stylistic evaluation. They do not represent the repertoire of ceramic vessels in use simultaneously at one specific point in time and should not be mistaken as reconstruction of 'life' assemblages (cf Orton *et al* 1993, 166). Each chronological group incorporates pottery types that altogether span several decades up to a century. Some of them certainly had overlapping life spans, while others may already have dropped out of the repertoire (Trinkaus 1986, 44f). It is impossible to clarify such details at present, since the chronological sequences covered by each excavation area are too short to determine the starting or drop-out point of any particular vessel type. Nevertheless, all three groups illustrate specific phases in the ceramic tradition of Sasanian Merv.

Before we set out the itinerary and structure of this discussion, it should be emphasised that we regard the pottery analysed here as a local product for the following reasons. According to the petrographic analysis, all of the fine wares correspond to the local geology (Joyner 1999, 7). The wide geographical distribution of similar deltaic alluvial deposits, as present in the raw material from the Merv ceramics, however, aggravates an exact determination of the clay provenance, and on petrographic grounds the possibility of a non-local production is not excluded (Joyner 1999, 6–7). Evidence provided by a number of sherds that show traces of over- and misfiring, such as fragments classified in fabric I1 (cf

Appendix 1), suggests a local manufacturing process for the pottery. This also seems plausible from a purely practical point of view, since a city on the scale of Merv could hardly have been supplied through imports, particularly in consideration of its geographical setting within the Karakum Desert. We therefore assume a local production in the vicinity of the city or at least within the oasis, despite the lack of excavated kilns for this period at Merv.

All analogies in shape from neighbouring areas are consequently regarded as evidence for movement of style and fashion in contrast to movement of pottery from a specific production centre through trade. Movement of style, however, is a complex phenomenon, and the various factors involved are difficult to assess, including the time lag between first appearances of a certain style in different areas. For this reason in particular, it seems unreliable to use parallels from other often distant sites to date individual pottery shapes at Merv.

Vessel forms related to coarse or cooking ware fabrics are omitted from the stylistic evaluation, since they were not part of the statistical analysis and will be discussed elsewhere (Puschnigg and Gilbert forthcoming).

The following assessment will concentrate on three main issues:

(a) Do the individual vessel types within each group share a common set of stylistic expressions?

(b) Are these stylistic expressions innovations in the pottery production, which appear characteristic for this particular phase, or do they represent the continuation of traditional forms?

(c) Are the stylistic features specific to each group regional or inter-regional in character?

A reference catalogue for the individual pottery types is given at the beginning of each section, followed by a brief discussion on the distinct chronological phases. Early and Middle Sasanian groups are considered together in the discussion, as the material derives from the same excavation area and the absolute time distance between the individual groups is uncertain at the moment.

In the catalogue every vessel type will first be examined stylistically, including rim shape, general vessel form and proportion, decoration and surface treatment. This will help to define type-specific characteristics that may be related to the vessel function as well as common features between the forms within each group, which may be regarded as the fashion of a particular period.

A comparison between the vessel types illustrated here and evidence from former YuTAKE excavations at Merv will demonstrate whether stylistically significant features are documented from earlier levels of occupation, or whether they represent innovations in ceramic production. Despite the relatively coarse and simplified chronological classification published in the excavation reports of the YuTAKE, it is usually clear when a new pottery type first occurs in a specific level (Filanovich 1974, 85). In the course of this comparison possible links with, or continuations of, earlier traditions in this area will emerge. As most of the YuTAKE publications are difficult to access from outside the former Soviet Union, the relevant illustrations are reprinted here in Appendix 3. The plan with locations of the different trenches, soundings and excavation areas is illustrated here once again for the purpose of orientation (Figure 6.1).

Finally, parallels from neighbouring areas are investigated. Areas for comparison are

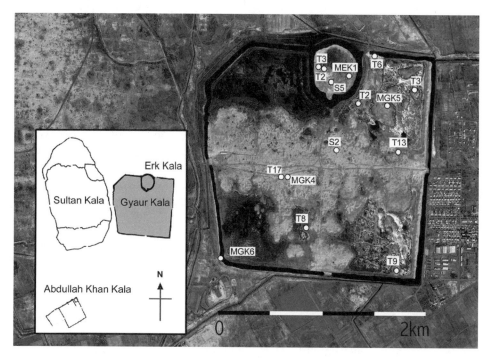

Figure 6.1: Plan of the location of the major YuTAKE trenches, soundings and IMP excavation areas.

situated inside the Sasanian Empire on the one hand and in the territories to the east of the Sasanian border on the other. The availability of comparable material is determined by the situation of archaeological research and publications. Since archaeological evidence from these areas is not homogeneous, any comparative study has to remain incomplete. The purpose of this preliminary stylistic assessment is to integrate the results of the statistical analysis to gain a first impression of the stylistic variation and orientation of the pottery. Comparisons discussed here are intended to illustrate possible inter-regional links and are therefore restricted to a minimum of parallels and close analogies. While the material published from the various projects over the years is still relatively sparse, it provides sufficient evidence to establish whether certain features are local or inter-regional.

In conclusion, the results of this assessment are evaluated with regard to the character-istics initially established for Sasanian pottery in the review of previous archaeological research in Iraq and Iran (Chapter 1). These were defined by a noticeable continuation of Parthian ceramic traditions into the first centuries of Sasanian rule and the development of a more distinctive style in later Sasanian times, possibly inspired by contemporary metal ware. As in the Partho–Sasanian transitional period, there appears to be an overlap between certain Late Sasanian and Early Islamic pottery types.

Most vessel types associated with the Early and Middle Sasanian periods are repre-sented in the statistical analysis and are referred to in the individual descriptions. A num-ber of former YuTAKE excavations, mostly in Gyaur Kala, cover a similar chronological period and provide a rich source for comparison. Apart from Trench 6, the 'Millers' quarter', a series of domestic buildings near the northern gate of Gyaur Kala most relevant for this phase comprise Trench 8, a stratigraphical test excavation south of the main occupational mound (Filanovich 1974, 94ff), and Trench 13, the 'merchant's house', interpreted as the dwelling of a well-established city merchant, according to the larger size of the structure and a number of iron blooms found there (cf Filanovich 1974, 77ff). Interesting references to related pottery shapes from earlier phases are illustrated from Trench 2, the 'Parthian workshop' situated southwest of IMP in Area 5, which was identified as an iron workshop after the discovery of a furnace and the large amount of iron slag and crucible fragments found in this trench (Usmanova 1963b, 172). Excavations in Erk Kala produced very little Early and Middle Sasanian material.

POTTERY TYPES FROM THE EARLY SASANIAN PERIOD

Handled bowl

Shape code

R13, miniature version: R189.

Semi-complete reference

Gyaur Kala, Area 5, context no 863, pottery find no 34579 (Plate 6 between pp 26 and 27).

Diameter

Rim 30–40 cm; base 8–10 cm, miniature version: rim 13 cm.

Fabric

A, G1.

Russian terminology

Often the general term *tagora* or *tagara* occurs in the literature, which simply means large dish or bowl (Sedov 1987, 54). In the YuTAKE reports on Merv the expression 'plate' or 'deep plate' is used.

Description

Double-handled bowl with everted rim (Figure 6.2). Rim part usually decorated with incised single wavy lines, combed wavy patterns, rows of impressions or a combination of several of these elements. Flat serpentine or wavy handles are generally attached to either side of the rim. One of the fragments showed some crenellation along the rim. The bowl stands on a low ringbase. Three fragments of a small 'miniature' version occurred in Area 5 (Herrmann *et al* 1998, 61, fig 3.1).

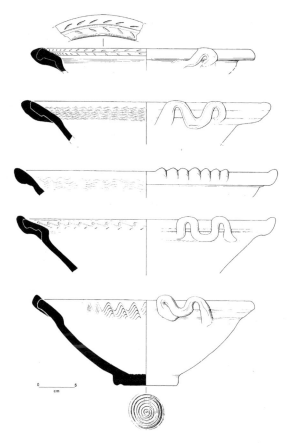

Figure 6.2: Fragments of handled bowls from MGK5.

Statistical grouping

In the statistical analysis the handled bowl appeared initially in a group with the trefoil-mouthed jug, but was subsequently presented as a separate group in stark contrast to the other Sasanian forms. This distinction seems coherent in configurations B – where the trefoil-mouthed jug and handled bowl were plotted closer to the residual shapes – and C, and suggests a chronological variation between the Sasanian groups. We therefore assume an earlier Sasanian date for the handled bowl, which is also supported by evidence produced from Kushano-Sasanian sites in northern Bactria (Uzbekistan).

Previous occurrences at Merv

Handled bowls are well documented at Merv and are usually referred to as 'plates with broad decorated rims'. Rutkovskaya classifies them as an innovation of the 2nd- to 3rd-century ceramic repertoire (Rutkovskaya 1962, 85). Fragments of this vessel type were found in the YuTAKE trenches 6 (Filanovich 1974, 62, fig 13; Katsuris-Buryakov 1963, 144),

8 (Filanovich 1974, 98, fig 26) and 13 in Gyaur Kala (Filanovich 1974, 84, fig 23) and in Trench 3 (Usmanova 1963a, 83, fig. 42) and Sounding no 5 in Erk Kala (Usmanova 1969, 26, fig. 8). The cultural layers with which they are associated are mostly dated to the Late Parthian or Partho–Sasanian transitional period, based on numismatic evidence and comparable ceramic material (cf Katsuris and Buryakov 1963, 152; Usmanova 1963, 83). In Trench 8 the handled bowls are dated to the 3rd to 4th centuries following analogies with other trenches at Merv and coin issues of Shapur II (309–379) (Filanovich 1974, 96–98, fig. 26). From the available evidence it is difficult to determine the starting date for this shape. In some reports it is described as an innovation of the end of the Parthian period, for which it appears to be diagnostic (cf Filanovich 1974, 61, 85). The bowls often occur in association with the juglets and handled jars described below, which were obviously perceived as part of the same repertoire (cf Filanovich 1974, 85; Katsuris and Buryakov 1963, 144, fig. 16). In view of the noticeable statistical differentiation between these shapes, however, their relationship does not appear that simple and requires further consideration (cf *Statistical grouping*, above). To judge from the material of the latest excavations, the bowls may belong to the third and fourth centuries.

Analogies from other areas

Parallels are published from sites along the Amu-darya and its tributaries, an area known as northern Bactria in Late Antique and Early medieval times, which comprised territories of the former Soviet Union, Southern Uzbekistan and Tadzhikistan, and the northern parts of Afghanistan. There is, however, variation in decorative techniques and patterns. Some bowls have incisions similar to that found at Merv, others are burnished or stamped. Stamped decoration appears to be characteristic for northern Bactria. Most bowls have vertical twisted handles. Other attachments to the bowl are usually crenellated, which might explain the crenellation on one of the specimens from Merv (Figure 6.2). The bowls are generally dated to the Late Kushan and Kushano-Sasanian periods (Lyonnet 1997, 196; Pidaev 1978, 96).

Southern Uzbekistan: Akkurgan, decoration incised, burnished and stamped (Pidaev 1978, 65f, 133, pl XI), Central Amu-Darya (Koshelenko 1985, 393, pl CV), Shodmon-Kala (Sedov 1987, pl XXVII, no 13), Kej-kobad-shakh, in the lower Kafirnigan valley (Sedov 1987, pl XXXIII, no 25), Dalverzin-Tepe, stamped decoration (Pugachenkova 1979, 80, fig 90).

Tadzhikistan: Yavanskoe gorodishche (Garavkala), decoration stamped, handles incised (Zeimal 1985, 141, no 382).

Northern Afghanistan: Ai Khanum, Archi, decoration incised (Lyonnet 1997, 239, 399, fig 60, nos 12, 13 – type O1 – 1/2).

Some scholars regard the handled bowls of Sasanian times as an advanced stage in a continuous development of this type from the Kushan period onward (Pidaev 1978, 96). Although related forms occurred earlier in the pottery assemblages, this particular bowl shape, with vertical handles or crenelated attachments, has recently been associated with Romano-Parthian influence growing stronger in northern Bactria at the beginning of the Kushano-Sasanian period (Lyonnet 1997, 196). A design identical to the bowls from Merv is shown on a fragment with handle attachment from Nineveh in the British Museum (BM: ANE Smith 2308), which represents the only documented specimen of this form within the western Sasanian empire so far. Details of its stratigraphical context are, however, unknown, so that any further interpretation has to remain open. No further analogies are published and despite the relative paucity of archaeological research in the central provinces of the empire (cf Chapter 1), it seems obvious that handled bowls never reached the same level of popularity in the west as in the northeastern border areas.

Although Roman and Western Parthian influence is not excluded, the presence of the single basic form elements, specifically kraters with identical handle attachments (cf Gardin 1973, fig 18; Litvinskii and Sedov 1983, 66–68, 210, pl V, nos 17 and 22, 223, pl XVIII, no 20; Lyonnet 1997, 424, pl IV.1b), in Central Asia from the Hellenistic period onward points to a strong local tradition of the handled bowl.

Trefoil-mouthed jug

Shape code

Ref4, Rref4.

Semi-complete reference

MGK5, context no 582, pottery find no 19204 (Plate 7).

Diameter

Rim 4–7cm.

Fabric

A, B3, G1, G2.

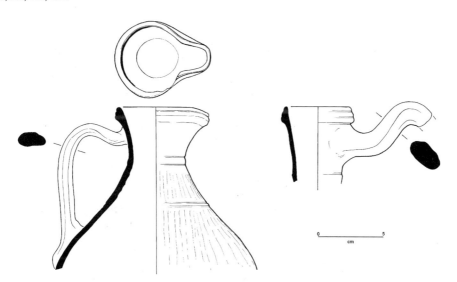

Figure 6.3: Trefoil-mouthed jugs from MGK5.

Russian terminology

Generally the term *kuvshin s einokhoevidnym ust'em* – 'jug with oinochoe-shaped opening' – is used (Filanovich 1974, 51).

Description

Trefoil-mouthed jug, rim divided by two grooves on the outside (Figure 6.3). Handle reaching from below the rim to the shoulder. A horizontal rib marks the middle height of the neck. The semi-complete specimen was red slipped and burnished vertically with two lines incised around the shoulder.

Statistical grouping

RRef4 was initially joined to one group with R13, the handled bowl (configuration B, context-by-form marginal table, membership list). The group was subsequently split during the computer reduction for configuration C, but still appears very close on the correspondence analysis plot (Figure 4.9). Both forms were distanced from the more contemporary material, which points to an earlier Sasanian date similar to that of the handled bowl.

Previous occurrences at Merv

Trefoil-mouthed jugs were found in several places at Merv, although they do not appear to be a dominant shape. Fragments of this type occurred in Sounding 2, Trench 2 and Trench 8, where they are associated with Parthian or Sasanian levels (Filanovich 1974, 51, YuTAKE Archive 1956; Filanovich 1974, 98, fig 26). Rutkovskaya divided oinochoe-shaped jugs into two groups: vessels of medium size decorated with a rib around the neck (Rutkovskaya 1962, 78, group no 5) and smaller specimens, which are usually plain (Rutkovskaya 1962, 77, fig 11, no 1, 80, group no 7). She assigned this shape generally to the 2nd and 3rd centuries (Rutkovskaya 1962, 67–99). As in MGK5, only neck and rim parts of the medium-sized trefoil-mouthed jugs were found in YuTAKE excavations, pointing to the fragile nature of this shape (Rutkovskaya 1962, 78). The smaller, plain version is not documented for MGK5.

Analogies from other areas

Trefoil-mouthed jugs are generally derived from the Greek *oinochoe*, which was widespread in Hellenistic times (Venco Ricciardi 1970, 474). Their appearance in Central Asia occurs in the Seleucid period (Gardin 1973, 148, pl 119.h). Different local variations developed through time, and with changing popularity the shape survived for a long while in the ceramic repertoire. Although originally a ceramic shape, this vessel form gained increasing popularity in metal and was a well-known type of Sasanian silver ware. Over its long period of production in metal and clay, both media are believed to have influenced each other reciprocally (Simpson 1997, 79; Venco Ricciardi 1970, 474). The decorative rib around the neck of some of the vessels has generally been related to metal ware

(Marshak 1961, 191; Simpson 1997, 76, fig 3, 79). For the earlier Sasanian period trefoil-mouthed jugs are documented in various provinces of the empire and in Northern Bactria.

Mesopotamia: Tell Mahuz (Venco Ricciardi 1970, 473f, fig 90, 22, 23).

Fars: Qasr-i Abu Nasr (Whitcomb 1985, 118, 127, fig 46.h).

Gurgan: Tureng Tepe (Lecomte 1987, 107f., pl 48.4, 55.18, 56.9).

Northern Bactria: Uzbekistan: Kara-Tepe, Old Termez (Stavisskii 1964, 53, fig 35), Zar-Tepe (Koshelenko 1985, 399, no 13).

Tadzhikistan: Aktepe II (Zeimal 1985, 146, no 409).

Specimens from northern Bactria are usually burnished, either vertically (Aktepe II) or show burnished ornaments (Kara-Tepe). The decorative rib around the neck occurs first on jugs found within the Sasanian Empire in Iraq and Iran, although most examples from Mesopotamia are dated to the Later Sasanian period (Simpson 1997, 79; Venco Ricciardi 1984, 50f, 55, fig 2.7). At Merv, however, the rib appears to be a standard feature of jugs, which certainly belong to an earlier Sasanian phase. The red burnished specimen from MGK5 seems close to the northern Bactrian jugs in its surface treatment. None of the trefoil-mouthed jugs mentioned forms a parallel to the jug type from Merv. In its mouth shape and neck the jug from Mesopotamia, now in the British Museum (WAA 118373), provides the best analogy. This specimen, however, is much smaller than those from MGK5 and is attributed to a later phase (Simpson 1997, 79).

Bowl

Shape code

R183, sR183.

Semi-complete reference

Gyaur Kala, Area 5, context no 765, pottery find no 31227 and context no 911, pottery find no 34079 (Plate 8).

Diameter

Rim 13–21cm, base 4–5cm.

Fabric

B2, B3, G1, G2.

Russian terminology

A number of different expressions are used for this bowl shape including *chasha s peregibom* (Pidaev 1978, 64) or *chasha s perekhvatom* (Sedov 1987, 54) – 'bowl with intercep-

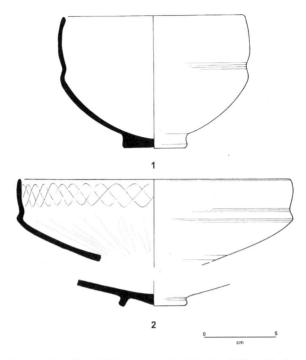

Figure 6.4: Bowl with waisted profile: (a) Plain version with high rim. (b) Burnished specimens.

tion'. Generally this type is regarded as part of the *kubkoobraznye chashi*, the goblet-shaped bowls (cf Pidaev 1978, 64).

Description

Bowl with waisted profile and simple rim. Two different versions are documented for Area 5: one appears generally smaller in diameter (13–16cm), shows a higher rim and a ringbase (Figure 6.4(a)). The other version is slightly larger (diameter 19–21cm) with a lower rim and a foot ring. Bowls of the second type are usually decorated on the inside (Figure 6.4(b)). A grid pattern of burnished lines is applied along the rim area, while the lower part displays an ornament of concentric spirals. This version was first identified in the 1998 season. Further research is needed to establish whether both variants are contemporary or reflect two consecutive stages in the development of this bowl shape.

Statistical grouping

In the statistical analysis R183 remained an independent group. Unfortunately, it is not well represented in the correspondence analyses of the marginal table 'context-form' in configurations C and D (Tables 4.39 and 4.55) and consequently an accurate chronological assessment on statistical grounds is not possible for this form. Its position between two more contemporary groups on the 'context-form' marginal table plots in configurations C and D (Figures 4.9 and 4.12) may point to a similar date range. No definite conclusions should be drawn at this stage, however. Due to the relatively early, Kushano-Sasanian, date of analogous shapes from northern Bactria, the bowl is included here among the earlier Sasanian forms.

Previous occurrences at Merv

Bowls of this type are not illustrated in any of the reports on previous YuTAKE excavations at Merv. Several trenches, however, produced a number of goblet-shaped bowls with related profiles (cf Usmanova 1963b, 186, fig 15). They seem to belong to an earlier level and are dated to the Parthian period (Usmanova 1963b, 190). A few fragments of this early type were found in Area 5 in 1999 (**Figure 6.5**). Although distinct from the waisted bowl of Sasanian times, this early shape may have influenced its development.

Analogies from other areas

Parallels are documented from Northern Bactria. The following is a list of representative analogies for each area:

Southern Uzbekistan: Airtam (Pugachenkova 1979, 74, fig 84), Akkurgan (cf Pidaev 1978, 64f, pl IX, 1–9, pl X, 1–13), Bezymyannoe (Sedov 1987, pl XXXII), Dalverzin-tepe (Pugachenkova 1978, 78, no 57), Darakhsha-tepe (Sedov 1987, pl XXXI, no 25), Shodmon-Kala (Sedov 1987, pl XXVII, nos 19, 21), Termez/Kara-Tepe (Staviskii 1964, fig 31A; 1982, 44, fig 15), Zar-Tepe (Koshelenko 1985, 399, pl CXI, nos 2, 3, 8).

Tadzhikistan: Aktepe II (Zeimal 1985, 146, no 410).

Afghanistan: Kunduz (Lyonnet 1997, 405, fig 66.3, type o3–2/2).

Most of these sites produced both versions of this shape with slight variations in the burnished decoration. Some of the vessels from Kara-Tepe were found in a funerary context (Staviskii 1982, 42f). The ornamental use of the technique of burnishing, which is usually applied evenly as a surface treatment, seems particularly popular in Central Asia during the Kushan and Kushano-Sasanian period. In Khoresm and northern Bactria the same range of burnished patterns also appears on other vessel types, such as jugs and jars from Toprak-Kala and Kara Tepe (cf Nerazik and Rapoport 1981, 75, fig 39, no 43; 78, fig 40, nos 9–10, 28; fig 43, nos 3, 43; Staviskii 1964, fig 35; 1982, 178, fig 14.a).

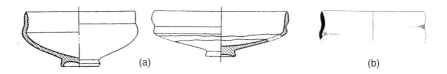

(a)   (b)

Figure 6.5: Related bowl shapes from earlier levels at Merv: (a) Specimens excavated in Gyaur Kala, Trench 2 (cf Usmanova 1963b, fig 20). (b) Fragment found in Area 5, context 1057.*

---

* Scales are omitted from the illustrations of comparative material, since published standards vary too much to be presented in consistent form.

Sedov, who studied changes in the ceramic material of Kobadian in northern Bactria from the Kushan to the Early medieval period, identified the bowls with waisted profile as the main innovation in the category of tablewares characteristic for the Post Kushan/ Kushano-Sasanian period (Sedov 1987, 55). He argues that the large scale of alterations in the ceramic repertoire cannot be accounted for purely by the development of local fashions (Sedov 1987, 56).

Lyonnet assumes a strong influence from Romano-Parthian pottery communicated through the deportation of prisoners from the eastern Roman *limes* area, following the Sasanian campaigns in the 3rd and 4th centuries (cf Lyonnet 1997, 239f). In other areas of the Sasanian Empire, however, this type is not documented (cf Boucharlat 1987, 205–209; Keall and Keall 1981, figs 19–20; Lecomte 1987, pl 46, 49–51 Trinkaus 1986, 53–75; Wenke 1975, figs 7–13). The bowl with waisted profile was also absent from Early Sasanian levels at Choche (personal communication Venco Ricciardi) and no earlier versions, such as those from the Parthian levels of Trench 2, Gyaur Kala, are attested from contemporary sites in Iran (cf Haerinck 1983). Ornamental burnish in the shape of a grid pattern, by contrast, is also shown on a jar from Gilan, northern Iran, dated to the Sasanian period (Iran Bastan Museum, inv no 19141).

Thus the bowl shape and its decorative pattern may represent independent traditions, which at times covered distinct geographical areas.

POTTERY TYPES FROM THE MIDDLE SASANIAN PERIOD

Double-handled jar (amphora)

Shape code

R30, sR30, R199.

Semi-complete reference

Several diagnostic parts of the vessel could be reconstructed from fragments to provide a complete profile (Figure 6.7, Plate 9). Rim to neck–shoulder junction – context no 917, pottery find no 34747; neck–shoulder junction and upper part of body – context no 560, pottery find no 18749 (Figure 6.6, Plate 9).

Diameter

Rim – 10–14cm, maximum diameter – 35–36cm, base – 10–14cm.

Fabric

A, B2, B3, G1, G2.

Russian terminology

Complete specimens of this shape are called *amphora* (Katsuris and Buryakov 1963, 144) or *amphoro-vidnyi sosud*, 'amphora-shaped vessel' (Filanovich 1974, 61).

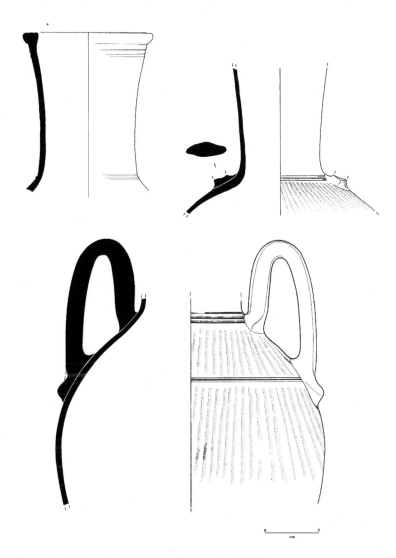

Figure 6.6: Reconstructable parts of double-handled jars from MGK5.

Description

Double-handled jar of ovoid shape with thickened rim (Figures 6.6 and 6.7). Two lines are incised below the rim. The neck–shoulder junction is marked by a rib, which often shows oblong impressions, as if produced by fingernails. The handles are the most diagnostic feature of this vessel type and reach from the neck–shoulder junction to the shoulder in a high loop. Lower handle attachments often bear the impression of a finger in order to secure the handle more effectively to the vessel wall.

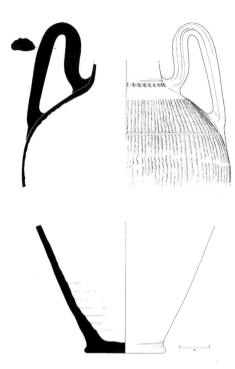

Figure 6.7: Drawn reconstruction of the body profile.

Characteristically, the upper part of the body to just below the maximum diameter is fluted. In addition, most of the vessels have one or two lines incised around the shoulder, at the height of the handle attachments. The base is flat or slightly concave with a thickened outside edge.

Statistical grouping

Group R30 constitutes one of the main groups of the more contemporary material from MGK5. It is contrasted with R13, the handled bowl, and Ref4, the trefoil-mouthed jug, on the one hand (configuration C, context-by-form marginal table, Figure 4.9), and R25, the juglet (see below) on the other (configuration D, context-by-form marginal table, Figure 4.12). A date of around the fourth to early fifth centuries is therefore suggested for this shape.

Previous occurrences at Merv

Although a number of double-handled jars have been found at Merv, this particular form is only documented for Gyaur Kala Trench 6 and probably Sounding 2 (Katsuris and Buryakov 1963, 144f, fig 16, 34; cf also Appendix 3, Figure A3.10). While Trench 6 produced a complete specimen of this type, only the rim and probably related base fragments have been found in Sounding 2 (Gertsman 1953, Appendix 3, Figure A3.1). Rutkovskaya in her ceramic study only refers to the striking handle shape, most probably using material from Trench 6 for illustrations (Rutkovskaya 1962, 77, fig 11, nos 18–19). A similar handle is reported from Trench 3 in Gyaur Kala (Dresvyanskaya 1974, 163, fig 8). The drawing, however, appears at a wrong angle and an unambiguous identification of the vessel type may thus not be possible.

In the archaeological literature amphora-shaped jars are commonly described as a new vessel type characteristic of the Partho–Sasanian transitional phase (cf Filanovich 1974, 61; Katsuris and Buryakov 1963, 144). Apart from the body profile and proportions, which distinguish them from the two-handled, almost biconical jars of the earlier Parthian period (cf Koshelenko 1985, 384, pl XCVI), the fluting of the vessel shoulder also appears to be a new technique of surface treatment not documented for pottery shapes of preceding periods (cf Usmanova 1963b). Related vessel shapes of similar chronological attribution are known from other areas at Merv. In Trench 8, situated near the southern gate of Gyaur Kala, the complete profile of a handled jar was retrieved (Filanovich 1974, 98, fig 26; cf Figure 6.8). It appears to have only one handle reaching from below the rim to the shoulder, but the vessel form, surface treatment and rim shape resemble the amphora from Trench 6. The date of this vessel is difficult to assess, although several analogous rim fragments have been found in Area 5 (cf Herrmann *et al* 1999, 12, fig 5, no 1). Specimens of this type of jar are not very well documented in the YuTAKE reports. Their fragmentary state and irregular occurrence in the recent excavations of MGK5 suggest a slightly earlier date.

A unique vessel of amphora-shaped appearance was excavated in Erk Kala, Trench 3 (Usmanova 1963a, fig 40; Figure 6.8(c)). The body shape, however, reflects a different form with strap handles reaching from the neck–shoulder junction via the rim in a high loop to the vessel body at the point of its maximum diameter. Rim and base shapes are different from the jars discussed above and the fluted surface treatment of the shoulder is missing. No details are given about the archaeological context of this jar, for which a general date of the 2nd to 4th centuries is suggested (cf Usmanova 1963, 81, fig 40). Since no analogies have

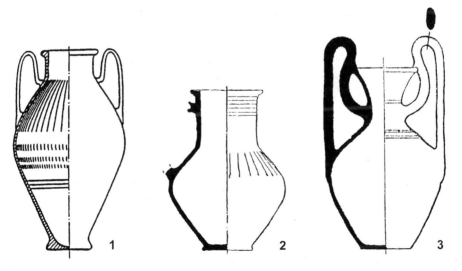

Figure 6.8: Handled jars found previously at Merv: (a) Jar from Trench 6 (Katsuris and Buryakov 1963, fig 16). (b) Jar from Trench 8 (Filanovich 1974, fig 26). (c) Jar from Erk Kala, Trench 3 (Usmanova 1963a, fig 40).

been found at Merv so far, it is difficult to put this vessel type in chronological relation to the double-handled jars from Trench 6 and MGK5.

Analogies from other areas

No parallels are found in neighbouring areas. Double-handled jars from northern Bactrian sites are quite different in character (cf Pidaev 1978, 134, pl XII, no 19) and no comparable material is published from northeastern Iran (cf Haerinck 1983; Lecomte 1987).

Some Parthian green-glazed wares found in western provinces near the Roman frontier show formal similarities with the jars from Merv (cf Toll 1946, 70ff., pls LI, LII). Apart from the vessel structure, the surface is fluted. The fluting is mostly applied to the shoulder area (Toll 1943, 9, 11), but sometimes covers the entire body (Ettinghausen 1938, pl 182; Simpson 1997, 77, fig 4). In contrast to the jars from Gyaur Kala, the handles of the green-glazed vases always start from the neck. Despite the geographical distance between the two areas, interactions cannot be excluded, particularly since some green-glazed Parthian vases or amphorae were apparently involved in long-distance trade (Haerinck 1999, 12). In context with the Merv jars, however, it needs to be stressed again that no imported vessels have been found.

Jar with perforated neck

Shape code

R42, sR42.

Semi-complete reference

Large parts of the upper body were found in Area 5, context no 850, pottery find no 33932, and context no 859, pottery find no 35966 (Figure 6.9, Plate 10).

Diameter

Rim 11–16cm.

Fabric

A, G1.

Russian terminology

This shape is not discussed individually in the Russian literature.

Description

Jar with short neck and bevelled, externally grooved rim (Figure 6.9). The vessel shoulder is usually fluted, and richly decorated with rows of impressions and bands of horizontal

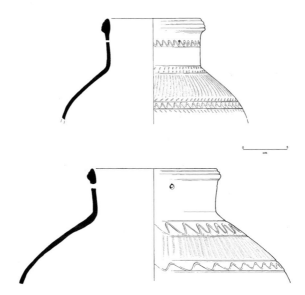

Figure 6.9: Jars with perforated neck from MGK5.

and wavy incised lines cutting across the fluting. How much of the body is generally covered by this surface treatment remains unknown at present. Occasionally incised decoration is also found on the neck. A characteristic of this vessel type appears to be the symmetrical perforation of the neck, which usually shows four holes below the rim. The holes were made prior to firing.

Statistical grouping

R42 was manually combined with R38 and R39 in one unit, which was initially included in the more contemporary group R30. The jar shape was subsequently presented as an independent group and differentiated from the amphora-shaped jar and the juglet (configuration D, context-by-form marginal table, Figure 4.12). The group was also contrasted with residual material (configurations C and D, context-by-form marginal tables, Figures 4.9 and 4.12). Considering all evidence, a fourth-century date close to the amphora-shaped jar seems plausible.

Previous occurrences at Merv

This shape is not discussed or shown in any of the YuTAKE reports. As pottery illustrations for the respective reports appear to be selective, subject to the authors' discretion, it is difficult to decide whether a particular shape was not regarded as representative for the purpose of discussion or whether it had not occurred in any of the excavations. Jars with a short neck and some kind of vertically scratched decoration are attested for Trench 6 (Katsuris and Buryakov 1963, 143, fig 14, nos 1 and 9, 145, fig 16, no 4). These vessels, however, are dated to the Late Sasanian period and appear to be different in the rim shape and neck, which is not perforated.

Parallels from other areas

Parallels to this type of jar are not illustrated from any of the areas included in this study. Vessels with perforated necks are rarely discussed in the archaeological literature in general, either, because their distribution is actually very sparse, or they are regarded as vessels of very specific function not representative of pottery assemblages. For the Sasanian period perforated jars are attested in the area of the central Amu-Darya, the area around the district of Chardzhou, northern Turkmenistan (Koshelenko 1985, 392–393, pls CIV, CV) and the Atrek Valley (Venco Ricciardi 1980, 70, fig L). None of the cited examples, however, shows close morphological similarities with the jars from Area 5. The jar from the Atrek Valley, which is dated to Late Sasanian times, resembles a shape documented at Merv, in Gyaur Kala Trench 2 and Trench 13, for the Parthian period (Filanovich 1974, 83, fig 22; Usmanova 1963, 195, fig 24, no 1). It is interesting to note that the perforations on the specimens found in Area 5 generally do not show any traces of wear and the exact function of the holes is not yet clear. Both vessels from Area 5 display an interesting pattern of decoration that appears to be a standard feature for this type of jar. The combination of fluting and incisions seems almost contradictory, since the incised or impressed patterns destroy the visual effect of the fluted surface. With regard to its surface treatment this vessel type is closely related to the double-handled jar discussed above. A similar concept of decoration is found again with the green-glazed vases from the western provinces of the Parthian Empire, although the single parts of the decoration, radiating and zigzag lines, are never applied across each other (Toll 1943, 9). Recent studies in pottery technology demonstrated a correlation between surface treatment and vessel function (Rice 1987, 232; Schiffer 1988, 27). While burnishing reduces the permeability of the surface, texturing has the opposite effect and improves the qualities of a vessel as a container for liquids, keeping the content cool by enhancing surface permeability. A functional aspect might also be considered for the rich decoration and surface treatment of some of the Merv jars, although further research is required to evaluate possible correlations. Considering their parallels with glazed pottery, the fluting of the vessels at Merv appears to have a primarily decorative character.

Juglet

Shape code

R25, Ref2, R25l (for a slightly larger version).

Semi-complete reference

Gyaur Kala, Area 5, context 774, pottery find nos 31832, 31833 (Plate 11).

Diameter

Rim 6–9cm, maximum diameter 10–14cm, base 3.5–5cm.

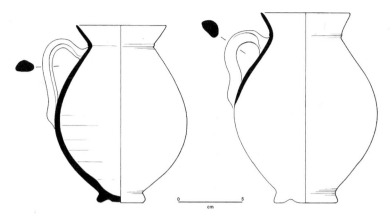

Figure 6.10: Juglets from MGK5.

Fabric

A, B2, B3, B4, G1, G2.

Russian terminology

The juglets are commonly described as *melkie kuvshiny* (Katsuris and Buryakov 1963, 143) or *malen'kie razdutye kubshiny* (Filanovich 1974, 85), 'small jugs' or 'small inflated jugs'. This expression, however, often includes a number of different jug shapes and is applied to small jugs in general, since the juglet discussed here was not perceived as a single vessel type.

Description

Juglet with everted rim and ringbase; neck–shoulder junction marked by a horizontal rib (Figure 6.10). Handle reaching from upper shoulder to middle height of the vessel. The surface is evenly burnished, vertically on the upper part and horizontally on the lower part of the body, producing a fine appearance. This shape is the best preserved pottery shape at Merv with altogether 14 semi-complete specimens.

Statistical grouping

In the statistical analysis the juglet remained a separate group. The group ~R25 was not very well captured by the early plots (configurations B and C, Tables 4.27 and 4.39), but appeared to be in contrast to group ~R30, the amphora-shaped jar, in the final configuration (configuration D, marginal table context-by-form, Figure 4.12). As this vessel type is generally the most complete from MGK5, it is regarded as probably contemporary with some of the occupational phases of structure C.

Previous occurrences at Merv

The juglet is well documented from YuTAKE excavations where, together with a variety of small jugs, it was regarded as a diagnostic shape for the Late Parthian and Early Sasanian periods. Juglets analogous to the ones illustrated here were found in Gyaur Kala Trench 6 (Katsuris and Buryakov 1963, 143f, fig 14, no 13, 145, fig 16, no 54), in Trench 13 (Filanovich 1974, 85) and in Trench 1 of the necropolis near Bayram-Ali (drawings arranged by Dresvyanskaya, YuTAKE 1965, Appendix 3, Figure A3.31). In the YuTAKE publications the juglet is often found associated with handled bowls and is clearly understood as part of the same ceramic repertoire. Both shapes are, however, differentiated in the computer analysis (configuration C, marginal table context-by-form, Figure 4.9).

Parallels from other areas

Direct parallels from other areas are not published. Small, burnished jugs with slightly everted rims appear to be popular in northern Bactria during the Kushano-Sasanian period (Staviskii 1982, pl 15), although similarities between these juglets and the ones from Merv are only vague and the specimens from Kara- and Zar-Tepe represent generally more closed forms. One specimen from Kara-Tepe with two handles and an incised line around the neck-shoulder junction shows a better analogy to the Merv juglets (Staviskii 1964, fig 33).

With regard to their basic vessel type, however, they seem more related to the mugs found at Ak-tepe, which occasionally have a rib around the neck–shoulder junction (Sedov 1987, pl XXII, nos 8, 13, 19). At Ak-tepe this shape is associated with the Kushano-Sasanian period and represents one of the new introductions attributed to this phase (Sedov 1987, 55). In this context the expression 'juglet' might be misleading, since the everted rim and small size make this vessel equally suitable for drinking.

Jug

Shape code

Ref1.

Semi-complete reference

MGK5, context no 560, pottery find no 18759 and context no 842, pottery find no 37112 (Figure 6.11, Plate 12).

Diameter

Maximum diameter 14cm.

Fabric

G1, G2.

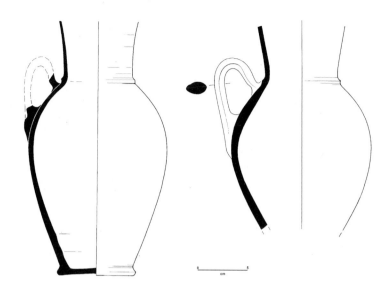

Figure 6.11: Jugs from MGK5.

Russian terminology

Not specifically mentioned in the literature.

Description

Jug of oval body shape with long, wide neck (Figure 6.11). Rim not preserved with the specimens found so far. Base flat or slightly concave with a thickened outside edge. A decorative rib marks the neck–shoulder junction. The body is usually plain but rarely shows a band of chattered lines around the lower part of the body.

Statistical grouping

Without any associated rim shape, this form is so far unquantifiable and could not be analysed statistically. We include it here due to the stylistic closeness to the previous shape. The semi-complete specimens provide additional evidence for a Sasanian date.

Previous occurrences at Merv

Parallels have not been discussed or illustrated in the reports of the YuTAKE excavations, although this implies that the shape was not perceived as an individual vessel type, rather than its absence from the archaeological record so far. Similar jugs are only documented from Trench 6 (Filanovich 1974, 62, fig 13; cf Appendix 3, Figure A3.16). Overall vessel shape and proportion appear close, except for the rib around the neck–shoulder junction, which is missing from these Trench 6 specimens (Filanovich 1974, 62, fig 13).

Parallels from other areas

Analogies from other areas are not known. As mentioned above, the jug appears to be close to its smaller counterpart, the juglet (see above), and may be regarded as representative of local ceramic production. Similar stylistic patterns are found on different, yet related vessel types. The plain body structure interrupted only by the rib around the neck–shoulder junction seems characteristic for one stylistic line within the ceramic repertoire of the Middle Sasanian phase. From this perspective, immediate analogies might not be expected.

Recent excavations at the southwestern section of the city walls of Gyaur Kala (IMP MGK6, cf Herrmann *et al* 1999, 15f) have produced another semi-complete specimen of this type, illustrating its established place within the utilitarian ceramic repertoire.

A QUESTION OF STYLE

Despite the reflection of various traditions and likely earlier (ie Parthian) sources of inspiration for some of the vessel types, they are all regarded here as manifestations of the pottery design and production of the first part of Sasanian rule at Merv. Although several of the vessels share specific features, each group appears to be heterogeneous and a number of subdivisions can be made. Most interesting in this respect are patterns of surface treatment and decoration. Two different techniques of surface treatment can be distinguished – burnishing and fluting. The even vertical and partly horizontal burnish is found on the trefoil-mouthed jug, the juglets and one of their related forms. It may have been applied simply to refine the surface appearance for aesthetic reasons, but it is equally possible that a functional purpose was involved, such as to stop liquids from penetrating through the surface quickly (cf Rice 1987, 232). Apart from the single rib marking the neck–shoulder junction of these vessels, they are undecorated. Fluting was used for the jars and double-handled jars. Here again a functional use of this technique may also be possible. Besides the fluting, both jar shapes show incised and impressed decorations, the jars with perforated neck usually richer with bands of incised or impressed patterns around the neck and shoulder. The two bowl shapes finally show distinct patterns of decoration, which appear to have served purely as embellishment. Handled bowls are incised or impressed, while the waisted bowls display an ornamental burnished decoration.

The vessel forms as such and most of the rim shapes do not show any immediate correlation, although the externally grooved rim found with the trefoil-mouthed jugs and the perforated jars seems to have a wider range of application (cf Appendix 2 and 3). A large proportion of the pottery types has close analogies to roughly contemporary material from northern Bactria, a stylistic link that seems to weaken in the Middle Sasanian phase. While the juglets show rather general similarities, some of the waisted bowls are effectively identical in shape, diameter and decoration. The handled bowl provides an illustrative example for local particularities, since techniques of decoration vary between both areas, while the vessel form is the same. Surprisingly, the ornamental use of burnishing was obviously common to both Merv and northern Bactria, whereas the stamped decoration remained limited to the latter. The trefoil-mouthed jug illustrates a certain amount of flexibility in the correlation between form and surface treatment, with one red burnished example which again has close analogies in Bactria. Most specimens of this shape, however, appear to be of light colour and plain.

The analogies visible in the ceramic material from Merv and northern Bactria may reflect a period of close relations between both areas following the Sasanian conquest of Bactria in the 3rd century and the installation of a Kushano-Sasanian king (Frye 1962, 203, 209). One of the coin issues minted at Merv during the reign of Shapur II has been related to this dynasty (Loginov and Nikitin 1993b, 249). This common political and administrative ground in itself was probably not the reason, but certainly provided the basis for an intense and fruitful cultural exchange between both territories: it is also documented in the spread of Buddhism from northern Bactria to Merv, where two sanctuaries were found by YuTAKE excavations (Pugachenkova and Usmanova 1995). We may assume that inspirations were generally reciprocal and certainly not confined to these two areas only. Innovations soon became subject to adaptation according to the demands of the local market, as is shown by the trefoil-mouthed jugs, where only the decoration was taken from Bactrian models.

At this stage of archaeological research it seems impossible to trace exactly the origins of every vessel type and shape. The introduction of a whole range of new shapes and decorative techniques is certainly more than a straight development of earlier ceramic forms; however, the mechanisms of change within the ceramic production may be more complex and heterogeneous than was first anticipated (cf Rice 1987, 464ff). We have seen certain parallels between material from Merv and the western part of the empire in Parthian and, possibly, Sasanian times (see double-handled jar and jar with perforated neck, above). The immediacy of the supposed contact underlying these parallels, however, is questionable and cannot be established, particularly since the pottery at Merv represents utilitarian plain wares produced locally.

What seems to be a unifying feature of the shapes presented here as Early and Middle Sasanian is that most of them, or at least their structural elements, are ultimately derived from Hellenistic pottery shapes (*oinochoe, krater, amphora*), which continued to be developed through the Parthian or Kushan period (Figure 6.12). In an indirect way this common retrospective orientation in the ceramic design produces the distinct stylistic expression which characterises the earlier phase of Sasanian pottery from Merv.

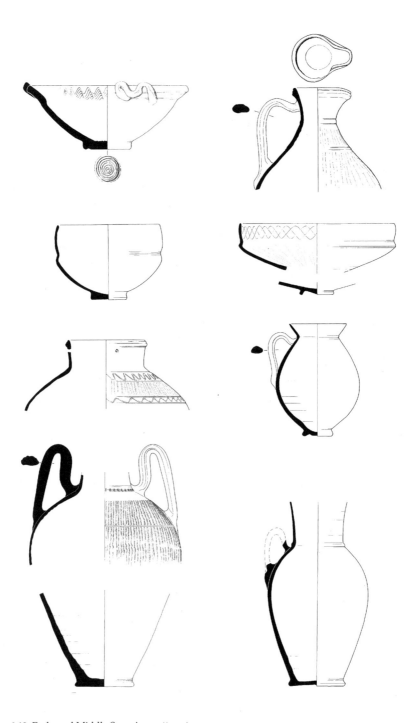

Figure 6.12: Early and Middle Sasanian pottery types.

— 7 —

POTTERY FROM LATE SASANIAN TIMES

PROBLEMS AND METHODOLOGY

As demonstrated by the complications experienced during the statistical analysis, the ceramic evidence of this period is much more difficult to understand, mainly due to the high degree of fragmentation throughout the assemblages. One of the two shape groups that emerged from the analysis was identified as 'more contemporary' on grounds of comparisons with the relative ceramic sequence evident from former YuTAKE excavations (Chapter 4). This group, however, is basically reduced to one vessel type. While this type provides a useful point of orientation, it is simply insufficient for a characterisation of the pottery production as a whole. As a result we have to consider additional evidence to gain a broader spectrum of the Late Sasanian pottery repertoire. The vessel types introduced in the following pages were chosen according to formal similarities with the statistically determined 'core' group and the stratigraphic distribution of these shapes as reflected in the YuTAKE reports. Single types are well defined through their archaeological context, both in the IMP and Soviet excavations in Gyaur Kala. Two discrete structures of public character are particularly suitable, since they show only a minor proportion of residual material of usually much earlier periods, which facilitates a clear differentiation. These structures are Trench 3, the 'Oval building', which was interpreted erroneously as a Christian monastery (Dresvyanskaya 1974) and Trench 9, the Buddhist stupa and Sangarama (Pugachenkova and Usmanova 1995). Material from kilns excavated near the southern gate of Gyaur Kala again provides an outlook into the Early Islamic period, which shows pottery shapes still reminiscent of Sasanian times (Zaurova 1962). Some kilns are dated by early Arab or Abbasid coins respectively that were partly incorporated into the brickwork (Zaurova 1962, 189).

Yet another problem arising from the high fragmentation of the Erk Kala material is the lack of semi-complete profiles to illustrate the vessel form. This applies in particular to the 'more contemporary' group, for which only rim sherds were found. Few related shapes are documented by rim fragments including neck–shoulder junctions, which roughly indicate the form of the vessel body. For most of the following vessel types illustrations are therefore confined to drawings. Attempts to reconstruct vessel profiles from better preserved pottery shapes with similar attributes remain tentative. Semi-complete specimens from former Soviet excavations are used as a reference where possible.

POTTERY TYPES FROM THE LATE SASANIAN PERIOD

Bowl

Shape code

R83, sR83.

Semi-complete reference

No semi-complete specimen has been found so far.

Diameter

Rim 14–24cm.

Fabric

A, G2.

Russian terminology

This shape has not been discussed within the Russian literature.

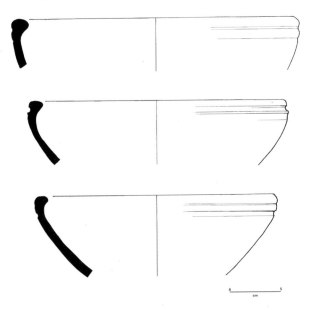

Figure 7.1: Rim fragments of bowls from MEK1.

Description

Bowl with inturned thickened rim, externally grooved (Figure 7.1). Apart from the rim profile this shape appears to be plain. The base shape is yet unidentified. Depending on the angle of the rim and wall profile, some specimens may also belong to a large type of jar, similar in form and structure to the jar shape codes R115 and R116, below (cf Figure 7.2).

Statistical grouping

R83 was eliminated during the simultaneous reduction of dimensions in the computer analysis and does not occur in the context-by-form marginal table of configuration A. The close analogy of the rim profile with R116, the 'more contemporary' group, however, justifies an attribution to Late Sasanian times.

Previous occurrences

This shape is rarely illustrated in the YuTAKE reports. Occurrences are only documented for Gyaur Kala Trench 9, the Buddhist sanctuary (Pugachenkova and Usmanova 1995, fig 12, nos 9–10) and Trench 17, point 3 (unpublished drawings, YuTAKE Archive: Galochkina 1963, Appendix 3, Figure 27). Although not illustrated in Dresvyanskaya's report (cf Dresvyanskaya 1974), fragments of this shape have also been collected during surface reconnaissance in 1997 in Trench 3, the 'Oval building' (IMP Archive), suggesting that the shape may have been more popular than indicated by the YUTAKE publications.

Analogies from different areas

Analogous shapes are rare. One of the bowl shapes illustrated for Tell Abu Sarifa is very close in its rim shape, although the rib underneath the rim is decorated (Adams 1970, fig 6, bz). The shape is regarded as Sasanian (Adams 1970, fig 6). Vague similarities in the rim shape are noticeable on some of the bowl shapes from Jibal (Keall and Keall 1981, fig 19, nos 1 and 31).

Jar

Shape code

R115, sR115, R116, sR116.

Semi-complete reference

No semi-complete specimen or reconstructable profile has been found.

Diameter

Rim 6–16cm.

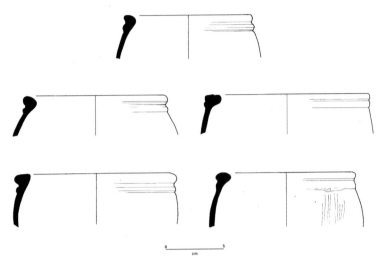

Figure 7.2: Rim fragments of the jar with convex neck from MEK1.

Fabrics

A, B2, G1, G2.

Russian terminology

This form is labelled *gorshok*, 'jar', in the literature (Rutkovskaya 1962, 106, under group 3).

Description

Hole-mouth jar with inturned, thickened rim (Figure 7.2). The rim appears to be divided externally by a groove, or a rib is applied below the rim, as is more appropriate in some cases. None of the fragments are preserved to an extent that would clarify the body profile of this shape. In Soviet publications it has been reconstructed as a simple jar without neck (Rutkovskaya 1962, 101, fig 13, no 5). With regard to the rim diameter, however, most of the vessels would be rather small and more likely to have survived in a more complete state. Fragments of similar hole-mouth jars recorded from Area 1 in Erk Kala and from the uppermost levels of Area 5 in Gyaur Kala showed handle attachments below the rim (cf Herrmann *et al* 1996, 6, fig 4, no 5), which indicates that the preserved part represents the rim and neck of the vessel. This is also supported by the pattern of breakage, mostly in the middle height of the neck or just above the neck–shoulder junction. In conclusion, we suggest that at least some fragments belong to a larger jar with convex neck as illustrated below (Figure 7.3; cf Filanovich 1974, 63, fig 17; cf also Dresvyanskaya 1974, 162, fig 7).

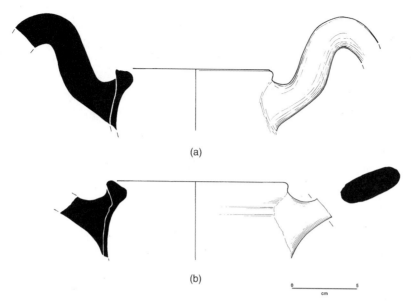

(a)

(b)

Figure 7.3: Hole-mouth shapes with handles attached below the rim: (a) MEK1; (b) MGK5.

Statistical grouping

Both shapes form the dominant part of the 'more contemporary' group ~R116 in configuration A (configuration A, marginal table context-by-form, Figure 4.4) and represent visibly the most popular of the Late Sasanian shapes. In some cases the rim profile is hardly distinguishable from R83, especially when sketched quickly without much detail in the rim orientation. Specimens that were only preserved up to 5 per cent often lack information on the rim diameter, so that a certain overlap between both shapes is likely, but would not have influenced the result of the analysis substantially.

Previous occurrences

The shape is well documented in the YuTAKE reports and occurred in Trench 3, the 'Oval building', in Gyaur Kala (Rutkovskaya 1962, 101, fig 13, no 5; cf Rutkovskaya 1962, 101, fig 13, no 5; cf. archive drawing, Rutkovskaya 1954, Appendix 3, Figure A3.9) and in Erk Kala, Trench 3 (Usmanova 1963a, 81, fig 40, nos 13, 83, fig 42, no 2) and Sounding 5 (Usmanova 1969, 29, fig 11). Since this type is generally poorly preserved, it seemed obviously undiagnostic at first and appears in different chronological contexts within the reports, ranging from Parthian (Usmanova 1963a, 81, fig 40) to Late Sasanian times (Rutkovskaya 1962, 99ff). Related shapes were obviously still in use in the post-Sasanian period, as is demonstrated by material found inside one of the kilns near the southern gate of Gyaur Kala (Zaurova 1962, 199, fig 18, no 2).

Analogies from other areas

No analogies of this vessel shape are published. Similar rim shapes, however, occur with hole-mouth jars from Qasr-i Abu Nasr, attributed to the Early Islamic period (Whitcomb 1985, 59, fig 20.c).

Jar with short neck

Shape code

R129, sR129, R130, sR130.

Semi-complete reference

No semi-complete specimen was found during the excavations in MEK1. The complete profile of this shape, however, is illustrated from Trench 3, the 'Oval building', in Gyaur Kala (Rutkovskaya 1962, 102, fig 14, no 7).

Diameter

Rim 5–13cm.

Fabric

A, B2, G1, G2.

Russian terminology

This jar is referred to as *kuvshin no vysokom poddone so sfericheskim tulovom*, 'jug on high stand with spherical body' (Rutkovskaya 1962, 103, group 3).

Description

Jar with short neck and inturned, thickened rim. The rim is usually grooved on the exterior, though the profile may vary to some extent. Neck and body profiles of the vessel form an uninterrupted, almost s-shaped curve without any demarcation of the neck–shoulder junction (Figure 7.4). The specimen found in Trench 3 suggests a globular body shape and a flat base in the shape of a high conical stand. Similar base shapes were found in MEK1 (Figure 7.5). They generally show a rib around the base–body junction, which is missing from the reference vessel, but is illustrated for base fragments found in the same levels in Trench 3 (cf Rutkovskaya 1962, 102, fig 14, no 16) and 6 (cf Katsuris and Buryakov 1963, 146, fig 17, nos 12 and 21). The rib around the base–body junction seems to be inspired by contemporary metal vessels (Harper 1993, 248f, catalogue nos 96, 97). In contrast to the previous shape R116, this jar type appears to have no handles.

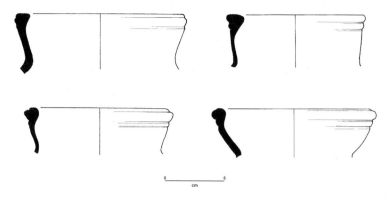

Figure 7.4: Jars with short neck from MEK1.

Figure 7.5: Semi-complete specimen found in YuTAKE, Trench 3, Gyaur Kala and related base shapes from MEK1.

Statistical grouping

The two shape codes R129 and R130, which essentially comprise two variations of the same vessel type, were manually grouped together, but subsequently dropped out of the analysis in the *srd* reduction. Rim shape and structure of this group, however, appear to be so close to the 'more contemporary' shapes R116 and R115 that they may be regarded as part of the Late Sasanian repertoire.

Previous occurrences

This particular jar type is recorded from Gyaur Kala Trench 3, the 'Oval building' (Rutkovskaya 1962, 102, fig 14, no 7), and Trench 6 (Katsuris and Buryakov 1963, 145, fig 16, no 8). While dated to Early Sasanian times in Trench 6 (Appendix 3, Figure A3.14), Rutkovskaya attributes the shape to the Late Sasanian period within the well-defined occupational levels of the single structure in Trench 3 (Rutkovskaya 1962, 100). In Erk Kala variations of this type were found in Trench 3 (Usmanova 1963, 84, fig 43, no 9) and Sounding 5 (Usmanova 1969, 29, fig 11), where they occurred together with the high conical base shapes mentioned above (Usmanov 1963, 81, fig 40, no 7; 1969, 29, fig 11). A divergence is again noticeable between the suggested dates of Early (Usmanova 1963, 84, fig 43) and Late Sasanian times (Usmanova 1969, 29, fig 11), which might be related to the high fragmentation of shapes and complex stratigraphy on the one hand, or to the general tendency to date structures early, to either the Parthian or the very Early Sasanian period on the other hand (cf Chapter 1).

Analogies from other areas

No parallels are published from other areas. One of the rim types illustrated in Keall and Keall shows general similarities, although this particular shape is depicted as a simplified type (Keall and Keall 1981, fig 29.4).

Jar with perforated neck

Shape code

R98, R98p (R98 perforated).

Semi-complete reference

A complete specimen of this vessel form was found during YuTAKE excavations in Erk Kala, Trench 2 (Plate 13 between pp 26 and 27). This reference vessel, however, appears to be slightly smaller than the fragments excavated in MEK1 with a rim diameter of 6cm and a height of 12.7cm.

Diameter

Rim 9–13cm.

Fabric

A.

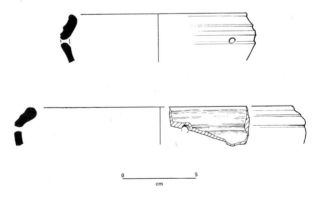

Figure 7.6: Jar rims from MEK1.

Russian terminology

This jar is not discussed as an individual vessel type.

Description

Hole-mouth jar with inturned rim (Figure 7.6). The vessel neck is externally ribbed and shows four regularly spaced pre-firing perforations. According to the reference vessel (Plate 13), this form has a flat base.

Statistical grouping

R98 occurred only three times in the contexts included in the analysis. It was manually grouped with R101 and R97, but dropped out of the *srd* reduction. In retrospect, this grouping was inconsistent, as R97 appears to be a different form (cf Appendix 2). As the jar with perforated neck, however, represents a rare shape in MEK1 assemblages, it did not contribute sufficiently to feature in the statistical analysis. Similarities with some of the previous forms, specifically with regard to the hole-mouth shape, and the discovery of a complete specimen within a well-defined Late Sasanian context, such as Trench 2 in Erk Kala, provide the chronological link to discuss the jar with perforated neck in this context.

Previous occurrences at Merv

This type of jar was found in Gyaur Kala, Trench 6, the 'Miller's Quarter'. Katsuris and Buryakov attribute this shape to pottery vessels from the third to fourth centuries AD (YuTAKE Archive, cf Appendix 3, Figure A3.18). One specimen is also illustrated among the pottery types from Gyaur Kala Trench 3, the 'Oval building'. This assemblage is dated by Dresvyanskaya to the fourth to sixth centuries AD (YuTAKE Archive, cf Appendix 3, Figure A3.8).

The complete specimen from Trench 2 (Plate 13), Erk Kala, which is now part of the YuTAKE finds collection of Asim Akhmedov (Williams *et al* 2003, 161–163), provided the necessary reference to identify the vessel form. With its hole-mouth shape, this jar is clearly associated with the stylistic traditions of the Late Sasanian vessel forms discussed above. At the same time, however, the four regular perforations link the shape to the Middle Sasanian jar with perforated neck, which appears to be its precursor. In contrast to this, however, the Late Sasanian jar is plain, apart from the ribbed neck.

Analogies from other areas

No parallels are published from Sasanian levels elsewhere.

Double-handled jar (amphora)

Shape code

R136, sR136, R137, sR137.

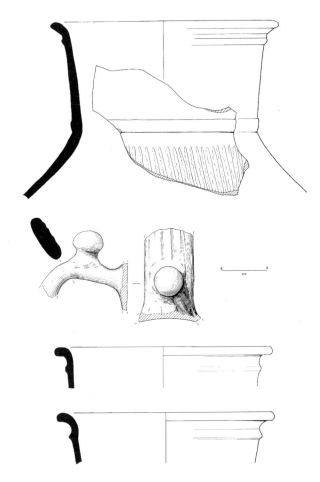

Figure 7.7: Fragments of the handled jar from MEK1.

Semi-complete reference

Parts of a near-complete specimen were found during the excavations in MEK1 (Figure 7.8 and Plate 14(a)). A complete and unbroken vessel of this type occurred in Trench 9, the Buddhist sanctuary (cf Pugachenkova and Usmanova 1995, 71, fig 21). This particular specimen, however, is delicately painted and represents an exclusive piece.

Diameter

Rim 19–24cm.

Fabric

A, G1.

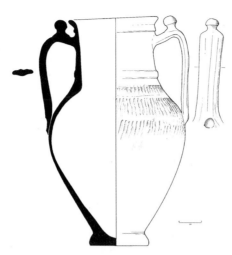

Figure 7.8: Drawing of the semi-complete specimen which was found in MEK1, context no 40 (cf Plate 14(a)).

Russian terminology

The characteristic rim shape is found on a number of vessels of varying size and diameter. For the double-handled jar illustrated here, the term *vaza*, vase, is used (Koshelenko 1966, 92–100). Recently the vessel has been referred to as an 'amphora-like vase' (cf Pugachenkova and Usmanova 1995, 71).

Description

Double-handled jar or amphora with everted rim. A single horizontal rib is applied to the neck just below the rim. The neck is slightly flared, sometimes almost straight and shows a rib around the neck–shoulder junction. The upper shoulder area of the vessel is fluted. To judge from the complete reference jars, the base is flat and splayed. Although this shape is usually poorly preserved, parallels found at Merv attest to two handles reaching from the neck to the vessel shoulder (Figure 7.8 and Plate 14). A rounded knob is attached to the top of the handle loop.

Statistical grouping

This shape formed a separate group before the computer reduction, but was unfortunately eliminated from the analysis. Since a relatively large number of fragments were recovered from MEK1 and the complete specimen of this type from Gyaur Kala, Trench 9, represents one of the most remarkable finds from Merv, we had hoped for further information on this shape from a statistical perspective. Unfortunately, the near-complete specimen from MEK1 came from a context that was unsuitable for statistical analysis. The vessel from Trench 9, now known as the 'Merv vase' (Plate 14(b)), is comparatively well dated through the archaeological context in which it was found, which is discussed below, and may be regarded as a 6th-century ceramic type.

Previous occurrences at Merv

The famous 'Merv vase' (Plate 14(b)) was discovered during excavations close to the northern facade of the Buddhist stupa in the southeast corner of Gyaur Kala (Pugachenkova and Usmanova 1995, 71f). Pugachenkova assigns the restoration of the northern part of the building, where the vessel was carefully bricked up, to the fifth phase of the stupa now dated according to coin finds in the foundation to the 6th century (Pugachenkova and Usmanova 1995, 56ff). The vase contained fragments of a Buddhist manuscript written in Brahmi on leaves of bark (Vorob'eva-Desyatovskaya 1983, 69) and obviously served as a reliquary. Another ceramic vessel with a much more extensive manuscript inside was found immured in the brickwork of a second stupa to the east of Gyaur Kala (Pugachenkova and Usmanova 1995, 76; Vorob'eva-Desyatovskaya 1983, 69). The association of the 'Merv vase' with 6th-century coins gives a general chronological setting, similar to the archaeological context of Area 1 in Erk Kala, where 6th-century coins were also found together with rims of the 'Merv vase' type (contexts no 200/group 22 and 281/group 11, cf Figure 5.7). Discussions of the painted vase tend to focus on its iconographic programme, so that its basic qualities as a ceramic vessel are mostly ignored (Grenet 1984, 266; Koshelenko 1966; Pugachenkova and Usmanova 1995, 71f). For the current analysis the iconography is relevant only insofar as it appears to be unrelated to its final use as Buddhist reliquary (cf Pugachenkova and Usmanova 1995, 72). Plain jars of a similar shape were also found in the necropolis near Bayram-Ali to the southwest of Gyaur Kala, where they were used as ossuaries (Ershov 1959, 188, pl 8, nos 1, 2). The typological relationship between the jars from the necropolis and the 'Merv vase' has already been recognised and the function of this vessel type was consequently interpreted primarily as an ossuary (cf Pugachenkova and Usmanova 1995, 72). This over-representation of complete specimens in funerary contexts, however, is misleading, since fragments of the same type also occur in Late Sasanian occupation levels, as in the recent excavations in Erk and Gyaur Kala (cf contexts no 40 in MEK1 and no 448 in MGK5), demonstrating that the jar was obviously produced as an everyday vessel for domestic use. Fragments of this shape from previous YuTAKE excavations are documented for Gyaur Kala, Trench 3, the 'Oval building' (Rutkovskaya 1962, 106, fig 17), Trench 9 (Pugachenkova and Usmanova 1995, fig 12) and Trench 17, Point 3 (Galochkina 1963; cf Appendix 3, Figure A3.27). Although the 'Merv vase' is exceptional in its rich and colourful decoration, singular fragments with figural painting found in late contexts of the recent excavations indicate the existence of a painted pottery tradition in Late Sasanian Merv (cf Herrmann *et al* 1996, Pl IId).

Regarding its basic structure, the 'Merv vase' has much in common with the handled jar from the preceding Middle Sasanian period (cf Chapter 6). Apart from the differences in rim shape and handle, the changes mainly concern the proportions of the structural elements: the neck diameter almost doubled, while the total height of the vessels remained basically unchanged. In contrast to the rounded contour of the Middle Sasanian jar, the maximum vessel diameter now lies in the upper third of the body height, lending it an egg-shaped appearance. Furthermore, the handles are broader and flatter in section, and the characteristic fluting of the upper body part is now reduced to a broad band around the upper shoulder. However, the principal components of the amphora-like storage vessel are preserved, and we might expect that the 'Merv vase' type of jar was used in much the same function as its predecessor from the Middle Sasanian period. The rounded handle knobs appear to be an accessory borrowed from metal jugs, where they serve as thumb-stop knobs (Simpson 1998, 338, 341, fig 203).

In 1996 a semi-complete double-handled jar was discovered by chance (it was hit by the lorry on the way to the excavation) on the surface near Area 4, close to the previous YuTAKE Trench 17 (Plate 15; for location cf Figure 6.1). The vessel, which is assumed to be from an Early Islamic context, still shows the basic elements of the 'Merv vase', illustrating the extraordinarily long continuation of this vessel type well into the post-Sasanian period.

Analogies from other areas

Parallels are not known in the literature. Similar forms with analogous rim shapes are, however, found with storage jars from Sasanian contexts in Fars. At Qasr-i Abu Nasr both large jars, similar in size and proportion to the 'Merv vase', and smaller versions have been found at the fortress (Whitcomb 1985, 118, 121, fig 43.d, fig 44.e, f, h). These jars are differentiated in surface treatment and patterns of decoration and usually have no handles. Whitcomb dates them to Late Sasanian and Early Islamic times (Whitcomb 1985, 118). Comparable vessels are also known from Qal'eh Dukhtar near Firuzabad, though they are of much larger proportions and different fabrics (Huff 1978, 144, figs 24, 26). The jars at Qal'eh Dukhtar are dated to Early Sasanian times according to their archaeological context and incised Pahlavi inscriptions on the shoulder of the vessels (Gignoux 1978, 148).

Jug

Shape code

R132, sR132.

Semi-complete reference

No semi-complete reference was found for this shape. A large part of the upper body was found in MEK1, context 99, pottery find no 2016 (cf Figure 7.9).

Diameter

Rim 5–6cm.

Fabric

A, G1, G2.

Russian terminology

This type is described as *kuvshin c venchikom v vide vertikal'nogo bortika*, 'jug with vertical collared rim' (Rutkovskaya 1962, 101, group 4).

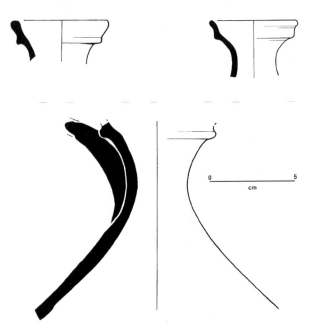

Figure 7.9: Jug rims and body fragments from MEK1.

Description

Jug with everted, collared rim. The neck appears to be slim with a smooth transition into the vessel shoulder. One of the fragments shows a handle attachment (Figure 7.9), which appears to be a standard feature (cf Rutkovskaya 1962, 101). The jug is very similar in style to the previous jar regarding the rim shape and body structure, which probably led to the confusion in Rutkovskaya's illustrations (Rutkovskaya 1962, 101, fig 13, no 12, 106, fig 17). Rim shapes analogous to the jug described here are depicted in Rutkovskaya's figure 17, but seem out of context and unmentioned in the discussion (Rutkovskaya 1962, 106, fig 17). No particular base shape is associated with this vessel type.

Statistical grouping

R132 was manually grouped with R135, but was subsequently deleted during the computer reduction. Its similarities with the large double-handled jar (cf Figure 7.8) characterises this shape as a Late Sasanian vessel type.

Previous occurrences at Merv

This jug is documented for Trench 3, the 'Oval building' (Rutkovskaya 1962, 106, fig 17) and Trench 9, the Buddhist sanctuary (Pugachenkova and Usmanova 1995, fig 12, no 35 and Appendix 3, Figures A3.21–2). In analogy to most of the previous shapes, we might expect that this jug was also found in other Late Sasanian contexts, such as Erk Kala,

Trench 3, Sounding 5, and Gyaur Kala, Trench 6, but was not chosen for illustration, since it was not perceived as an individual vessel type.

Analogies from other areas

Parallels are not documented for this vessel type. Jugs from the assemblages of Qasr-i Abu Nasr and Hajiabad, however, show basic similarities in the rim shape (Azarnoush 1994, 199, fig 177, c; Whitcomb 1985, 127, fig 46, c). These vessels are dated to the Middle Sasanian period (Azarnoush 1994, 214; Whitcomb 1985, 118).

Jar

Shape code

R126.

Semi-complete reference

No reconstructable profile has been found, either during previous or current excavations. Well-preserved fragments illustrate the upper body profile of this jar (**Figure 7.10**).

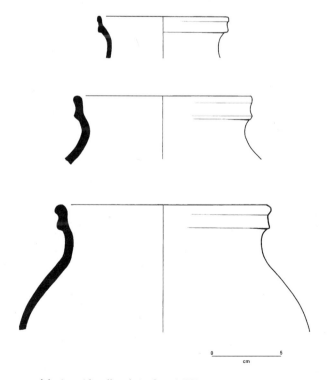

Figure 7.10: Fragments of the jar with collared rim from MEK1.

Diameter

Rim 9–15cm.

Fabric

A.

Russian terminology

This jar is described as *krinka*, 'narrow jar' (Rutkovskaya 1962, 106, group 1, fig 17).

Description

Jar with collared rim and low neck, which immediately curves out to the shoulders (Figure 7.10). The rim is usually structured by a single broad and shallow groove on the exterior. Rutkovskaya defined a relatively broad group of wide-necked vessels, including a number of different rim types of jars and jugs (Rutkovskaya 1962, 106, group 1, fig 17), while she overlooked the overlap between the jar with collared rim depicted in her illustration (Rutkovskaya 1962, 106, fig 17) and the group of jugs she describes earlier (Rutkovskaya 1962, 101, group 4, fig 13, no 12). No specific base shape has yet been identified for this form.

Statistical grouping

Only three fragments of the shape R126 occurred in the contexts selected for analysis. Since the shape forms a very small group, it was deleted from the further analysis in the final configurations. R126 also dropped regularly out of the trial reductions and seemed unsuitable for merging with other shapes. The general resemblance in the rim shape between this jar and the previous group justifies its inclusion in this discussion.

Previous occurrences

Fragments of this type occurred in Gyaur Kala in Trench 3, the 'Oval building' (Rutkovskaya 1962, 101, fig 13, no 12, fig 17) and Trench 9, the Buddhist sanctuary* (cf Appendix 3, Figure A3.21, nos 2, 13 and 22). A similar jar shape is illustrated for Sounding 5 in Erk Kala (Usmanova 1969, 29, fig 11). All these specimens are dated to the Late Sasanian period (Rutkovskaya 1962, 99ff.; Pugachenkova and Usmanova 1995, fig 12; for comparable rim shapes cf no 35; Usmanova 1969, 29, fig 11). With minor modifications this jar type apparently survived into post-Sasanian times, as indicated by its occurrence in the rubbish dumps associated with the potters' kilns in the vicinity of the southern city walls of Gyaur Kala (Zaurova 1962, 203, fig 21, nos 29, 30).

---

* Z I Usmanova kindly provided me with additional, unpublished pottery drawings from Trench 9, for which I am very grateful.

Analogies from other areas

No parallels may be found in the literature. Some jars excavated at Hajiabad show similar features in the rim and body shape, though far less pronounced than at Merv (cf Azarnoush 1994, fig 174.c–e).

TOWARDS A SASANIAN STYLE

Despite the deficiencies of the statistical analysis with regard to the material from Erk Kala MEK1, a number of forms could be retrieved through alternative methods. The vessel shapes discussed above certainly do not represent the complete assemblage of Late Sasanian wares, though their distribution and also the consistency of the core group ~R116 within the statistical calculations suggest that they probably form a significant part of the repertoire of this period.

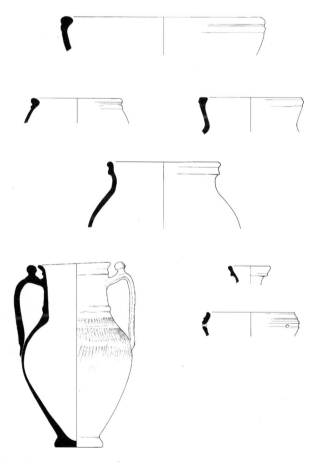

Figure 7.11: Late Sasanian pottery types.

Considering the Late Sasanian pottery shapes as a group, a greater homogeneity is immediately noticeable in the material. The close similarity between a wide range of rim shapes makes an unambiguous attribution to specific vessel types often impossible (cf bowl and jar, Figures 7.1 and 7.2). Common features, however, are not restricted to the rim, but also apply to the general design of the forms. The vessel profile seems smoothed, often lacking a marked break at the neck–shoulder junction. In general the pottery appears to be less decorated than in the preceding phases. Embellishment is reduced to the horizontal rib or groove respectively, which is employed to emphasise the orifice of the vessel or sometimes still the neck–shoulder junction (Figure 7.11), or to a band of chattered decoration around the shoulder. A new distinct element is introduced with the convex shape of the neck, which adds to the curvature of the profile.

Many shapes appear at first unrelated to the previous phase. This perceived discontinuity makes any assessment, which is based on style, of the time distance between the two groups of pottery practically impossible. To judge from the archaeological evidence of the upper most levels at MGK5 and YuTAKE, Trench 6 (Katsuris and Buryakov 1963, 145, fig 16; cf also Appendix 3, Figures A3.10; Herrmann *et al* 1996, 5–6, fig 4), both groups, identified here as Middle and Late Sasanian pottery, represent consecutive phases.

On closer examination, links between some vessel types of both groups are noticeable, particularly with the double-handled jar or amphora, the 'Merv vase', and the perforated jar. While functional divisions persist, stylistic expressions change considerably. This again impairs the validity of a system of use classification for ceramic shapes in a fine chronological analysis. The general sparsity of open vessel forms, however, is remarkable and cannot be explained by the erratic nature of the archaeological evidence alone. Other materials may have temporarily replaced fired clay as a medium for these vessels. In the early Islamic period, at least, they are an important part of the repertoire again.

The changes visible in Late Sasanian pottery may well reflect what has been described in the literature as 'the development of a Sasanian style' (Venco Ricciardi 1984, 53). Unlike the previous phase, no immediate geographical link can be established for the Late Sasanian material. Parallels are hardly found for this period and the few analogies cited here are scattered over a larger territory, though the closest similarities apparently occur within the heartland of the Sasanian Empire. At present it is difficult to assess the significance of the comparisons made, since published material from inside the Sasanian territories is scant for this late period. The links to the eastern neighbour, northern Bactria, so strongly visible in the Middle Sasanian material, however, seem completely dissolved.

Many of the Late Sasanian shapes are still recognisable in the post-Sasanian/Early Islamic ceramic material from the kiln structures in the southern part of Gyaur Kala, a legacy similar to that observed for the Late Parthian and Early Sasanian transition.

— 8 —

SO WHAT HAVE WE GAINED?

The primary objective of this work was a chronological analysis of the ceramic material from recent excavations at Merv. While numismatic evidence suggested a Sasanian date for the occupational levels of the buildings revealed, the pottery assemblages appeared to contain chronologically diverse material. Problems of material reuse within mudbrick architecture were therefore given special consideration. Despite the obvious secondary nature of deposits, an attempt was made to analyse the material without prior selection of theoretically defined categories of assemblages or stylistically classified form groups. As archaeological problems and potential difficulties inherent in the data set had been defined beforehand, analytical methods were thought advanced enough to produce a chronological sequence based on the assumed dominance of primary components at least in parts of the assemblages. A quantitative approach was therefore chosen, since the key to any chronological differentiation appeared to be the proportional comparison of pottery types between assemblages. Based on the measure of estimated vessel equivalents (*eves*) different methods of assemblage comparison were used to determine the most suitable approach.

At the end of a series of different analytical applications we concluded that no seriation of the individual assemblages was possible based on the dominant pottery types of secondary deposits. Results did not immediately show a consistent ceramic chronology. A refined gradation of differences in the depositional history of the contexts proved unfeasible and no coherent pattern emerged regarding stratigraphic position of the deposits or their function. Systematic distinctions between contexts according to the degree of reuse of their material content remain hypothetical for the moment. Variations between statistically significant groups of contexts, fabrics and forms, however, were clearly shown. Examining these variations with the help of the archaeological evidence on Merv resulted in a chronological interpretation and built the first steps towards a pottery sequence.

In the conventional analysis, variations between assemblages were explored through a number of tables showing two- and three-way interactions between variables. Broad patterns of interaction were noticeable and the quantitatively relevant groups of variables, according to their respective definition, were identified. Fabric types seemed to change over time reflecting a trend towards lighter, higher fired fine wares, while forms showed an increasing prevalence of closed and larger vessel forms. Due to the sparsity of the data set, however, the analysis had to remain on a fairly coarse level unsuitable to trace or examine individual groups. Regarding the variable 'context', only differences between the two excavation areas were studied. Internal variation or changes throughout the stratigraphic sequence of each area could not be defined, though. The grouping of the variable 'form' was not taken beyond a basic classification of form categories, which in view of the largely continuous use of the principal vessel forms during the time periods concerned (Parthian–Sasanian) were not appropriate for a finer chronological distinction or further stylistic comparisons. As far as the variable 'ware' is concerned, no special arrangements were necessary, as fabric diversity was limited and the single groups were left unchanged. The conventional analysis proved useful to get a first impression of possible chronological trends. Results, however, lacked the detail of information required to assess individual ceramic shapes or contexts. Another disadvantage of the conventional approach lay in the lack of a formal significance test with regard to the observed variations. Without informed choice the focus of the discussion regarding certain form or fabric groups might therefore be occasionally misplaced.

From a practical point of view, this type of analysis is reasonably easy to conduct. No further technical requirements are needed. The tables were mostly retrieved through database queries. Residual values, however, had to be calculated separately. Alterations to the data set (eg the exclusion of certain groups of variables) required the whole table to be recalculated. Two-way tables seemed relatively easy to interpret, but only provided an incomplete picture of the data variation. A thorough analysis of the three-way table, on the other hand, was more difficult and had to remain tentative in many respects.

The qualitative seriation was conducted to explore possibilities of manual data reduction, specifically with regard to the variable 'form', in preparation for the 'Pie-slice' analysis. Since this seriation was not used as a principal analytical tool, it is discussed only briefly here. Applied to this data set the qualitative seriation more than any theoretical consideration demonstrated the necessity of a quantitative approach. In the qualitative seriation both excavation areas appeared in an uninterrupted sequence. The internal structure of the data, however, was not clear and the sequence of pottery shapes was difficult to understand in view of the high variability of the data set. Only the variables 'context' and 'form' were considered in the seriation. The single shapes and contexts remained unmodified for this analysis. A number of contexts subsequently appeared out of their stratigraphic order. Larger contexts also tended to obscure chronological patterns. The subsequent manual seriation provided a useful supportive device for the grouping of shape codes, as three distinct patterns of occurrence were observed. An assessment based on the presence or absence of single shapes by context, however, was unable to account for the complex structure of this data set.

The application of the computer program 'seriate', part of the statistical package 'iagraves' (Chapter 4, Figure 4.1) was unproblematic and seriation diagrams are comparatively easy to understand. There is also accessible literature on the interpretation of such diagrams for urban seriation (cf Carver 1985).

Compared to the previous approaches, the 'Pie-slice' analysis generally operates on a more sophisticated level of statistics. This is, however, also reflected in the wealth of information provided with each calculation. Configurations often proved to represent only one further step in a series of analyses, gradually exploring the structure and variability of the data set. Inevitably, the analysis took more time than the other methods employed, but also produced more conclusive results and valuable insights into the role of different variables. As the program could handle relatively large tables and had facilities for coherent data reduction, variables could be studied in more detail. This helped to identify individual groups of fabrics and shapes significant to the variation of the data set, which were then assessed in their chronological relationship. Absolute dates for these groups had to be determined through archaeological evidence or by analogies to previous excavations. The groups themselves and the variation between them, however, were proposed by 'Pie-slice'.

Among those shape groups, the Late Sasanian jars (~R116) from MEK1 were previously not recognised as chronologically diagnostic in former Soviet excavations. This may also be related to their mostly fragmentary state. Many pottery shapes significant for MGK5 were already identified by the YuTAKE, including the handled bowl (R13), the double-handled jar (R30) and the juglet (R25), but were perceived as contemporary in the Soviet literature, representing simultaneous innovations to the ceramic repertoire of the Late Parthian or Early Sasanian period. Following the differentiated picture, which emerged during the 'Pie-slice' analysis, it appears plausible that these shapes were gradually introduced and belong to different phases of the Early and Middle Sasanian period. While the general chronological trend towards closed vessel forms noted in the conventional analysis was confirmed by the 'Pie-slice' configurations, the increase in vessel size seemed less consistent. Such development is certainly documented for the double-handled jar (amphora) from the Middle Sasanian to the Early Islamic period. Many large closed forms from MEK1, however, are in effect residual shapes, belonging to the Yaz III-type pottery of the Late Achaemenid and to the Parthian period. These would have contributed to the impression of an increase in size without being distinguishable from later pottery shapes in the conventional analysis given the basic classification system of vessel forms applied.

As far as fabric groups are concerned, the broad pattern of a gradual increase in firing temperature, already established in the single two- and three-way tables, was also noticeable in the correspondence analysis plots. The 'Pie-slice' analysis, however, provided a better insight into the fabric variations, in particular those of MGK5. With regard to fabric G1, a marked difference is noticeable between the two approaches. This proportionally large fabric group showed little variation in the conventional analysis and was assumed to suggest an overlap between the two excavation areas, while in the 'Pie-slice' analysis G1 displayed significant variations both between the excavations MEK1 and MGK5 and within the assemblages of MGK5. In addition, assemblages from both excavation areas were found to be distinct. The difference in the assessment of fabric G1 may be linked to the fact that patterns illustrated by the residuals of the conventional analysis were particularly strong for smaller groups, which made variations of the larger group G1 appear to be less striking (Chapter 3, Table 3.4(b)).

Certain associations and mergers that occurred during the computerised data reduction provided further information on links between groups of variables. It should be noted, however, that small groups are naturally less diverse and therefore more likely to be merged with larger groups, although this may be based on the lack of diversity rather than genuine similarity. Consequently, the archaeological background of the single mergers should be studied individually. Groupings and associations of the variable 'context' were occasionally unexpected. Despite the known secondary nature of the deposits, a clearer division between contexts with overwhelmingly residual material and those with a greater proportion of contemporary pottery was expected. This was also believed to be possibly related to the function of contexts, such as walls and in-built structures as opposed to repair layers or infills. Besides a visible tendency regarding the association of wall contexts with residual shapes, no specific difference was noticed. Contemporary and residual components were not as clearly distinguishable as was first assumed. All deposits turned out to be strongly affected by residuality and the differences in proportions of reused material were relatively vague.

Apart from the detailed information on single groups of variables, interactions between them were characterised. Naturally, expectations and ideas developed with the progress of excavations, and the recording of assemblages and interactions of the variable 'form' in particular were assumed to be significant. The comprehensive results presented in the quasi-log-linear analysis, however, further improved the understanding of the inter-dependence between the variables 'ware' and 'form'. In this respect, the changes of models observed between the first configuration concerning MEK1 and MGK5, and those of MGK5 alone, are very interesting (Chapter 4, Tables 4.17, 4.45 and 4.61). Interactions of the variable 'context' were noted throughout.

With its comprehensive statistical applications, 'Pie-slice' is not easy to operate for a novice. Initially, the interpretation of quasi-log-linear models and correspondence analysis plots required some practice and familiarisation, and the guidance of a statistician or experienced user may be necessary. After a period of experimentation and the develop-ment of a coherent approach in handling the manual data reduction, no further problems were encountered with the understanding and interpretation of the results. The practical advantage of 'Pie-slice' in comparison with the conventional analysis is that changes to the tables are conducted on a temporary configuration interface without altering the actual data. Marginal tables are automatically recalculated by the computer, opening up the pos-sibility of exploring the data set without much effort or loss of time. The various control mechanisms of the quasi-log-linear analysis, the M5 models or rejection of the data set, ensure that results and their interpretation are valid and founded with the archaeological realities of the assemblages. Patterns of interaction are explicitly shown (eg Chapter 4, Table 4.17), whereas the interpretation of the three-way table in the conventional analysis (Tables 3.4(a) and 3.4(b)) is much more complicated and may be prone to errors. Apart from the statistical advantages, the level of detail ultimately makes the results of the corre-spondence analysis compatible with conventional typological methods of examination, as shown in the stylistic assessment.

Finally, the stylistic assessment focused on vessel forms attributed to the Sasanian period and sought to visualise the distinct phases in the development of the pottery as exemplified by the individual shape groups contributing to the various configurations of the 'Pie-slice' analysis. Three chronologically distinct phases were indicated by the correspondence analysis plots, in correlation with the dates established for the buildings in MGK5 and MEK1 labelled as Early, Middle and Late Sasanian. Design and sources of inspiration for the Early and partly also the Middle Sasanian phase are guided by a com-mon interest in earlier traditions. For most of the Sasanian Empire, the initial stages of pottery production have been described as a continuation of Parthian wares. At Merv, however, some new shapes (eg the handled bowl or trefoil-mouthed jug) seem to have appeared fairly early on in Sasanian times, though this new style in pottery production was based on a combination of different formal elements and decorative techniques developed in the preceding periods. As recent excavations did not cover the Late Parthian or the beginning of the Sasanian occupation at Merv, it is at present impossible to determine whether local traditions prevail or inspirations drew on a wider sphere of influence. The early Sasanian pottery forms, however, are closely linked to the pottery style of northern Bactria, the neighbouring territory to the east. Some Middle Sasanian forms, such as the double-handled jar or the jar with perforated neck, appear already disconnected from this phenomenon and no eastern parallels are found for any of the Late Sasanian vessels. The increasing independence in pottery style may also reflect the fading of Hellenistic traditions in this region, which still bore heavily on the early Sasanian forms.

A marked stylistic transformation characterises the pottery repertoire in the later Sasanian phase. The design appears more uniform, extending over a wide range of closed and possibly also open forms. Some of the Middle Sasanian vessel types are still in use, specifically the double-handled jar and the jar with perforated neck, though shaped and decorated in the new fashion. Several vessel types apparently continued to be produced and developed into Islamic times. A certain parallelism is visible here to the general trend established for the Early Sasanian period. This transposed scheme of political changes and visible alterations in the material culture seems plausible, since generally no immediate break in population structure or culture is involved. Only after some time a new identity develops in response to political changes.

Skeuomorphic features occur sporadically on ceramic vessels, as in the ribs around the neck of the earlier, and in the base shape and handle knobs of the later phase. On the whole, however, contemporary metal ware does not appear to have dominated the pottery design at any point in time.

Considering the archaeological context and the primary research objectives of this study, the quantitative approach offered by the 'Pie-slice' computer package proved to be most successful. The primarily exploratory character of the analysis corresponded well to the low level of knowledge about the pottery from Merv, while the basic models employed by the quasi-log-linear analysis helped to better understand the variations observed. Different circumstances may require different methodologies, and a combination of a variety of approaches, including statistical, scientific and stylistic assessments, will naturally produce a more comprehensive picture. Chronology was the main concern of this work, but in future the research focus will shift to include other aspects of pottery production at Merv.

— APPENDIX 1 —

FABRIC TYPE SERIES

This catalogue illustrates the fabric type series used for pottery recording in the field and for the statistical analysis. It is based on the classification system originally set up for the International Merv Project by St John Simpson (Chapter 2). The series was primarily designed to detect chronological changes in the use of fabrics against the background of the relative petrographic homogeneity expected from clays of the local alluvial plain. Fabric types are therefore not only defined by differences in the composition of clays and tempering, but also with regard to colourings resulting from various firing conditions. The term 'fabric' is not used in a strictly petrographic sense.

Inconsistencies of classification criteria and possible confusion were, however, noted, and as part of a comprehensive scientific research programme (Williams *et al* 2003, 163–165) the fabric type series is currently being revised to take account of the qualitative differences regarding the individual classification criteria (Puschnigg and Gilbert forthcoming).

The fabric types described below are restricted to those occurring with pre-Islamic material.

FABRIC CODE: A

Description

White or pale yellow fabric with pale greenish tinge; some fine dark sand inclusions; rare fine voids; wheel-thrown; hard fired.

Figure A1.1: Fabric A.

Colour
Surface:
Sherd body: 5Y 8/2, 5Y 8/3.

Classification
Fineware.

Petrography
Group 4 after Joyner (Chapter 4, Table 4.62), silty quartz and biotite mica fabric.

Comment
This fabric probably corresponds to the greenish-grey fabric mentioned in Soviet literature on Merv.

-----cm

FABRIC CODE: B1

Description

Usually yellowish-red fabric and interior with paler reddish-yellow zone close to the exterior; the exterior surface is rarely yellowish, but usually very pale brown or pale yellow; cores rare; other rare examples with heavily reduced fabrics ranging from greyish-brown to very dark greyish-brown on one wall; vessels often coil-built and thick-walled, occasionally with red slip on the exterior; hard fired.

Figure A1.2: Fabric B1.

Colour
Surface: 10YR 8/3–8/4; 2.5Y 8/4
Sherd body: 5YR 5/6–5/8; 7.5 YR 6/6–6/8 closer to exterior; rarely 10YR 5/2, 10YR 3/2.

Classification
Fineware.

Petrography
This fabric was not part of the preliminary petrographic analysis.

Comment
Fabric B1 was used to classify fragments of large storage vessels only. It does not appear to represent a statistically independent observation and was consequently left out of all analyses.

-----cm

FABRIC CODE: B2

Description

Reddish fabric with cream/buff surfaces; some fine sand and rare calcareous inclusions; as B1, but vessels are wheel-thrown and not thick-walled.

Figure A1.3: Fabric B2.

Colour

Classification
Fineware.

Petrography
This fabric was not part of the preliminary petrographic analysis.

Comment
Probably identical with 'red fabric with light or white slip' mentioned in Soviet literature at Merv.

FABRIC CODE: B3

Description

Reddish-yellow fabric with similar surface; sparse well-sorted dark and pale sand inclusions; rare voids, wheel-thrown, hard-fired.

Figure A1.4: Fabric B3.

Colour
Surface: similar to body
Sherd body: 5YR 6/8.

Classification
Fineware.

Petography
Group 4 after Joyner (Chapter 4, Table 4.62), silty quartz and biotite mica fabric.

Comment
Probably identical with 'red fabric' mentioned in Soviet literature on Merv.

FABRIC CODE: B4

Description

Figure A1.5: Fabric B4.

Colour

Classification
Fineware.

Petrography
Coincides with group 4 after Joyner (Chapter 4, Table 4.62), silty quartz and biotite mica fabric (pilot project completed by Ann Feuerbach, Institute of Archaeology, UCL).

Comment

-----cm

FABRIC CODE: C

Description

Usually light reddish-brown fabric, exterior varies from this to light yellowish-brown to light brownish-grey, often partially blackened; occasionally sooted all over the exterior; abundant fine-coarse vitrified clay ('slag') and some grog temper, inclusions measuring up to 4mm across; interior surfaces usually paler, with traces of smoothing; handmade; hard-fired; somewhat brittle; wall thickness varies from 0.6 to 1cm.

Figure A1.6: Fabric C.

Colour
Surface: 10YR 6/4, 10YR 6/2
Sherd body: 5YR 6/3.

Classification
Coarse/cooking ware.

Petrography
Group 1 after Joyner (Chapter 4, Table 4.62), slag-tempered fabric.

Comment

-----cm

FABRIC CODE: D

Description

Usually grey, rarely pale yellow or reddish-yellow with grey core or grey with light grey – light yellowish-brown interior surface; exterior often blackened; handmade; hard-fired; somewhat brittle; wall thickness varies from 0.4 to 1.3cm.

Figure A1.7: Fabric D.

-----cm

Colour
Surface: 2.5Y 7/2, 10YR 6/4
Sherd body: 2.5Y N6/–N5, 2.5Y 8/4, 7.5YR 7/6.

Classification
Coarse/cooking ware.

Petrography
Group 2 after Joyner (Chapter 4, Table 4.62), calcite-tempered fabric.

Comment

FABRIC CODE: E

Description

Usually pink or reddish-yellow fabric, often with white or very pale brown surfaces, but fabric also varies from reddish yellow to very pale brown, pale olive with a pale greenish tinge or dark brown; exterior surfaces blackened in many cases; poorly sorted and containing abundant coarse organic and occasional grog inclusions; handmade; relatively hard-fired yet crumbly and somewhat brittle; wall thickness 0.6 to 1.9cm.

Figure A1.8: Fabric E.

-----cm

Colour
Surface: 10YR 8/2, 10YR 8/3
Sherd body: 7.5YR 7/4, 7.5YR 7/6; 7.5YR 6/6– 10YR 7/4, 5Y 6/4, 10YR 4/3.

Classification
Coarse/cooking ware.

Petrography
Group 3 after Joyner (Chapter 4, Table 4.62), grog-tempered fabric.

FABRIC CODE: G1

Description

Light brown or very pale brown fabric with pale yellow or light yellowish-brown surfaces, occasionally pinkish towards one surface; some fine burnt-out organic and fine dark sand inclusions; wheel-thrown; hard-fired.

Figure A1.9: Fabric G1.

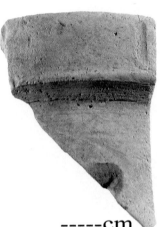

Colour
Surface: 2.5Y 7/4, 10YR 6/4–2.5Y
Sherd body: 7.5YR 6/4, 10YR 7/4.

Classification
Fineware.

Petrography
Group 4 after Joyner (Chapter 4, Table 4.62), silty quartz and biotite mica fabric.

Comment
Some sherds are marginal A/G1.

FABRIC CODE: G2

Description

Light brown or very pale brown fabric with similar surfaces; some fine burnt-out organic and fine dark sand inclusions; wheel-thrown; hard-fired.

Figure A1.10: Fabric G2.

Colour
Surface: similar to body
Sherd body: 7.5YR 6/4, 10YR 7/4.

Classification
Fineware.

Petrography
Group 4 after Joyner (Chapter 4, Table 4.62), silty quartz and biotite mica fabric.

Comment
Some sherds merge to fabric B2.

FABRIC CODE: I1

Description

Accidentally reduced ware; grey or light grey fabric; rare very dark grey core with olive surfaces and outer core, or brown with paler surfaces; some fine organic inclusions; wheel-thrown; hard-fired.

Colour
Surface: rare 5Y 5/3
Sherd body: 5Y 5/1, 5Y 7/1–2; rare 5Y 3/1, 10YR 5/3.

Classification
Fineware.

Petrography
This fabric was not part of the pre-liminary petrographic analysis.

Comment
Accidentally reduced fineware!

FABRIC CODE: I2

Description

Deliberately reduced; grey or light-grey fabric and surfaces; some fine organic inclusions; surfaces usually lightly burnished although this has sometimes worn off; wheel-thrown; hard-fired.

Figure A1.11: Fabric I2.

Colour
Surface:
Sherd body: 5Y 5/1, 5Y 7/1–2.

Classification
Fineware.

Petrography
Group 4 after Joyner (Chapter 4, Table 4.62), silty quartz and biotite mica fabric.

Comment
Probably identical with grey or dark-grey fabric with black slip mentioned in Soviet literature on Merv.

FABRIC CODE: K

Description
Burnished red slip, occasionally worn off.

Figure A1.12: Fabric K.

Colour

Classification
Fineware.

Petrography
Group 4 and group 5 after Joyner (Chapter 4, Table 4.62), silty quartz and biotite mica fabric and fine red fabric.

Comment
Group of mixed fabrics with identical surface treatment!

FABRIC CODE: X

Description
Unidentified fabric; fragments either lost in storage before fabric typing or numbering illegible. In use only for processed records on computer database and in the Pie-slice program.

— APPENDIX 2 —

POTTERY FORMS

The following catalogue is restricted to those rim shapes which occurred in the statistical analysis. It provides a visual guide to the pottery discussed in the statistical analyses (Chapters 3 and 4). A comprehensive catalogue of all shape codes will be published elsewhere (Puschnigg and Gilbert forthcoming). The rim codes were numbered continuously, starting from 1 (R1, R2), in the order of first encounter during pottery processing. The numbering system only serves for reference purposes. It is not hierarchical and does not reflect any relationships between shapes, either functional or typological. A brief description is included for each code.

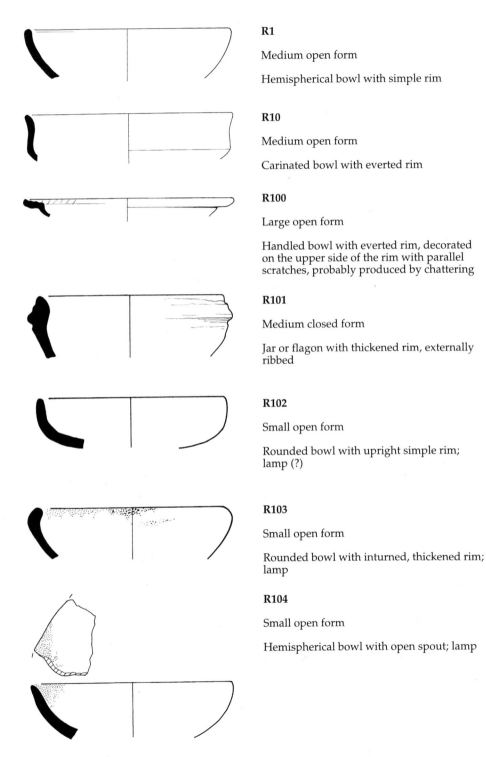

R1

Medium open form

Hemispherical bowl with simple rim

R10

Medium open form

Carinated bowl with everted rim

R100

Large open form

Handled bowl with everted rim, decorated on the upper side of the rim with parallel scratches, probably produced by chattering

R101

Medium closed form

Jar or flagon with thickened rim, externally ribbed

R102

Small open form

Rounded bowl with upright simple rim; lamp (?)

R103

Small open form

Rounded bowl with inturned, thickened rim; lamp

R104

Small open form

Hemispherical bowl with open spout; lamp

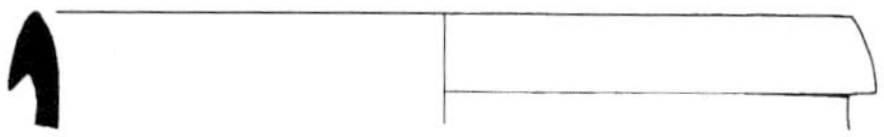

R106

Large closed form

Jar with hooked rim and carinated base

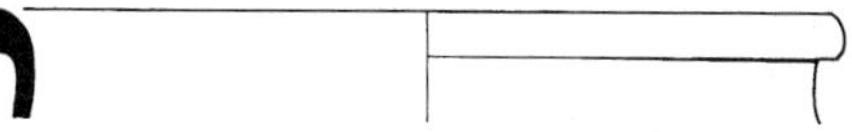

R107

Large closed form

Jar with hooked rim and carinated base

R108

Large closed form

Jar with collared rim and carinated base

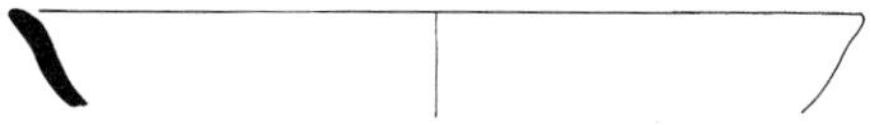

R11

Medium open form

Rounded bowl with everted rim

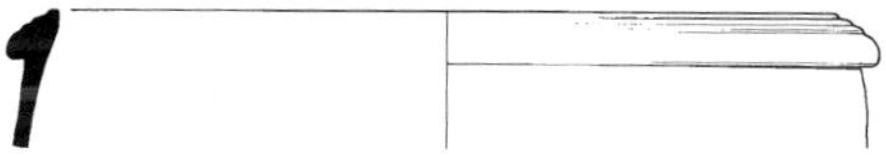

R112

Medium closed form

Jar with clubbed rim, externally grooved

R113

Large closed form

Jar with thickened inturned rim

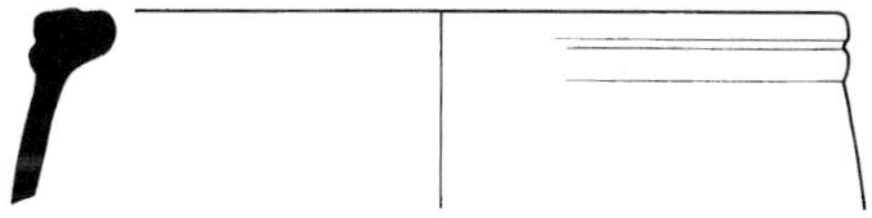

R115

Large closed form

Hole-mouth jar with thickened inturned rim, flat on top, externally grooved

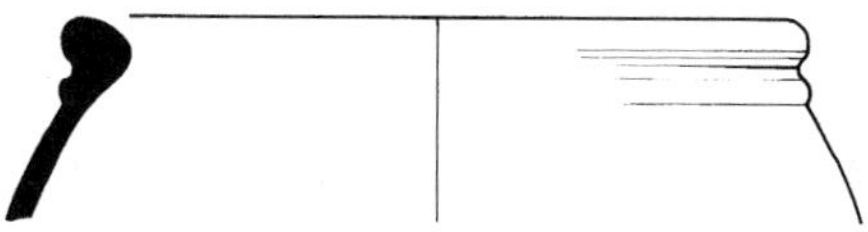

R116

Large closed form

Hole-mouth jar with thickened inturned rim, externally grooved

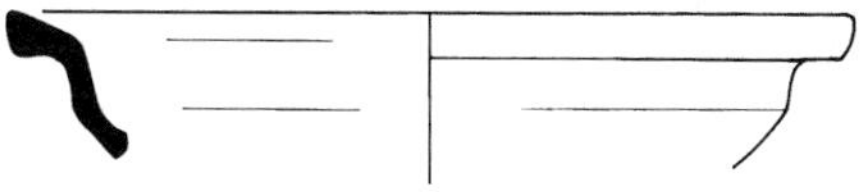

R12

Medium open form

Bowl with everted thickened rim

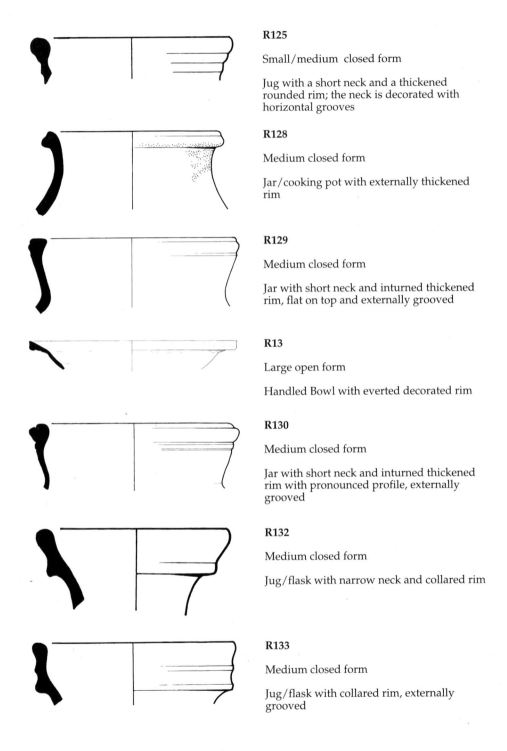

R125

Small/medium closed form

Jug with a short neck and a thickened rounded rim; the neck is decorated with horizontal grooves

R128

Medium closed form

Jar/cooking pot with externally thickened rim

R129

Medium closed form

Jar with short neck and inturned thickened rim, flat on top and externally grooved

R13

Large open form

Handled Bowl with everted decorated rim

R130

Medium closed form

Jar with short neck and inturned thickened rim with pronounced profile, externally grooved

R132

Medium closed form

Jug/flask with narrow neck and collared rim

R133

Medium closed form

Jug/flask with collared rim, externally grooved

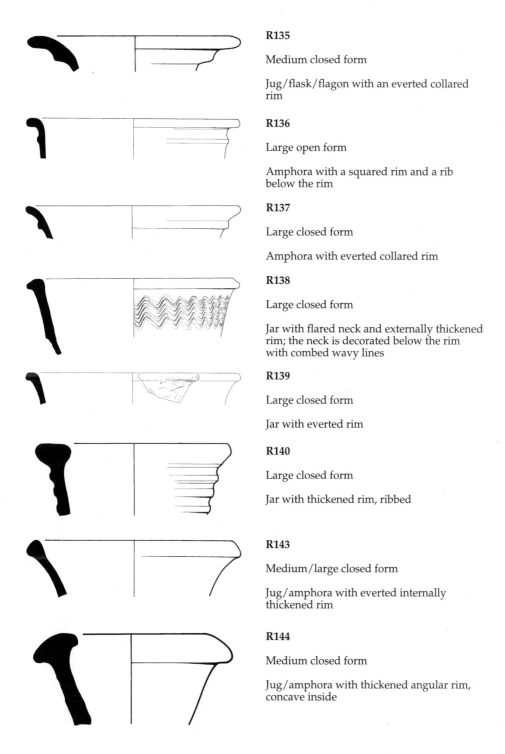

R135

Medium closed form

Jug/flask/flagon with an everted collared rim

R136

Large open form

Amphora with a squared rim and a rib below the rim

R137

Large closed form

Amphora with everted collared rim

R138

Large closed form

Jar with flared neck and externally thickened rim; the neck is decorated below the rim with combed wavy lines

R139

Large closed form

Jar with everted rim

R140

Large closed form

Jar with thickened rim, ribbed

R143

Medium/large closed form

Jug/amphora with everted internally thickened rim

R144

Medium closed form

Jug/amphora with thickened angular rim, concave inside

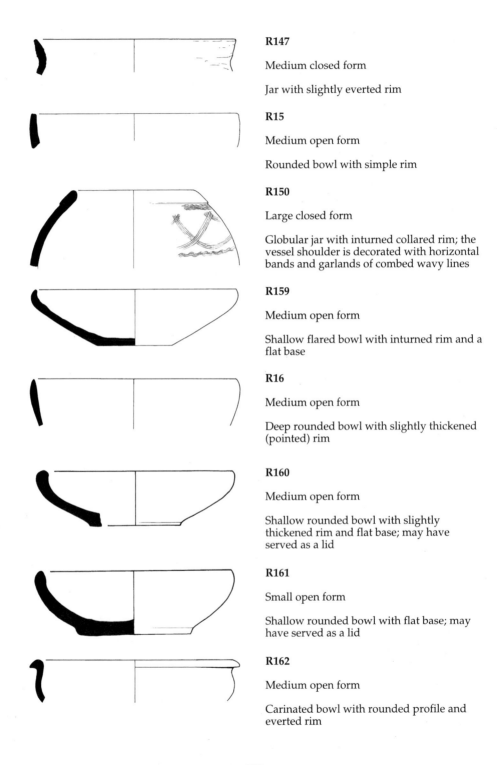

R147

Medium closed form

Jar with slightly everted rim

R15

Medium open form

Rounded bowl with simple rim

R150

Large closed form

Globular jar with inturned collared rim; the vessel shoulder is decorated with horizontal bands and garlands of combed wavy lines

R159

Medium open form

Shallow flared bowl with inturned rim and a flat base

R16

Medium open form

Deep rounded bowl with slightly thickened (pointed) rim

R160

Medium open form

Shallow rounded bowl with slightly thickened rim and flat base; may have served as a lid

R161

Small open form

Shallow rounded bowl with flat base; may have served as a lid

R162

Medium open form

Carinated bowl with rounded profile and everted rim

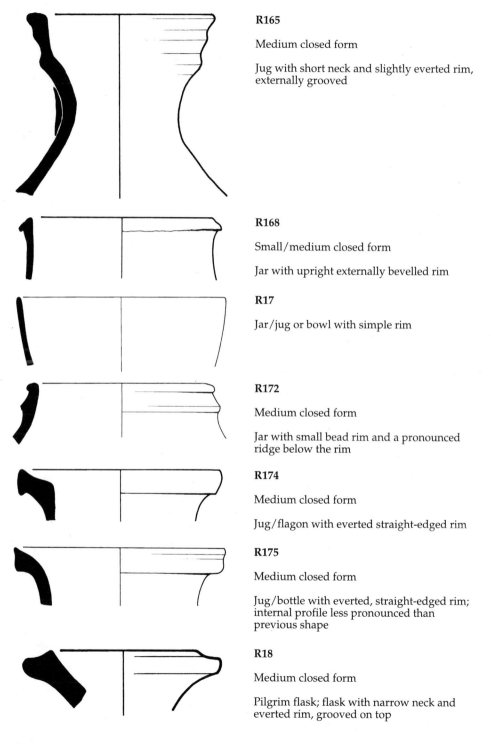

R165

Medium closed form

Jug with short neck and slightly everted rim, externally grooved

R168

Small/medium closed form

Jar with upright externally bevelled rim

R17

Jar/jug or bowl with simple rim

R172

Medium closed form

Jar with small bead rim and a pronounced ridge below the rim

R174

Medium closed form

Jug/flagon with everted straight-edged rim

R175

Medium closed form

Jug/bottle with everted, straight-edged rim; internal profile less pronounced than previous shape

R18

Medium closed form

Pilgrim flask; flask with narrow neck and everted rim, grooved on top

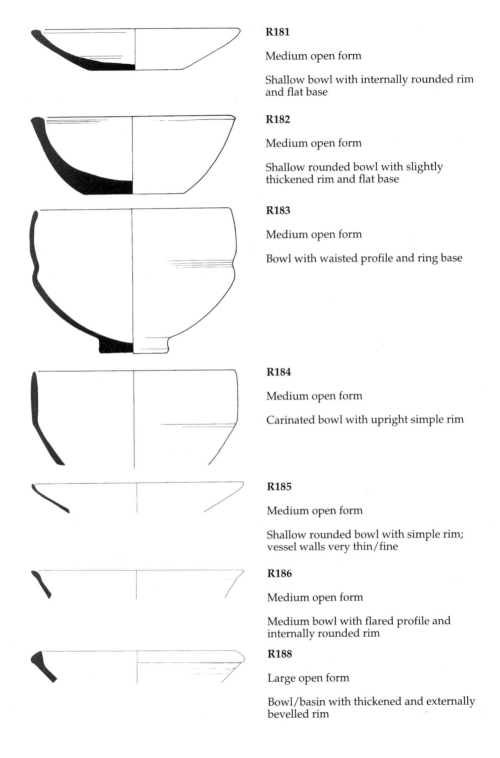

R181

Medium open form

Shallow bowl with internally rounded rim and flat base

R182

Medium open form

Shallow rounded bowl with slightly thickened rim and flat base

R183

Medium open form

Bowl with waisted profile and ring base

R184

Medium open form

Carinated bowl with upright simple rim

R185

Medium open form

Shallow rounded bowl with simple rim; vessel walls very thin/fine

R186

Medium open form

Medium bowl with flared profile and internally rounded rim

R188

Large open form

Bowl/basin with thickened and externally bevelled rim

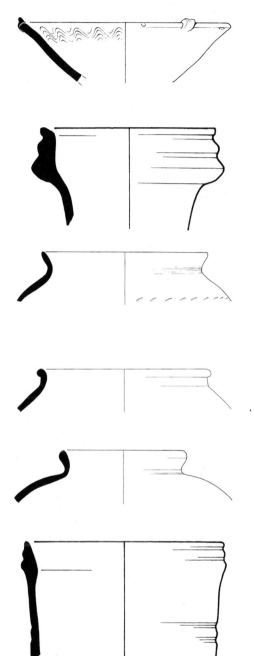

R189

Medium open form

Rounded bowl with slightly everted rim, decorated on the inside with combed wavy lines; the bowl rim is further decorated with two handle attachments

R19

Medium closed form

Bottle/jug with upright thickened rim, externally grooved

R191

Medium closed form

Globular jar (cooking pot) with everted rim; shoulder often decorated with a row of impressions produced by a pointed tool (stabbing)

R193

Medium closed form

Jar with upright beaded rim

R194

Medium closed form

Globular jar with slightly everted thickened rim

R198

Medium closed form

Jug with slightly thickened bevelled rim, externally grooved; the neck is decorated with a horizontal rib

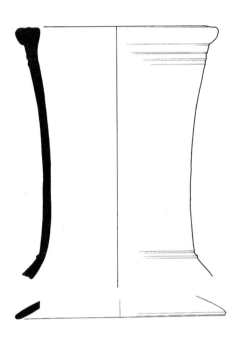

R199

Large closed form

Amphora with a flared neck and a thickened rim, flat on top; two incised horizontal lines decorate the neck below the rim

R2

Medium open form/lid

Shallow bowl with flat rim; probably served as a lid

R20

Medium closed form

Bottle with externally thickened reed rim

R203

Medium open form

Pan with almost upright, simple rim

R204

Medium open form/lid

Conical lid with flat rim

R206

Medium closed form

Jar with thickened and bevelled rim, externally grooved; the neck is perforated

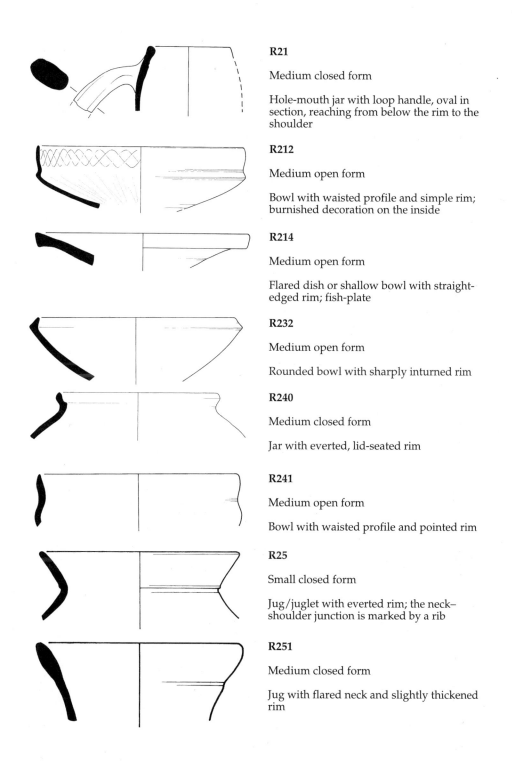

R21

Medium closed form

Hole-mouth jar with loop handle, oval in section, reaching from below the rim to the shoulder

R212

Medium open form

Bowl with waisted profile and simple rim; burnished decoration on the inside

R214

Medium open form

Flared dish or shallow bowl with straight-edged rim; fish-plate

R232

Medium open form

Rounded bowl with sharply inturned rim

R240

Medium closed form

Jar with everted, lid-seated rim

R241

Medium open form

Bowl with waisted profile and pointed rim

R25

Small closed form

Jug/juglet with everted rim; the neck–shoulder junction is marked by a rib

R251

Medium closed form

Jug with flared neck and slightly thickened rim

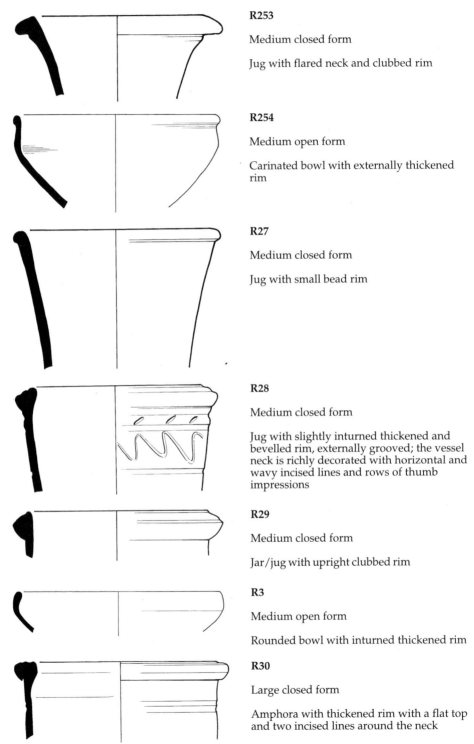

R253

Medium closed form

Jug with flared neck and clubbed rim

R254

Medium open form

Carinated bowl with externally thickened rim

R27

Medium closed form

Jug with small bead rim

R28

Medium closed form

Jug with slightly inturned thickened and bevelled rim, externally grooved; the vessel neck is richly decorated with horizontal and wavy incised lines and rows of thumb impressions

R29

Medium closed form

Jar/jug with upright clubbed rim

R3

Medium open form

Rounded bowl with inturned thickened rim

R30

Large closed form

Amphora with thickened rim with a flat top and two incised lines around the neck

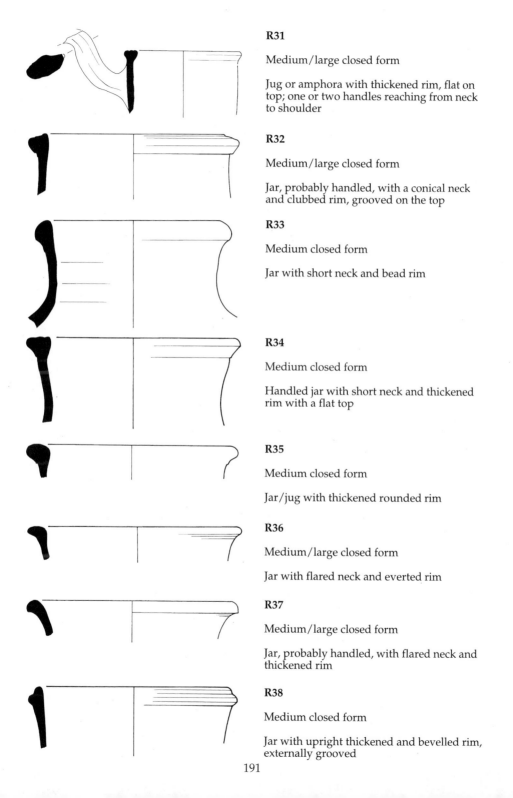

R31

Medium/large closed form

Jug or amphora with thickened rim, flat on top; one or two handles reaching from neck to shoulder

R32

Medium/large closed form

Jar, probably handled, with a conical neck and clubbed rim, grooved on the top

R33

Medium closed form

Jar with short neck and bead rim

R34

Medium closed form

Handled jar with short neck and thickened rim with a flat top

R35

Medium closed form

Jar/jug with thickened rounded rim

R36

Medium/large closed form

Jar with flared neck and everted rim

R37

Medium/large closed form

Jar, probably handled, with flared neck and thickened rim

R38

Medium closed form

Jar with upright thickened and bevelled rim, externally grooved

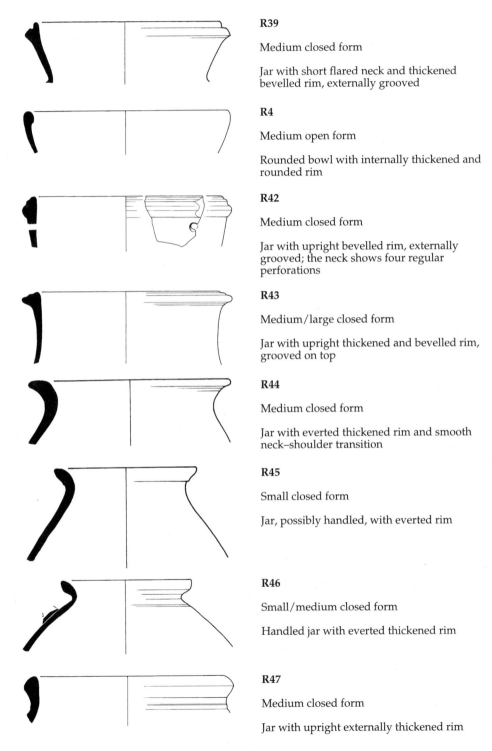

R39

Medium closed form

Jar with short flared neck and thickened bevelled rim, externally grooved

R4

Medium open form

Rounded bowl with internally thickened and rounded rim

R42

Medium closed form

Jar with upright bevelled rim, externally grooved; the neck shows four regular perforations

R43

Medium/large closed form

Jar with upright thickened and bevelled rim, grooved on top

R44

Medium closed form

Jar with everted thickened rim and smooth neck–shoulder transition

R45

Small closed form

Jar, possibly handled, with everted rim

R46

Small/medium closed form

Handled jar with everted thickened rim

R47

Medium closed form

Jar with upright externally thickened rim

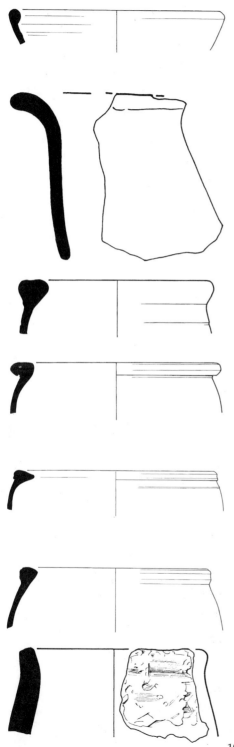

R5

Medium open form

Flared bowl with internally thickened and rounded rim

R52

Jar/bowl with everted rim; the hole vessel seems to be relatively thin-walled

R53

Small closed form

Neckless jar with inturned thickened rim with a flat top

R55

Medium closed form

Neckless jar with inturned rim and a pronounced external thickening, flat on top; the rim–shoulder transition is marked by a groove

R56

Medium closed form

Neckless jar with inturned and thickened straight-edged rim; the lower rim edge forms a small rib

R57

Medum closed form

Neckless jar with slightly inturned thickened and straight-edged rim

R59

Small/medium closed form

Jar with slightly everted simple rim

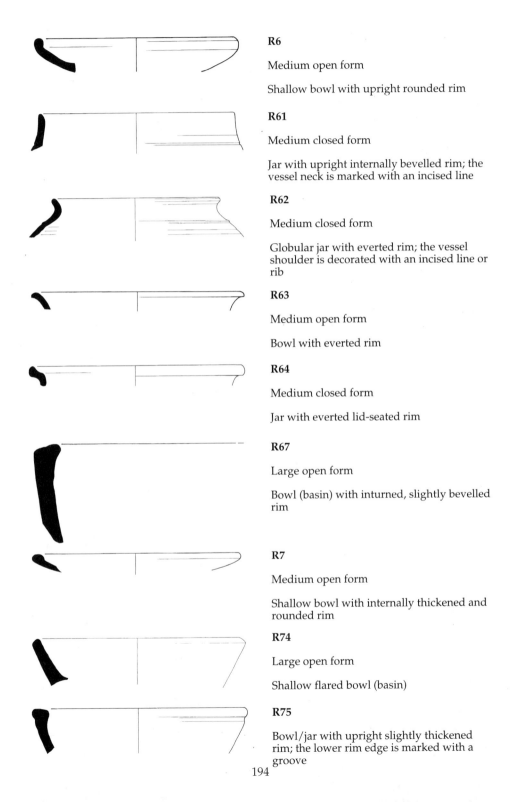

R6

Medium open form

Shallow bowl with upright rounded rim

R61

Medium closed form

Jar with upright internally bevelled rim; the vessel neck is marked with an incised line

R62

Medium closed form

Globular jar with everted rim; the vessel shoulder is decorated with an incised line or rib

R63

Medium open form

Bowl with everted rim

R64

Medium closed form

Jar with everted lid-seated rim

R67

Large open form

Bowl (basin) with inturned, slightly bevelled rim

R7

Medium open form

Shallow bowl with internally thickened and rounded rim

R74

Large open form

Shallow flared bowl (basin)

R75

Bowl/jar with upright slightly thickened rim; the lower rim edge is marked with a groove

R76

Large closed form

Hole-mouth jar with a rim thickened on either side

R77

Bowl or hole-mouth jar with slightly inturned thickened rim

R78

Large open form

Rounded bowl with thickened rim, flat on top and externally grooved

R79

Large open form

Flared bowl (basin) with everted thickened rim, externally grooved

R8

Medium open form

Rounded bowl with inturned bevelled rim

R80

Large open form

Flared bowl (basin) with everted rim

R81

Large open form

Flared bowl (basin) with a slightly thickened rim, grooved on top

R83

Hole-mouth jar or bowl with inturned thickened rim, externally grooved

R84

Medium open form

Shallow rounded bowl

R85

Medium open form

Rounded bowl

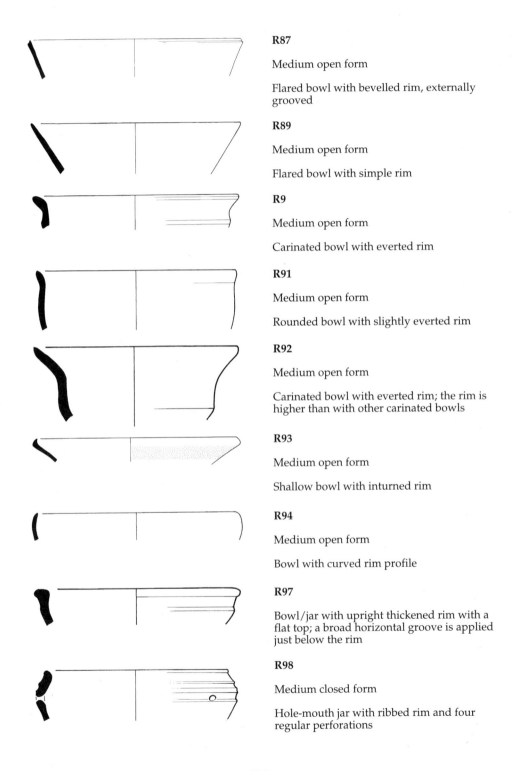

R87

Medium open form

Flared bowl with bevelled rim, externally grooved

R89

Medium open form

Flared bowl with simple rim

R9

Medium open form

Carinated bowl with everted rim

R91

Medium open form

Rounded bowl with slightly everted rim

R92

Medium open form

Carinated bowl with everted rim; the rim is higher than with other carinated bowls

R93

Medium open form

Shallow bowl with inturned rim

R94

Medium open form

Bowl with curved rim profile

R97

Bowl/jar with upright thickened rim with a flat top; a broad horizontal groove is applied just below the rim

R98

Medium closed form

Hole-mouth jar with ribbed rim and four regular perforations

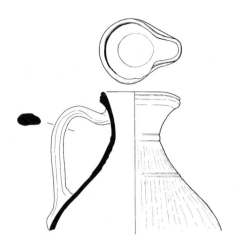

Ref4

Medium closed form

Trefoil-mouthed jug with bevelled rim, externally grooved; the handle, oval in section, reaches from below the rim to the shoulder; a horizontal rib marks the middle height of the neck; the semi-complete specimen was red slipped and vertically burnished with two lines incised around the shoulder

— APPENDIX 3 —

YuTAKE POTTERY DRAWINGS

The following illustrations show a selection of pottery drawings from YuTAKE excavations, which are relevant to the discussions in the chronological and stylistic analyses. Most of the original plates are stored in the YuTAKE archive in Ashgabad, except for those from Gyaur-Kala, Trench 9, which are kept with Zamira Usmaova in Tashkent. This appendix contains only drawings from Gyaur-Kala excavations, many of which have been used in the published reports. They are illustrated here as a visual reference to facilitate immediate comparisons. Names in brackets refer to the authors of the drawings and publications, where appropriate.

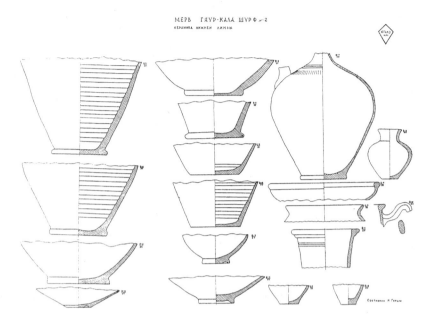

Figure A3.1: (above) Gyaur Kala, sounding 2. Pottery from the lower lens (N Gertsman, YuTAKE 1953)

Figure A3.2: (below) Gyaur Kala, Trench 2. Pottery from the stratigraphic sounding no 4 (M Mershchiev; cf Usmanova 1963b, fig 20)

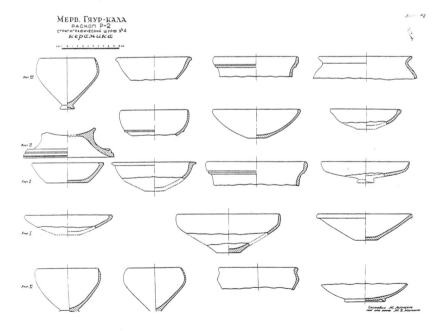

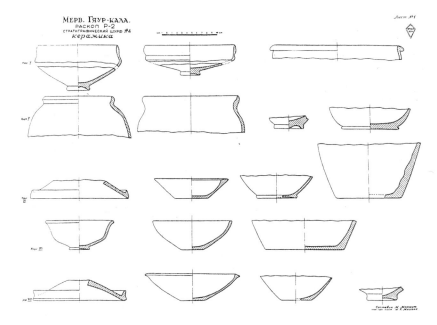

Figure A3.3: (above) Gyaur Kala, Trench 2. Pottery from the stratigraphic sounding no 4 (M Mershchiev; cf Usmanova 1963b, fig 20)

Figure A3.4: (below) Gyaur Kala, Trench 2, sounding 3, level XII. Pottery from the second century BC, (Z Usmanova; cf Usmanova 1963b, fig 24)

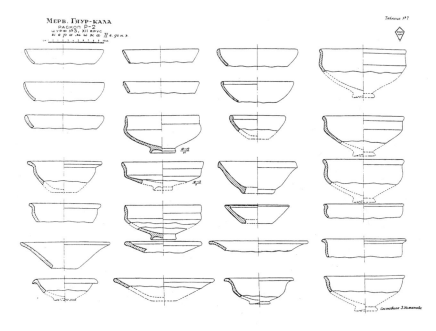

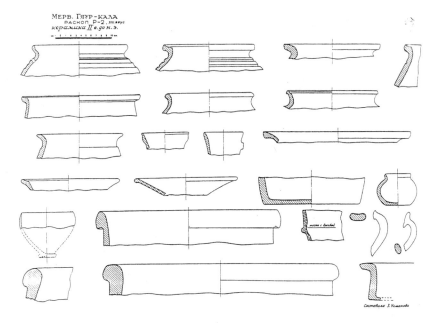

Figure A3.5: (above) Gyaur Kala, Trench 2, level XIII. Pottery from the second century BC (Z Usmanova; cf Usmanova 1963b, fig 24)

Figure A3.6: (below) Gyaur Kala, Trench 2. Pottery from the first to second centuries AD (Z Usmanova; cf Usmanova 1963b, fig 16)

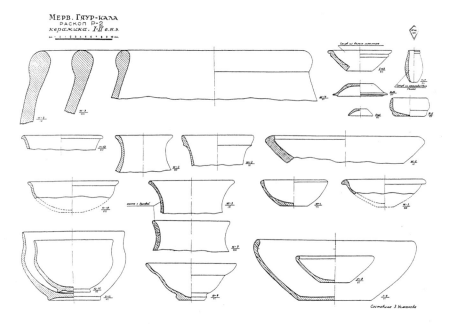

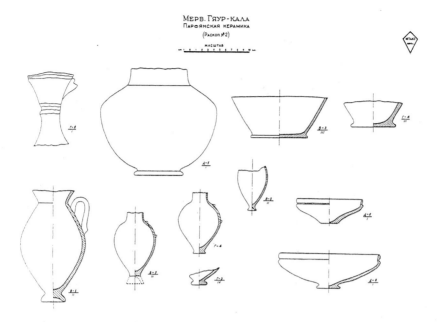

Figure A3.7: (above) Gyaur Kala, Trench 2. Parthian pottery

Figure A3.8: (below) Gyaur Kala, Trench 3. Pottery from the fourth to sixth centuries (G Dresvyanskaya, cf Dresvyanskaya 1974, fig 7)

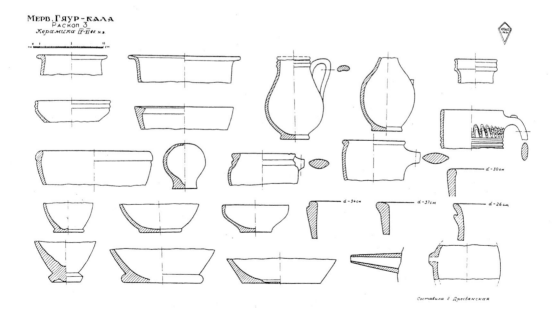

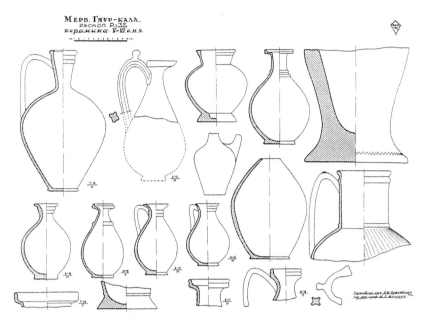

Figure A3.9: (above) Gyaur Kala, Trench 3. Pottery from the fifth to sixth centuries AD (L M Rutkovskaya, cf Rutkovskaya 1962, fig 14)

Figure A3.10: (below) Gyaur Kala, Trench 6. Partho-Sasanian pottery from the second to third centuries AD (K Katsuris, cf Katsuris and Buryakov 1963, fig 16)

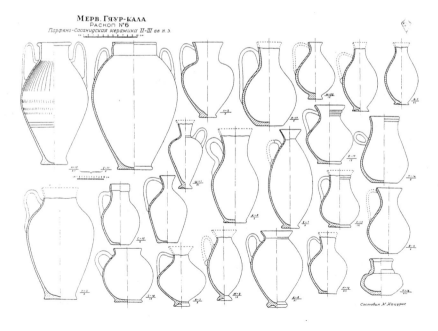

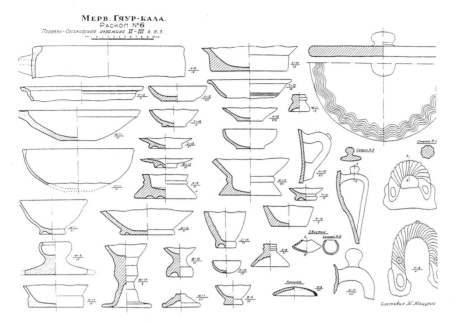

Figure A3.11: (above) Gyaur Kala, Trench 6. Partho-Sasanian pottery from the second to third centuries AD (K Katsuris, cf Katsuris and Buryakov 1963, fig 17)

Figure A3.12: (below) Gyaur Kala, Trench 6. Partho-Sasanian pottery from the second to third centuries AD (K Katsuris, Katsuris and Buryakov 1963, fig 13)

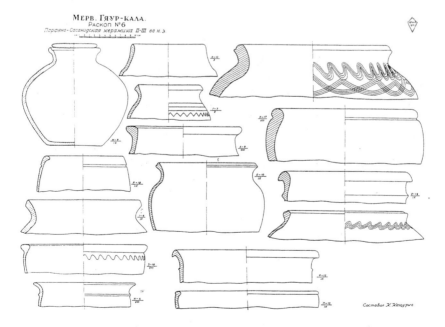

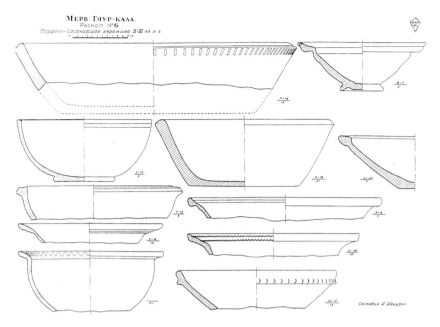

Figure A3.13: (above) Gyaur Kala, Trench 6. Partho-Sasanian pottery from the second to third centuries AD (K Katsuris, cf Katsuris and Buryakov 1963, fig 13)

Figure A3.14: (below) Gyaur Kala, Trench 6. Partho-Sasanian pottery from the second to third centuries AD (K Katsuris; cf Katsuris and Buryakov 1963, fig 16)

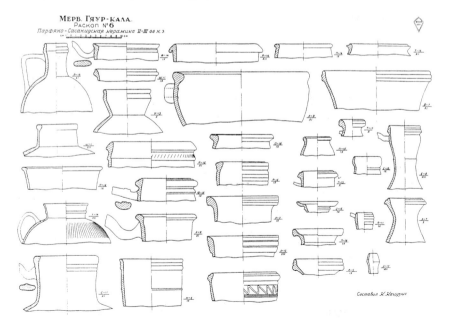

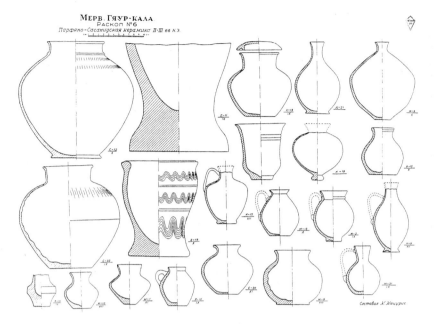

Figure A3.15: (above) Gyaur Kala, Trench 6. Partho-Sasanian pottery from the second to third centuries AD (K Katsuris; cf Katsuris and Buryakov 1963, fig 14)

Figure A3.16: (below) Gyaur Kala, Trench 6. Pottery from the second to fourth centuries AD (D P Varkhotova; cf Filanovich 1974, fig 13)

Figure A3.17: (above) Gyaur Kala, Trench 6. Pottery from the third to fourth centuries AD (D P Varkhotova; cf Filanovich 1974, fig 13)

Figure A3.18: (below) Gyaur Kala, Trench 6. Pottery from the third to fourth centuries AD (D P Varkhotova; cf Filanovich 1974, fig 14)

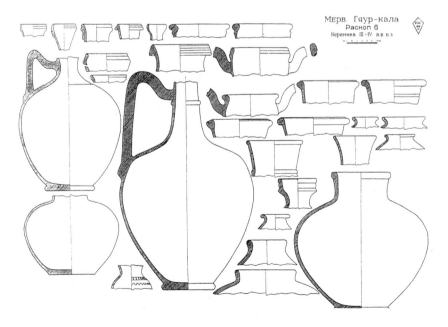

Figure A3.19: (above) Gyaur Kala, Trench 6. Pottery decoration (D P Varkhotova)

Figure A3.20: (below) Gyaur Kala, Trench 8. Pottery from the fifth to sixth centuries AD (cf Filanovich 1974, fig 26)

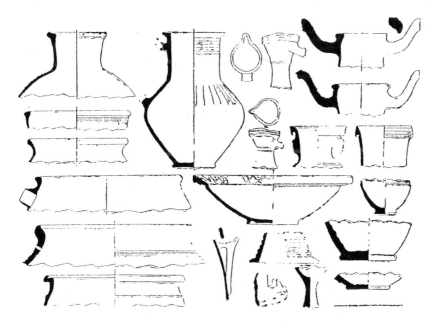

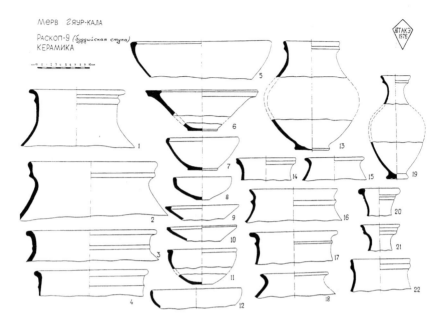

Figure A3.21: (above) Gyaur Kala, Trench 9, Sangarama. Pottery (YuTAKE 1976)

Figure A3.22: (below) Gyaur Kala, Trench 9, Sangarama. Pottery (YuTAKE 1976)

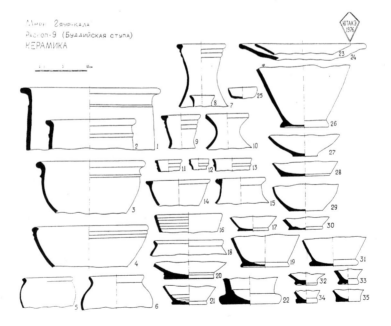

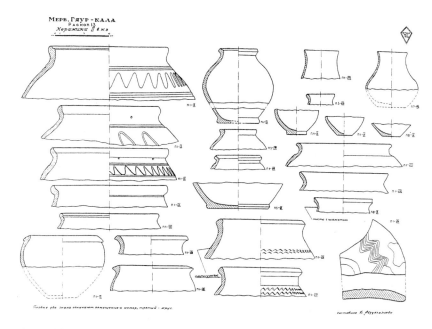

Figure A3.23: (above) Gyaur Kala, Trench 13. Pottery from the second century AD (B Abdulgazieva; cf Filanovich 1974, fig 22)

Figure A3.24: (below) Gyaur Kala, Trench 13. Pottery from the second century AD (B Abdulgazieva; cf Filanovich 1974, fig 22)

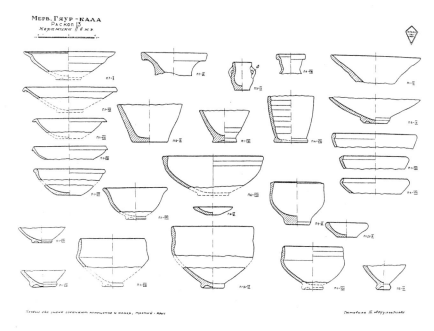

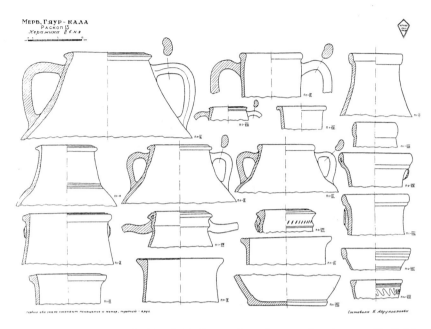

Figure A3.25: (above) Gyaur Kala, Trench 13. Pottery from the second century AD (B Abdulgazieva; cf Filanovich 1974, fig 23)

Figure A3.26: (below) Gyaur Kala, Trench 13. Pottery from the second to third centuries AD (B Abdulgazieva; cf Filanovich 1974, fig 23)

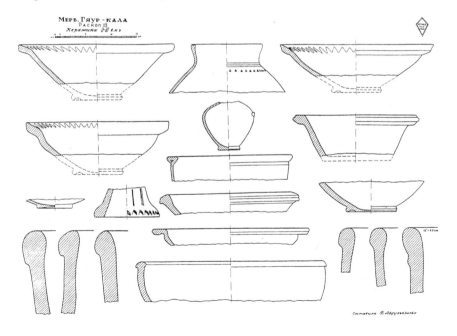

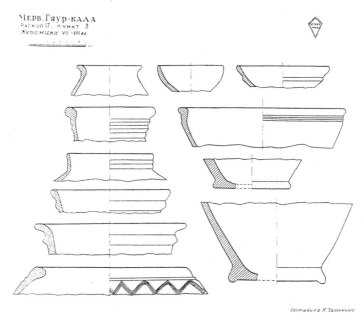

Figure A3.27: (above) Gyaur Kala, Trench 17, punkt 3. Pottery from the seventh to eighth centuries AD (N Galochkina, YuTAKE 1963)

Figure A3.28: (below) Gyaur Kala, Potter's quarter near the southern gate. Pottery from kiln no 2 (Zaurova 1962, fig 18)

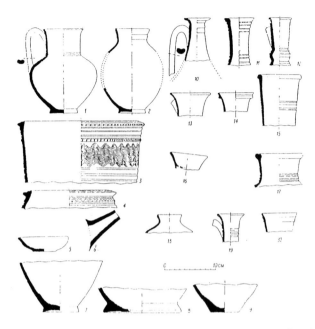

Figure A3.29: (above) Gyaur Kala, Potter's quarter near the southern gate. Pottery from kiln no 1 (Zaurova 1962, fig 19)

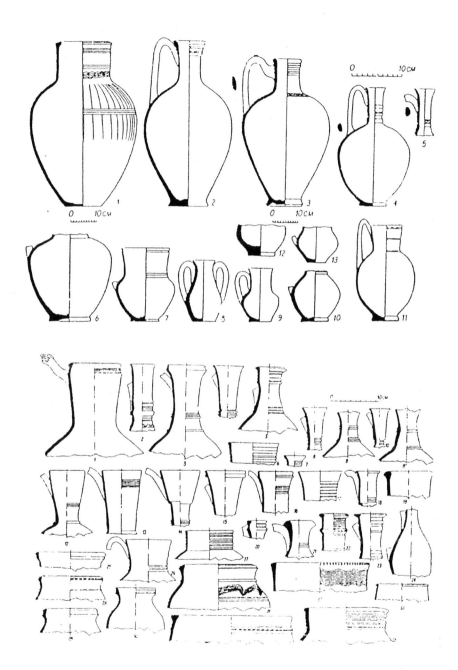

Figure A3.30: (above) Gyaur Kala. Potter's quarter near the southern gate. Pottery from kiln no 2 (Zaurova 1962, fig 17; pottery from the dump of the kilns from the seventh to eighth centuries (cf Zaurova 1962, fig 21)

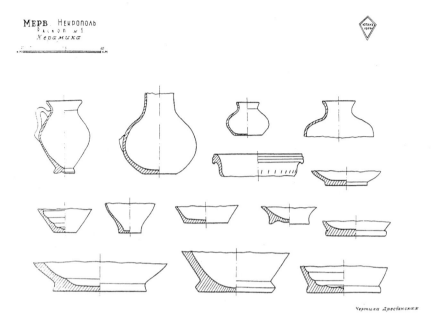

Figure A3.31: (above) Merv, Necropolis, Trench 1 (G Dresvyanskaya, YuTAKE 1965)

ШУРФ H9

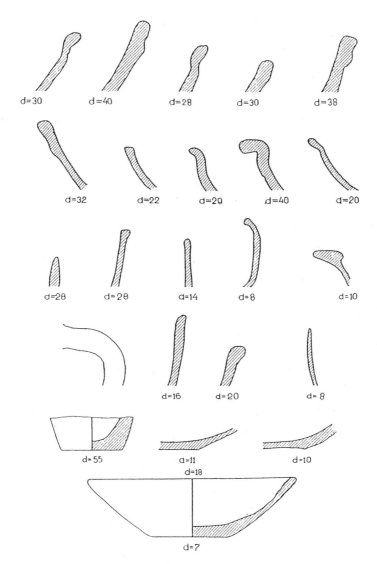

Figure A3.32: (above) Merv, Necropolis, sounding 9

APPENDIX 3

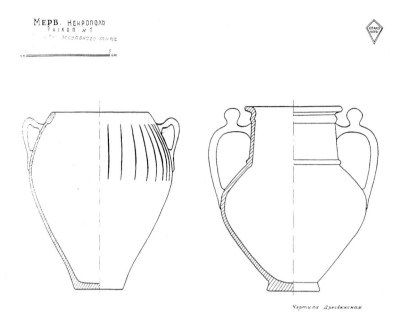

Figure A3.33: (above) Merv, Necropolis, Trench 1. Ossuary-type vessels (G Dresvyanskaya, YuTAKE 1965)

Figure A3.34: (below) Merv, Necropolis, Trench 3. Ossuaries of the fifth to sixth centuries AD (G Dresvyanskaya, YuTAKE 1967)

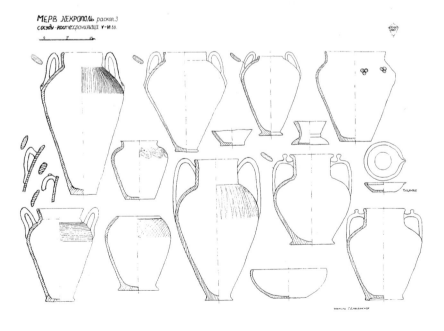

BIBLIOGRAPHY

ABBREVIATIONS

AA:	Archäologischer Anzeiger (Berlin)
AMI:	Archäologische Mitteilungen aus Iran (Berlin)
CDAFI:	Cahiers de la Délégation archéologique française en Iran (Paris)
CSCO:	Corpus Scriptorum Christianorum Orientalium (Louvain)
EncIr:	Encyclopaedia Iranica (Costa Mesa)
KSIIMK:	Kratkie Soobshcheniya (o dokladach i polevych issledovaniyach) Instituta istorii material'noy kul'tury AN (Moskva)
Materialy YuTAKE:	Materialy Yuzhno-Turkmenistanskoi Arkheologicheskoi Kompleksnoi Ekspeditsii (Ashkhabad)
MDAFA:	Mémoires de la Délégation archéologique française en Afghanistan (Paris)
SA:	Sovetskaya Arkheologiya (Moskva)
Trudy TashGU:	Trudy Tashkentskogo Gosudarstvennogo Universiteta (Tashkent)
Trudy YuTAKE:	Trudy Yuzhno-Turkmenistanskoi Arkheologicheskoi Kompleksnoi Ekspeditsii. Trudy Instituta istorii, arkheologii i etnografii AN Turkmenskoi SSR (Ashkhabad)
VDI:	Vestnik Drevnei Istorii (Moskva)

REFERENCES

Adams, R McC, (1962) 'Agriculture and Urban Life in Early Southwestern Iran' *Science* 136, 109–122

Adams, R McC, (1970) 'Tell Abu Sarifa. A Sassanian – Islamic Ceramic Sequence from South Central Iraq', *Ars Orientalis* IX, 87–119

Adams, R McC, (1981) *Heartland of Cities. Surveys of Ancient Settlement and Land Use on the Central Floodplain of the Euphrates*, Chicago: University of Chicago Press

Adams, R McC and Hansen, D P, (1968) 'Archaeological Reconnaissance and Soundings in Jundi Shahpur', *Ars Orientalis* VII, 53–70

Alram, M, (1986) 'Nomina Propria in Nummis', *Iranisches Personennamenbuch* IV, 186–216, Wien: Verlag der Österreichischen Akadademie der Wissenschaften

Arzoumanian, Z, (1982) 'A Critique of Sebeos and his History of Heraclius, A Seventh-century Document', in Samuelian, Th J, *Classical Armenian Culture. Influences and Creativity*, 68–78, Chico, CA: Scholars Press

Azarnoush, M, (1994) *The Sasanian Manor House at Hajiabad, Iran*. Monografie di Mesopotamia III, Firenze: Le Lettere

Bader, A, Callieri, P and Khodzhaniyazov, T, (1998a) 'Survey of the "Antiochus' Wall". Preliminary report on the 1993–1994 campaigns', in Gubaev, A, Koshelenko, G and Tosi, M, *The Archaeological Map of the Murghab Delta. Preliminary Reports 1990–95*, 159–186, Roma: IsIAO

Bader, A, Gaibov, V and Koshelenko, G, (1998b) 'The Seleucid Period', in Gubaev, A, Koshelenko, G and Tosi, M, *The Archaeological Map of the Murghab Delta. Preliminary Reports 1990–95*, 187–188, Roma: IsIAO

Baharal, D, (1996) *Victory of Propaganda. The Dynastic Aspect of the Imperial Propaganda of the Severi: The Literary and Archaeological Evidence* AD 193–235, BAR International Series 657, Oxford: Tempvs Reparatvm

Baxter, M J, (1994) *Exploratory Multivariate Analysis in Archaeology*, Edinburgh: Edinburgh University Press

Bishop, Y M M, Fienberg, S E and Holland, P W, (1975) *Discrete Multivariate Analysis*, Cambridge, MA: MIT Press

Blochet, E, (1895) 'Liste géographique des villes de l'Iran', *Recueil de Travaux relatifs à la Philologie et à l'Archéologie egyptiennes et assyriennes pour servir de bulletin a la Mission Française du Caire XVII*, Paris: Bouillon

Boucharlat, R, (1987) *Les Niveaux Post-Achéménides à Suse, Secteur Nord*, CDAFI 15, Paris: Association Paleorient

Boucharlat, R and Haerinck, E, (1992) 'Ceramics XII, The Parthian and Sasanian periods', *EncIr* V, 305–307

Boucharlat, R, and Lecomte, O, (1987) *Fouilles de Tureng Tepe. 1. Les Periodes Sassanides et Islamiques*. Mémoire 74, Paris: Recherche sur les Civilisations ADPF

Brock, S P, (1995) 'Bar Shabba, Mar Shabbay, first Bishop of Merv', in Tamcke M, Schwaigert W and Schlarb E, *Syrisches Christentum weltweit. Studien zur syrischen Kirchengeschichte, Festschrift Professor Hage*, 190–201, Münster: LIT

Carver, M O H, (1985) 'Theory and Practice in Urban Pottery Seriation', *Journal of Archaeological Science* 12(5) 353–366

Cattani, M and Genito, B (1998) 'The Pottery Chronological Seriation of the Murghab Delta from the End of the Bronze Age to the Achaemenid Period: A Preliminary Note', in Gubaev, A, Koshelenko, G and Tosi, M, *The Archaeological Map of the Murghab Delta. Preliminary Reports 1990–95*, 75–87, Roma: IsIAO

Chabot, J B, (1902) *Synodicon Orientale, ou Recueil de Synodes Nestoriens*. Publé, Traduit e Annoté après le MS Syriaque 332 de la Bibliothèque Nationale et le MS KVI, 4 du Musée Borgia, à Rome, Paris: Imprimerie Nationale

Christensen, A P, (1993) *The Decline of Iranshahr. Irrigation and Environment in the History of the Middle East 500* BC to AD 1500, Copenhagen: Museum Tusculanum Press

Christensen, A P and Johansen, C F, (1971) 'Les poteries héllenistiques et les terres sigilées orientales', *Hama III, 2. Fouilles et recherches de la Fondation Carlsberg 1931–1938*, Copenhague: Nationalmuseet

Cremaschi, M, (1998) 'Palaeohydrography and Middle Holocene Desertification in the Northern Fringe of the Murghab delta', in Gubaev, A, Koshelenko, G and Tosi, M, *The Archaeological Map of the Murghab Delta. Preliminary Reports 1990–95*, 15–25, Roma: IsIAO

Demirji, M S, (1987) *Researches on the Antiquities of Saddam Dam Basin Salvage, and other Researches*, State Organization of Antiquities and Heritage, Baghdad, Iraq

Dresvyanskaya, G Ya, (1974) 'Oval'nyi' dom khristianskoi obshchiny v starom Merve', *Trudy YuTAKE* XV, 155–181

Duncan, R J, Hodson, F R, Orton, C R, Tyers, P A and Vekaria, A (1989) 'Data Analysis for Archaeologists', The Institute of Archaeology programs, University College London

Dutt, N, (1978) *Buddhist Sects in India*, 2nd edn, Delhi: Motilal Banarsidass

Errington, E and Cribb, J, (1992) *The Crossroads of Asia*, Cambridge: Ancient India and Iran Trust

Ershov, S A, (1959) 'Nikotorye Itogi arkheologicheskogo Izucheniya Nekropolya s ossuarnymi Zakhoronenyami v Raione Goroda Bairam-Ali (Raskopki 1954–1956 gg)', *Trudy Instituta Istorii, Arkheologii iEtnografii. Materialy po arkheologii Turkmenistana* V, 160–204

Ettinghausen, R, (1938) 'Parthian and Sasanian pottery', in Pope A U, *A Survey of Persian Art, Sasanian Periods* Vol 2, 664–680, London, New York: Oxford University Press

Fiey, J M, (1979) *Communotés syriaques en Iran et Iraq des origines à 1552*, London: Variorum Reprints

Filanovich, M I, (1974) 'Gyaur Kala', *Trudy YuTAKE* XV 15–139

Fowden, G, (2001) 'Varieties of Religious Community', in Bowersock G W, Brown P and Grabar O, *Interpreting Late Antiquity. Essays on the Postclassical World*, 82–106, Cambridge (MA) and London: Belknap Press of Harvard University Press

Frye, R N, (1962) *The Heritage of Persia*, London: Readers' Union

Frye, R N, (1984) *The History of Ancient Iran*, Handbuch der Altertumswissenschaft III, 7, München: Beck

Frye, R N, (1996) *The Heritage of Central Asia*, Princeton, NJ: Markus Wiener Publishers

Gardin, J-C, (1973) 'Les céramique', in *Fouilles d'Aï Khanoum I, 2*, MDAFA XXI, 121–188, Paris: Klincksieck

Genito, B, (1998) 'The Iron Age in the Merv oasis', in Gubaev, A, Koshelenko, G and Tosi, M, *The Archaeological Map of the Murghab Delta. Preliminary Reports 1990–95*, 89–95, Roma: IsIAO

Gignoux, Ph, (1978) 'Pithos-Inschriften von Qal'a-ye Dukhtar', *AMI* 11, 147–150

Gignoux, Ph, (1984) 'L'organisation administrative sassanide: le cas du marzban', *Jerusalem Studies in Arabic and Islam* IV, 1–29, Jerusalem: Hebrew University

Gignoux, Ph, (1988) 'Pour une évaluation de la contribution des source arméniennes à l'histroire sassanide', *Acta Antiqua Academiae Scientiarum Hungaricae* XXXI 1985–1988, Fasc 1–2, 53–65, Budapest

Gignoux, Ph, (1991) 'A propos de quelques inscriptions et bulles sassanides', in *Histoire et Cultes de l'Asie Centrale préislamique, actes du Colloque international du CNRS, Paris, 22–28 novembre 1988*, 65–69, Paris: Editions du Centre national de la recherche scientifique

Gillman, I and Klimkeit, H-J, (1999) *Christians in Asia before 1500*, Richmond: Curzon Press

Gnoli, G, (1985) 'The Quadripartition of the Sasanian Empire', *East and West*, Vol 35 nos 1–3, 265–270

Gnoli, G (1989) *The Idea of Iran: an Essay on its Origin*, Rome: Istituto Italiano per il Medio ed Estremo Oriente

Göbl, R, (1971) *Sasanian numismatics*, Braunschweig: Klinkhardt und Biermann

Grenet, F, (1984) *Les pratiques funeraires dans l'Asie Centrale sedentaire*, Paris: Editions du Centre national de la recherche scientifique

Gubaev, A, Koshelenko, G and Tosi, M (1998) *The Archaeological Map of the Murghab Delta. Preliminary Reports 1990–95*, Roma: IsIAO

Guidi, I, (1903) 'Chronicon anonymum de ultimis regibus Persarum' *CSCO* Vol 2, Scriptores Syri Tomus 2, Chronica Minora I, Louvain 1955, Réimpression anastatique Guidi 1903, Louvain: L. Durbecq

Gyselen, R, (1989) *La Géographie administrative de l'empire Sasanide. Les témoignages sigillographiques*, Paris: Groupe pour l'Étude de la Civilisation du Moyen-Orient

Gyselen, R, (1995) 'Les Sceaux des Mages de l'Iran sassanide', in *Au Carrefour des Religions. Mélanges offerts à Philippe Gignoux*. Res Orientalis VII, 121–150, Bures-sur-Yvette: Groupe pour l'Étude de la Civilisation du Moyen-Orient

Haerinck, E, (1983) *La céramique en Iran pendant la période parthe*, Gent: Imprimerie orientaliste

Haerinck, E, (1999) 'Les échanges par la voie maritime du golfe Persique', *Dossiers d'Archéologie* 243 (5/1999) 12–13

Harper, P O, (1993) 'La vaisselle en métal', in *Splendeur des Sassanides*, 95–108, Exhib cat Bruxelles: Musées royaux d'Art et d'Histoire: Crédit communal

Herrmann, G, (1999). *Monuments of Merv. Traditional Buildings of the Karakum*, London: The Society of Antiquaries

Herrmann, G, Masson, V M, Kurbansakhatov, K, *et al*, (1993) 'The International Merv Project. Preliminary Report on the First Season (1992)', *Iran* XXXI, 39–62

Herrmann, G, Kurbansakhatov, K, *et al*, (1994) 'The International Merv Project. Preliminary Report on the Second Season (1993)', *Iran* XXXII, 53–75

Herrmann, G, Kurbansakhatov, K, *et al*, (1995) 'The International Merv Project. Preliminary Report on the Third Season (1994)', *Iran* XXXIII, 31–60

Herrmann, G, Kurbansakhatov, K, and Simpson, St John (1996) 'The International Merv Project. Preliminary Report on the Fourth Season (1995)' *Iran* XXXIV, 1–22

Herrmann, G, Kurbansakhatov, K, Simpson, St John *et al* (1997) 'The International Merv Project. Preliminary Report on the Fifth Season (1996)', *Iran* XXXV, 1–33

Herrmann, G, Kurbansakhatov, K, Simpson, St John *et al* (1998) 'The International Merv Project. Preliminary Report on the Sixth Season (1997)', *Iran* XXXVI, 53–75

Herrmann, G, Kurbansakhatov, K, Simpson, St John *et al* (1999) 'The International Merv Project. Preliminary Report on the Seventh Season (1998)', *Iran* XXXVII, 1–24

Herrmann, G, Kurbansakhatov, K, Simpson, St John *et al* (2000) 'The International Merv Project. Preliminary Report on the Eighth Season (1999)', *Iran* XXXVIII, 1–31

Herrmann, G, Kurbansakhatov, K, Simpson, St John *et al* (2001) 'The International Merv Project. Preliminary Report on the Ninth Season (2000)', *Iran* XXXIX, 9–52

Hobbs, R, (1995) 'Roman Coins from Merv, Turkmenistan', *Oxford Journal of Archaeology* 14, 97–102

Horne, L, (1983) 'Recycling an Iranian village: Ethnoarchaeology in Baghestan', *Archaeology* 1983 (July/August), 16–20

Horne, L, (1994) *Village Spaces. Settlement and Society in Northeastern Iran*, Washington, DC: Smithsonian Institute Press

Howard-Johnston, J, (1995) 'The Two Great Powers in Late Antiquity: A Comparison', in Cameron, A, *The Byzantine and Early Islamic Near East*, Vol III, *States, Resources and Armies*, 157–226, Princeton, NJ: Darwin Press

Huff, D, (1978) 'Ausgrabungen auf Qal'a-ye Dukhtar bei Firuzabad 1976', *AMI* 11, 117–147

Huff, D (1986), 'Sasanian Archaeology and Architecture', *EncIr* II, 302–308

Joyner, L, (1999) 'Petrographic Analysis of Parthian and Sasanian Ceramics from Merv, Turkmenistan', Unpublished report, The British Museum, Department of Conservation, Documentation and Science, DSR Project 7081

Kaim, B, (2002) 'Un temple du feu sassanide découvert à Mele Hairam (Turkménistan méridional)', *Studia Iranica* 3, 215–230

Katsuris, K and Buryakov, Yu, (1963) Izuchenie remeslannogo kvartala antichnogo Merva u severnykh vorot Gyaur-Kaly', *Trudy YuTAKE* XII, 119–163

Keall E J, and Keall, M J, (1981) 'The Qal'eh-i Yazdigird Pottery: A Statistical Approach', *Iran* 19, 33–80

Kennet, D (2004) *Sasanian and Islamic Pottery from Ras al-Khaimah*, Society for Arabian Studies Monographs no 1, BAR S1248, Oxford: Archaeopress

Kirsta, B T, (1984) 'Poverkhnostnye Vody', in Atamamedov, N V, *Turkmenskaya Sovetskaya Sotsiyalisticheskaya Respublika*, 37–44, Ashkhabad: Glavnaya redaktsiya Turkmenskoi sovetskoi entsikloedii

Kleiss, W, (1986) 'Beobachtungen an der Wallanlage von Leilan in West-Azerbaidjan', *AMI* 19, 211–218

Kleiss, W, and Kroll, St, (1992) 'Survey in Ost-Azerbaidjan 1991', *AMI* 25, 1–46

Klejn, L S, (1997) *Das Phänomen der Sowjetischen Archäologie*. Gesellschaften und Staaten im Epochenwandel 6, Frankfurt am Main: Peter Lang

Koshelenko, G A, (1966) 'Unikal'naya vaza iz Merva', *VDI* 1, 92–100

Koshelenko, G A, (1985) *Drevneishie Gosudarstva Kavkaza i Srednei Azii*, Moskva: Izdatel'stvo Nauka

Koshelenko, G, Bader, A and Gaibov, V, (1995) 'The Beginnings of Christianity in Merv', *Iranica Antiqua* XXX, Festschrift K Schippmann II, 55–70, Leiden: Brill

Krikorian, K M, (1982) 'Sebeos, Historian of the Seventh Century', in Samuelian Th J, *Classical Armenian Culture. Influences and Creativity*, 52–67, Chico, CA: Scholars Press

Kühnel, E, (1933) *Die Ausgrabungen der 2. Ktesiphon-Expedition*, Berlin: Islamische Kunstabteilung der Staatlichen Museen

Landshut, S, (1971) *Karl Marx. Die Frühschriften*, 6th edn, Stuttgart: Kröner

Langdon, S and Harden, D B, (1934) 'Excavations at Kish and Barghutiat', *IRAQ* 1, 1–136

Lecomte, O, (1987) 'La céramique sassanide', in Boucharlat, R and Lecomte, O, *Fouilles de Tureng Tepe. 1. Les Periodes Sassanides et Islamiques*. Mémoire 74, 93–119, Paris: Recherche sur les Civilisations ADPF

Lerner, J A, (1977) 'Christian Seals of the Sasanian Period', *Uitgaven van het Nederlands Historisch-archaeologisch Instituute Istanbul* XII, Istanbul: Nederlands Historisch-Archaeologisch Instituut te Istanbul

Litvinskii, B A and Sedov, A V (1983) *Tepai-shakh. Kul'tura I svyazi kushanskoi Baktrii*, Moskva: Izdatel'stvo Nauka

Loginov, S D and Nikitin, A B (1993a) 'Sasanian Coins of the Third Century from Merv', *Mesopotamia* XXVIII, 225–246

Loginov, S D and Nikitin, A B (1993b) 'Coins of Shapur II from Merv', *Mesopotamia* XXVIII, 247–269

Loginov, S D and Nikitin, A B (1993c) 'Sasanian Coins of the late 4th–7th centuries from Merv', *Mesopotamia* XXVIII, 271–312

Loginov, S D and Nikitin, A B (1993d) 'Post-Sasanian Coins from Merv', *Mesopotamia* XXVIII, 313–317

Lyonnet, B, (1997) 'Céramique et peuplement du Chalcolithique à la conquête Arabe', *Prospections archéologiques en Bactriane orientale (1974–1978)* vol 2, Paris: Éditions Recherche sur les Civilisations

MacDowall, D W, (1979) 'The Monetary Systems and Currency of Central Asia', in Harmatta J, *Prolegomena to the Sources on the History of Pre-Islamic Central Asia*, Budapest: Akadémiai Kiadó

Marshak, B I, (1961) 'Vlyanie torevtiki na sogdiiskuyu keramiku VII–VIII vekov', *Trudy Gosudarstvennogo Ermitazha* V, 177–201, Leningrad

Marquart, J, (1901) *Eranshahr nach einer Geographie des Ps Moses χorenac'I*, Berlin

Masson, M E, (1963) 'K izucheniyu proshlogo starovo Merva' *Trudy YuTAKE* XII, 7–19

Masson, M E, (1966) 'Sredneaziatskaya arkheologicheskaya nauchnaya shkola Tashkenskogo gosudarstvennogo universiteta', *Trudy TashGU* 295, 29–52

Masson, M E, (1980) 'Kratkii ocherk po istorii izucheniya gorodishch starogo Merva do 1946 g', *Trudy YuTAKE* XVII, 10–37

Moorey, P R S, (1978) *Kish Excavations 1923–1933*, Oxford: Clarendon Press

Naumann, R and Huff, D, (1975) 'Takht-i Suleiman. Bericht über die Ausgrabungen 1965–1973', *AA* 90, 109–180

Nautin, P, (1982) 'L'Auteur de la "Chronique Anonyme de Guidi": Élie de Merw', *Revue de l'Histoire des Religions* 199, Fasc 1, 303–314

Negro Ponzi, M M, (1968) 'Sasanian Glassware from Tell Mahuz (North Mesopotamia)', *Mesopotamia* III–IV, 293–384

Nerazik, E E and Rapoport, Yu A, (1981) *Gorodishche Toprak-Kala (Raskopki 1965–1975 gg)*, Moskva: Ixdatel'stvo Nauka

Neusner, J, (1986) *Israel and Iran in Talmudic Times (A Political History)*, Lanham, MD: University Press of America

Nöldeke, Th, (1893) 'Die von Guidi herausgegebene syrische Chronik', *Sitzungsbericht der phil.- hist Classe der kaiserl Akad d Wiss*, Bd 128, Abh IX, Wien

Orton, C and Tyers, P, (1990) 'Statistical Analysis of Ceramic Assemblages', *Archeologia e Calcolatori* 1, 81–110

Orton, C and Tyers, P, (1993) 'A user's guide to Pie-slice', Institute of Archaeology, London

Orton, C, Tyers, P and Vince, A, (1993) *Pottery in Archaeology*, Cambridge Manuals in Archaeology, Cambridge: Cambridge University Press

Ovezov, D M, (1970) *Akademik Akademii nauk Turkmenskoi SSR Mikhail Evgen'evich Masson*, Ashkhabad: Izdatel'stvo Akademii nauk Turkmenskoi SSR

Pidaev, Sh P, (1978) *Poseleniya kushanskogo vremeni severnoi Baktrii*, Tashkent: Izdatel'stvo Fan

Piotrovskii, B B, (1949) 'Razvedochnye raboty na Gyaur Kala v starom Merve', *Materialy YuTAKE* 1, 35–41

Pugachenkova, G A, (1979) *Iskusstvo Baktrii epokhi Kushan*, Moskva: Izdatel'stvo Iskusstvo

Pugachenkova, G A and Usmanova, Z I, (1995) 'Buddhist monuments in Merv', in Invernizzi, A, *In the land of the Gryphons. Papers on Central Asian Archaeology in Antiquity*, 51–81, Firenze: Casa Editrice Le Lettere

Pumpelly, R, (1908) *Explorations in Turkestan. Expedition of 1904, Prehistoric Civilizations of Anau* I, Washington, DC: Carnegie Institution

Puschnigg, G, (2000) *A Diachronic and Stylistic Assessment of the Ceramic Evidence from Sasanian Merv*, unpublished Ph.D., University College London

Rahbar, M, (1998) 'Découverte d'un monument d'époque sassanide à Bandian, Dargaz (Nord Khorassan). Fouilles 1994 et 1995', *Studia Iranica* 27, 213–250

Rawlinson, H G, (1912) *Bactria: the History of a Forgotten Empire*, London: Probsthain

Rice, P M, (1987) *Pottery Analysis. A Sourcebook*, Chicago, IL: University of Chicago Press

Roodenberg, J J, and Thissen, L C, (2001) *The Ilipinar Excavations II*, Uitgaven van het Nederlands

Historisch-Archaeologisch Instituut te Istanbul XCIII, Leiden: Nederlands Instituut voor het Nabije Oosten

Rutkovskaya, L M, (1962) 'Antichnaya keramika drevnego Merva', *Trudy YuTAKE* XI, 41–116

Rubin, Z, (1995) 'The Reform of Khusro Anushirvan', in Cameron, A, *The Byzantine and Early Islamic Near East* III. States, Resources and Armies, 227–298, Princeton, NJ: Darwin Press

Rye, O S, (1981) *Pottery Technology. Principles and Reconstruction*, Manuals in Archaeology 4, Washington, DC: Taraxacum

Salvatori, S, (1998) 'Margiana Archaeological Map: The Bronze Age Settlement Pattern', in Gubaev, A, Koshelenko, G and Tosi, M, *The Archaeological Map of the Murghab Delta. Preliminary Reports 1990–95*, 57–66, Roma: IsIAO

Sarre, F, (1921) *Die Keramik im Euphrat- und Tigrisgebiet*, Berlin: Reimer

Scher, A (1908–1918) *Histoire nestorienne inédite*: (chronique de Séert), Paris: Firmin-Didot, 1950–2003, Volumes reprinted from edn originally published: Paris: Firmin-Didot, 1907–1918

Schiffer, M B, (1987) *Formation Processes of the Archaeological Record*, Albuquerque: University of New Mexico Press

Schiffer, M B, (1988) 'The Effects of Surface Treatment on Permeability and Evaporative Cooling Effectiveness of Pottery', in Farquhar, R M, Hancock, R G V and Pavlish, L A, *Proceedings of the 26th International Archaeometry Symposium held at University of Toronto, Toronto, Canada May 16th to May 20th, 1988*, 23–29, Toronto: Archaeometry Laboratory, University of Toronto

Schmidt, E, (1937) *Excavations at Tepe Hissar, Damghan*, Philadelphia, PA: The University Museum

Schmidt, H, (1908) 'The Excavations in Ghiaur Kala (Old Merv)', in Pumpelly, R, *Explorations in Turkestan*, 187–210, Washington, DC: Carnegie Institution

Schmidt, J H, (1934) 'L'expédition de Ctésiphon en 1931–32', *Syria* 15, 1–23

Schnyder, R, (1975) 'Keramik- und Glasfunde vom Takht-i Suleiman 1959–1968', *AA* 90, 180–196

Schwaigert, W, (1989) 'Das Christentum in Huzistan im Rahmen der frühen Kirchengeschichte Persiens bis zur Synode von Seleukia-Ktesiphon im Jahre 410', unpublished Ph.D., Marburg/Lahn

Sedov, A V, (1987) *Kobadian. Na poroge rannego srednevekov'ya*, Moskva: Izdatel'stvo Nauka

Shaw, B D, (2001) 'War and Violence', in Bowersock, G W, Brown, P and Grabar, O, *Interpreting Late Antiquity. Essays on the Postclassical World*, Cambridge (MA) and London: Belknap Press of Harvard University Press

Simpson, St J, (1996) 'From Tekrit to the Jaghjagh: Sasanian Sites, Settlement Patterns and Material Culture in Northern Mesopotamia', in Bartl, K and Hauser, St R, *Continuity and Change in Northern Mesopotamia from the Hellenistic to the Early Islamic* Period, 87–126, Berlin: Dietrich Reimer

Simpson, St J, (1997) 'Partho-Sasanian Ceramic Industries in Mesopotamia', in Freestone, I and Gaimster, D, *Pottery in the Making. World Ceramic Traditions*, 74–79, London: British Museum Press

Simpson, St. J, (1998) 'Gilt-silver and Clay: A Late Sasanian Skeuomorphic Pitcher from Iran', *in Entlang der Seidenstraße. Frühmittelalterliche Kunst zwischen Persien und China in der Abegg-Stiftung*, Riggisberger Berichte 6, 335–380, Riggisberg: Abegg-Stiftung

Stavisski, B Y, (1964) 'Kara-Tepe – Buddiiskii peshchernyi monastyr' v starom Termeze', *Materialy sovmestnoi arkheologicheskoi ekspeditsii na Kara-Tepe* 1, Moskva

Stavisski, B Y, (1982) 'Osnovnye itogi izucheniya Kara-Tepe 1974–1977 gg', *Materialy sovmestnoi arkheologicheskoi ekspeditsii na Kara-Tepe* 5, 7–50, Moskva

Stavisky, B Y, (1996) *Buddiiskie Kompleksy Kara-Tepe v Starom Termeze. Osnovnye Itogi Rabot. 1978–1989 gg*, Moskva: Vostochnaia literatura

Sycheva, N S, (1975) 'Keramika Kara-Tepe', *Materialy sovmestnoi arkheologicheskoi ekspeditsii na Kara-Tepe* 4, 88–148, Moskva

Tafazzoli, A, (2000) *Sasanian Society*, New York: Bibliotheca Persica Press

Thierry, F, (1993) 'Sur les Monnaies Sassanides trouvées en Chine', in Rika Gyselen, *Circulation des Monnaies, des Marchandises et des Biens,* Res Orientalis V, 89–139, Bures-sur-Yvette: Groupe pour l'Étude de la Civilisation du Moyen-Orient

Thomson, R W, (1982) *Elishe. History of Vardan and the Armenian War,* Cambridge, MA: Harvard University Press

Thomson, R W and Howard-Johnston, J, (1999) *The Armenian History Attributed to Sebeos,* Liverpool: Liverpool University Press

Toll, N, (1943) *The Excavations at Dura-Europos, Final Report IV: Pt I, Fasc I, The Green Glazed Pottery,* New Haven, CT: Yale University Press

Toll, N, (1946) *The Excavations at Dura-Europos, Preliminary Report of the Ninth Season of Work, 1935–1936: Pt II, The Necropolis,* New Haven, CT: Yale University

Trever, K V, (1954) 'Kushani, Khioniti i Ephtaliti v armyanskim Istochnikam IV–VII vv', *SA* XXI, 131–147

Trinkaus, M K, (1981) 'The Partho–Sasanian Northeast Frontier. Settlement in the Damghan Plain, Iran', Dissertation in Anthropology, University of Pennsylvania, Philadelphia

Trinkaus, M K, (1983) 'Pre-Islamic Settlement and Land Use in Damghan, Northeast Iran', *Iranica Antiqua* XVIII, 119–144

Trinkaus, M K, (1986) 'Pottery from the Damghan Plain, Iran: Chronology and Variability from the Parthian to the Early Islamic Periods', *Studia Iranica* 15, 24–88

Usmanova, Z I, (1963a) 'Erk Kala (po materialam YuTAKE 1955–1959 gg)', *Trudy YuTAKE* XII, 20–94

Usmanova, Z I, (1963b) 'Raskopki masterskoi remeslennika parfyanskogo vremeni na gorodishche Gyaur Kala', *Trudy YuTAKE* XII, 164–200

Usmanova, Z I, (1969) 'Novye dannye k arkheologicheskoi stratigrafii Erk-Kaly', *Trudy YuTAKE* XIV, 13–55

Vaidov, R M, (1954) 'Rannesrednevekovoe gorodishche Sudagylan (Mingechaur)', *KSIIMK 54*

Vanden Berghe, L, (1993) 'Historique de la découverte et de la recherche', in *Splendeur des Sassanides,* 13–18, Exhib catalogue, Musées royaux d'Art et d'Histoire, Bruxelles: Crédit communal

Venco Ricciardi, R, (1967) 'Pottery from Choche', *Mesopotamia* II, 93–104

Venco Ricciardi, R, (1970) 'Sasanian Pottery from Tell Mahuz (North Mesopotamia)', *Mesopotamia* V–VI, 429–482

Venco Ricciardi, R, (1980) 'Archaeological Survey in the Upper Atrek Valley (Khorassan, Iran): Preliminary Report', *Mesopotamia* XV, 51–72

Venco Ricciardi, R, (1984) 'Sasanian Pottery from Choche (Artisans' Quarter) and Tell Baruda', in Boucharlat, R and Salles, J-F, *Arabie Orientale, Mésopotamie et Iran Méridional. De L'age du Fer au Début de la Période Islamique.* Mémoire 37, 49–57, Paris: Recherche sur les Civilisations ADPF

Vorob'eva-Desyatovskaya, M I, (1983) 'Pamyatniki pis'mom kharoshtkhi i brakhmi iz sovetskoi Srednei Azii', in *Istoria i kul'tura Tsentral'noi Azii,* Moskva: Izdatel'stvo Nauka

Wenke, R, (1975) 'Imperial Investments and Agricultural Developments in Parthian and Sasanian Khuzestan', *Mesopotamia* 10–11, 31–217

Wenke, R, (1987) 'Western Iran in the Partho-Sasanian Period: The Imperial Transformation', in Hole, F, *The Archaeology of Western Iran. Settlement and Society from Prehistory to the Islamic Conquest,* 251–277, Washington, DC: Smithsonian Institution

Wenke, R J and Pyne, N M (1990) 'Some Issues in the Analysis of Sasanian Iran', in *Contribution à l'Histoire de l'Iran, Mélanges Offerts à Jean Perrot,* Paris: Editions Recherche sur les Civilisations

Whitcomb, D S, (1985) *Before the Roses and Nightingales. Excavations at Qasr-i Abu Nasr, Old Shiraz,* New York: Bradford D Kelleher

Wiesehöfer, J, (2001) *Ancient Persia: From 550 BC to 650 AD,* London: I B Tauris

Wiessner, G, (1967) 'Zu den Subskriptionslisten der ältesten christlichen Synoden in Iran', in Wießner, G, *Festschrift für Wilhelm Eilers,* 288–298, Wiesbaden: Harrassowitz

Williams, T, Kurbansakhatov, K *et al,* (2003) 'The Ancient Merv Project, Turkmenistan. Preliminary Report on the Second Season (2002)', *Iran* XLI, 139–170

Wright, W (1882) *The Chronicle of Joshua the Stylite, Composed in Syriac* AD *507*, with a translation into English and notes, Cambridge

Wright, H T, (1979) 'Archaeological Investigations in Northeastern Khuzestan, 1976', *Museum of Anthropology, The University of Michigan, Technical Reports* 10, Ann Arbor: University of Michigan Press

Zaurova, E Z, (1962) 'Keramicheskie Pechi VII–VIII vv na gorodishche Gyaur Kala starogo Merva', *Trudy YuTAKE* XII, 174–216

Zeimal', E V, (1985) *Drevnosti Tadzhikistana. Katalog Vystavki*, Dushanbe: Izdatel'stvo Donish

Zeimal, E V, (1996) 'The Circulation of Coins in Central Asia during the Early Medieval Period (Fifth–Eighth Centuries AD)', *Bulletin of the Asia Institute: The Archaeology and Art of Central Asia. Studies from the Former Soviet Union. New Series/Vol 8 1994*, Michigan

Zhukovsky, V A, (1894) 'Drevnosti Zakaspiiskogo kraya. Razvaliny starogo Merva', *Materialy po arkheologii Rossii*, St Peterburg: Tipografiya glavnogo upravleniia udielov

INDEX

THE ANCIENT MERV PROJECT

This volume is a product of the Ancient Merv Project, a long-running collaboration between the Institute of Archaeology, University College London, and the Ministry of Culture, Turkmenistan.

Previous volumes on Ancient Merv include

Herrmann, G (1999) *Monuments of Merv: traditional buildings of the Karakum*. London: Society of Antiquaries of London

Herrmann, G (2002) *The monuments of Merv: a scanned archive of photographs and plans*. London: Institute of Archaeology, UCL and the British Institute of Persian Studies

Numerous interim reports are available in the journals *MIRAS* and *Cultural Values* (both published in Turkmenistan) and *Iran*, the Journal of British Institute of Persian Studies (http://www.bips.ac.uk/journal.html).

Additional volumes from the Ancient Merv Project are in preparation, including works on the ceramics from Merv, a Late Sasanian House in Erk Kala, the defences of Gyuar Kala, the Islamic defences, the medieval Islamic city, and the Islamic stucco.

For more details on the project and its publications visit the Ancient Merv Project website at www.ucl.ac.uk/merv

Author **Gabriele Puschnigg** is a Research Fellow at the Institute of Archaeology, University College London, and Assistant Director of the Ancient Merv Project.